D1084765

Public Policies for Distressed Communities

Public Policies for Distressed Communities

Edited by
F. Stevens Redburn
U.S. Department of Housing
and Urban Development
Terry F. Buss
Youngstown State University

LexingtonBooks
D.C. Heath and Company
Lexington, Massachusetts
Toronto

The Policy Studies Organization gratefully thanks the Ohio Department of Mental Health for its financial aid to the symposium on which this book is based. However, no one other than the individual authors is responsible for the ideas advocated here.

Library of Congress Cataloging in Publication Data
Main entry under title:

Public policies for distressed communities.

Includes index.
1. Community development—Government policy—United States. 2. Community development—United States—Finance. 3. Regional economics. 4. Regional development—Government policy—United States. 5. Urban development—Government policy—United States. I. Redburn, F. Stevens. II. Buss, Terry F.
HN90.C6P8   361.6   80-8393
ISBN 0-669-04105-x   AACR2

Copyright © 1982 by D.C. Heath and Company

Published simultaneously in Canada

Printed in the United States of America

International Standard Book Number: 0-669-04105-x

Library of Congress Catalog Card Number: 80-8393

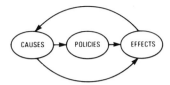

Policy Studies Organization Series

General Approaches to Policy Studies

Specific Policy Problems

Analyzing Poverty Policy
  edited by Dorothy Buckton James
Crime and Criminal Justice
  edited by John A. Gardiner and Michael Mulkey
Civil Liberties
  edited by Stephen L. Wasby
Foreign Policy Analysis
  edited by Richard L. Merritt
Economic Regulatory Policies
  edited by James E. Anderson
Political Science and School Politics
  edited by Samuel K. Gove and Frederick M. Wirt
Science and Technology Policy
  edited by Joseph Haberer
Population Policy Analysis
  edited by Michael E. Kraft and Mark Schneider
The New Politics of Food
  edited by Don F. Hadwiger and William P. Browne
New Dimensions to Energy Policy
  edited by Robert Lawrence
Race, Sex, and Policy Problems
  edited by Marian Lief Palley and Michael Preston
American Security Policy and Policy-Making
  edited by Robert Harkavy and Edward Kolodziej
Current Issues in Transportation Policy
  edited by Alan Altshuler
Security Policies of Developing Countries
  edited by Edward Kolodziej and Robert Harkavy
Determinants of Law-Enforcement Policies
  edited by Fred A. Meyer, Jr., and Ralph Baker
Evaluating Alternative Law-Enforcement Policies
  edited by Ralph Baker and Fred A. Meyer, Jr.
International Energy Policy
  edited by Robert M. Lawrence and Martin O. Heisler
Employment and Labor-Relations Policy
  edited by Charles Bulmer and John L. Carmichael, Jr.
Housing Policy for the 1980s
  edited by Roger Montgomery and Dale Rogers Marshall
Environmental Policy Formation
  edited by Dean E. Mann
Environmental Policy Implementation
  edited by Dean E. Mann
The Analysis of Judicial Reform
  edited by Philip L. Dubois
The Politics of Judicial Reform
  edited by Philip L. Dubois
Critical Issues in Health Policy
  edited by Ralph Straetz, Marvin Lieberman, and Alice Sardell

Contents

Introduction

F. Stevens Redburn and
Terry F. Buss

The 1980s are likely to see a major restructuring of the economy of this nation and the world. In the process, industries and communities that were the growth centers of previous decades will experience economic crisis. This restructuring—presaged in this country by the decaying productivity of certain basic manufacturing industries—will mean that many places can no longer provide sufficient incomes or jobs for their people or maintain the quality of existing public amenities. As disinvestment proceeds, these communities will face the challenge of finding new economic and social roles, reducing the effect of job losses, and maintaining the quality of life within rigid fiscal limits.

In the United States, national policy toward economically distressed areas has been ambivalent and limited in scope (Levitan and Zickler 1977). In the 1960s and 1970s, small-scale area-development programs (for example, Appalachian Regional Commission (ARC), Economic Development Administration (EDA), and Office of Economic Opportunity (OEO) Community Action Program) were launched, the first two emphasizing infrastructure improvements. In the last administration, new efforts (for example, Urban Development Action Grants (UDAG) and EDA business loans) were undertaken to aid distressed urban areas. (Other forms of local economic assistance, such as the Comprehensive Employment Training Act (CETA) and the Community Development Block Grant program, were less obviously targeted at distressed areas or aimed at redevelopment.) These programs were criticized, on the one hand, as too small to address the economic problems of these communities seriously and, on the other hand, as wasteful shell games, producing a suboptimal geographic pattern of national investment. Even this commitment to relatively small-scale area-development efforts appears to be faltering. The absence of consensus regarding targeted development reflects intellectual polarization, which produces different calculations of the efficacy of such assistance.

Terms of the Debate

Discussion of the wisdom of area-development policies is now highly polarized. Many question distressed-area aid on grounds of national economic efficiency; at the extreme, some criticize even ameliorative policies such as urban public-housing subsidies, welfare assistance, and CETA as "well-intentioned" but "continuing to attract and residentially trap larger numbers of disadvantaged in our urban cores while offering them little hope for meaningful or permanent employment" (Kasarda 1980). This debate is represented in this book by Elliott Sclar and Martin Katzman (chapters 2 and 3) who, by way of different analytical frameworks, reach opposite conclusions on the efficacy of targeting public subsidies to distressed areas.

A basic difference between the two polar positions derives from the manner in which each calculates the costs and benefits of public and private investment. Opposition to area-targeted development is based on a model that assumes the free flow of private capital at its most productive use maximizes national economic growth and provides both new work opportunities for the geographically mobile faction of the labor force and increased income to those caught in the backwash of economic change. Advocates of area aid, on the other hand, use a broader framework for calculating the costs of regional shifts. They note that while some people may relocate to places of opportunity, highly integrated, culturally based communities, and nurturing family and neighborhood networks cannot. In estimating effects on national productivity, advocates weigh more heavily than others the costs of reproducing at today's prices public capital and housing that, though often antiquated, can continue to support efficient economic activity and high levels of social amenity. Finally, some advocates of distressed-areas aid challenge the market economists' assumption that the profit-maximizing behavior of large (especially multinational, oligopolistic, and conglomerate) firms necessarily contributes to national productivity.

The possible trade-off between overall economic efficiency and aid to distressed communities is a particularly timely question because of the national economy's recent poor performance and pending decisions about how to restructure the nation's productive capacity (see Schwartz and Choate 1980). Chapter 1 suggests that reconciling the objectives of a national industrial policy with those of area redevelopment will not be easy. However, the writers also warn that "if the persons and places adversely affected by industrial change are not compensated for their losses and reestablished in alternative economic opportunities, then they will bring political pressure to bear on government to halt the process of economic change."

Aside from fundamental differences of values and paradigms, debate over area development is complicated by negative evaluations of existing federal assistance programs to communities in economic crisis. For example, Barsh and Gale (chapter 4) criticize those policies for failing to distinguish the development needs of urban and rural areas, for pitting rural areas against the cities in competition for aid, and for conflicting and uncoordinated activity. Vaughan and Sekera in chapter 6 question whether federal programs such as UDAG are achieving their stated goals and argue instead for a development approach that emphasizes building local capacity. Looking beyond area economic assistance, Harrison and Bluestone (chapter 10) doubt that much progress can be made toward orderly economic planning without far-reaching changes in tax, tariff, and antitrust policy.

Dealing with the Effects of Area Economic Crisis

Whatever is or is not done to aid long-term redevelopment of distressed areas, the hardships created in the short run by major plant closings (and similar situations) deserve public attention. Chapter 11, by Foltman, provides practical advice on the management of plant closings. Previous work by scholars such as Brenner (1973) and Cobb and Kasl (1977) have greatly contributed to our understanding of how much job loss and unemployment cost individuals and communities. Chapters 13 and 14, by Catalano and Dooley and by Liem, extend and synthesize this research. By adopting a mental-health perspective, they are able to take full measure of personal costs of economic change and to base policy judgments on more than the narrow production criteria used in some analyses.

Another sophisticated dimension sometimes missing in discussions of area-development policy concerns the unique problems of particular regions. Two case studies, chapters 5 and 8 (by Burton and Alpert of the Redwood Forest region of northern California and by Cooke and Rees of South Wales, United Kingdom) illustrate the value of closely examining the causes of local economic crisis and deriving solutions tailored to local needs. At the same time, each case is representative of a larger class of situations: one, the carelessly exploited resource-based economy, and the other, the declining heavy-industry region.

Innovations in public policy require innovations in conceptualization and analysis. The work of Kunde and Berry (chapter 15) constitutes a practical synthesis of these two levels of creativity. Their chapter is a progress report on changes in the way urban area leadership looks at and allocates public investments. Similarly, Davidson and Pryde, and Long and Wittmaier (chapters 7 and 9) emphasize particular innovations in the way local economic crisis is interpreted and addressed. Blasi and Whyte (chapter 12) examine the various forms of worker ownership, which they and others see as a possible way to improve productivity and humanize the work place. Lindberg also deals with the problems of forming effective local partnerships for development that include the public, private, and community/volunteer sectors (chapter 18). In chapter 17, Kanter discusses the politics of state development-policy deals with the practical limits on public efforts to revitalize distressed areas. Finally, Bergman (chapter 16) discusses the problems and prospects of community-development planning in the wake of major plant shutdowns. For these authors, the situations of such localities represent not only crisis but opportunity.

The Chinese ideogram for crisis, as Jane Jacobs noted in her classic work on the economy of cities, is composed of the symbols of danger and opportunity. Those caught up in economic crisis can easily see the danger; it is a much harder, intellectually demanding task to discover the opportunity. The chapters that follow represent such an effort. Their common source of strength is the energy devoted to thinking in new ways about an old and recurring problem: What happens to places and people when the economy shifts and they are left behind; and what should be done about it?

References

Brenner, H. *Mental Illness and the Economy.* Cambridge, Mass.: Harvard University Press, 1973.

Cobb, S. and S. Kasl. *Termination: The Consequences of Job Loss.* Washington, D.C.: National Institute of Occupational Safety and Health, HEW, 1977.

Kasarda, J. "The Implications of Contemporary Redistribution Trends for National Urban Policy." *Social Science Quarterly* 61 (1980):373-400.

Levitan, S. J. Zickler. *Too Little But Not Too Late: Federal Aid to Lagging Areas.* Lexington, Mass.: Lexington Books, D.C. Heath, 1977.

Schwartz, G. and P. Choate. *Being Number One: Rebuilding the U.S. Economy.* Lexington, Mass.: Lexington Books, D.C. Heath, 1980.

**Part I
Overview of
Major Policy Issues**

1 National Industrial Policy and Economically Distressed Communities

Marc Bendick, Jr., and
Larry C. Ledebur

Introduction

It is widely perceived that the nation's industrial engine is faltering. The dramatic reduction in productivity gains throughout the 1970s and the absolute productivity decline in the last year of the decade have been highly publicized (Denison 1979; Kendrick 1979; Norsworthy et al. 1979; Tatom 1979). The nation's balance of trade has deteriorated as a result of both the increasing cost of energy imports and the declining international competitiveness of some U.S. products. Sales and employment have declined precipitously in the nation's major manufacturing industries, (notably automobiles and steel) and ripple effects of these contractions have spread to other industrial sectors. The combination of these events has generated concern about the economy's capacity to (1) overcome the stagflationary curse of simultaneous recession and inflation; (2) provide employment opportunities for an expanding labor force; and (3) generate income adequate to meet both the rising aspirations of individuals and the nation's many social objectives (Thurow 1980).

This industrial malaise has evoked a spate of calls for national policies that would revitalize the nation's economic base. Individual policies differ, but there are two major underlying themes. The first is the contention that many of the nations that are trade competitors of the United States actively subsidize the competitiveness of their products in international markets. Therefore, it is argued, the United States must implement comparable programs to offset these artificial advantages. The second contention is that traditional macroeconomic demand policies alone no longer represent adequate government management of the American economy; some form of direct intervention into the supply side of economic activity is required.

While there is some agreement concerning why industrial assistance policies are needed, consensus does not extend to the type of policies that should be implemented. The following four categories reflect the range of policies frequently advocated (Bendick 1981).

3

Industry-Neutral Approaches. One set of analysts, often called *supply-side* economists, advocate broad-scale policies designed to stimulate productivity in the private sector. Their proposals include a variety of tax incentives for savings and industrial investment, as well as reduction of regulatory and reporting requirements which are considered burdensome and costly to industry (Shapiro and White 1977). This approach in part corresponds to traditional American emphasis on creating a general climate of profitability and private investor confidence and does not involve particularized incentives or assistance targeted to specific industries.[1]

Cooperative Productivity-Enhancement Approaches. Adherents of this *social compact* approach seek to move beyond traditional adversarial relationships to establish cooperative commitment for industrial rejuvenation among business, labor, and government. For example, the new auto industry committee, composed of leaders from the major automotive firms, the United Auto Workers, and government regulatory agencies, is designed as a cooperative vehicle for planning a three-year recovery program for the industry. A similar tripartite committee for the economy as a whole was proposed by President Carter. He suggested a National Industries Board with chairmanship shared by the chairman of the board of the Dupont Corporation and the president of the AFL-CIO.

Industrial Bailout Approaches. Since the most visible signs of industrial distress are those of the rapid contraction—and in some cases, threatened bankruptcy—of several major American industrial corporations, it is not surprising that one major proposed approach to industrial aid is to provide direct government assistance to firms and industries in current distress. Extensive ad hoc federal financial underwriting of the Chrysler Corporation and the Lockheed Corporation through mechanisms such as loans and loan guarantees exemplify this approach, as does longer-term federal managerial assistance to reorganize bankrupt railroads (the Conrail Corporation).

Winner Industries Approaches. Perhaps the most controversial proposals for industrial policies are those which advocate that the federal government identify industries which are potential major loci of productivity gains, employment growth, and international competitiveness and then provide active financial (and other) backing to their development (Schwartz and Choate 1981). Japan is an overseas prototype for this approach. The Ministry of International Trade and Industry, the Ministry of Finance, the major banks, and the major industrial corporations work together under an explicit plan to develop certain industrial sectors for the sake of the nation's prosperity (Tresize 1976).

Whatever specific forms of industrial policy initiative are eventually adopted, one thing is clear from these myriad proposals: considerations of economic efficiency—of production costs, technological progress, market responsiveness, and profitability—have suddenly won a prominent place in national policy debates and have become criteria for judging government actions. Poverty suddenly became a public issue in 1964, as did energy a decade later. During the 1980s, *economic efficiency* will enjoy a similar priority in public policy.

Trade-offs with Subnational Development Objectives

While the primary considerations motivating industrial policy are those of economic efficiency, subnational economic development policies which focus on lagging regions or economically distressed central cities spring instead from consideration of equity. Typical criteria taken to indicate a need for local-economy concern have been low income, high unemployment rates, and high rates of out-migration. When economic efficiency has been used as a rationale for subnational development efforts, consideration has usually been restricted to underutilized and immobile resources, including public infrastructure investment such as schools and roads (Burggraf 1980). The more dominant theme is that public inducements to locate industrial plants in other than where the private market would dictate will detract from economic efficiency, but that the sacrifice is justified by equity gains.

This difference in motivation for the two types of programs generates two questions, each of which can be investigated empirically:

Does pursuit of either kind of policy typically imply significant trade-offs in terms of the aims of the other?

Could each type of policy be designed to support the aims of the other?

These questions are expressed pragmatically and programmatically in specific issues such as: Which industries should receive support? What kinds of firms should be supported within industries? What kind of aid should be supplied? Should support be devoted primarily to creating new economic activities and jobs or preventing the loss of those already in existence. By examining the patterns in which aid would be distributed under different sets of objectives, it is possible to demonstrate empirically that the problem of trade-offs is a serious one.

To do so, we utilize data from the 1972 Census of Manufactures for the twenty manufacturing industries distinguished at the two-digit level of aggregation in the Standard Industrial Classification (SIC).[2] To represent the efficiency-oriented goals of industrial policy, we use the percentage change in value added to an industry from 1967 to 1972 as an indicator;

industries experiencing large changes in added value were experiencing either large increases in productivity, rapid rises in the price per unit of their output, or rapid influxes of capital or labor. Hence, they are examples of growing industries where it might be economically efficient to place new investment. In contrast, to represent the equity-focused goals of subnational development policy, we use the average number of jobs associated with one million dollars of capital invested in the industry. Many of the industry-promotion instruments available to government are subsidies to capital, and this indicator represents the quantity of employment which might potentially be created by application of these instruments.

Table 1-1 indicates the effect, in terms of these two indicators, of targeting aid to the five industries which rank highest by each of the indicators. The set of five industries selected to maximize the percentage change in value added averaged a 55.1 percent change in value added over the period 1967 to 1972. In contrast, the set of five industries selected to maximize the number of jobs associated with each one million dollars of capital investment averaged only 40.8 percent on this same criterion, approximately one-quarter less. On the other hand, that latter set of five industries generated an average of sixty-one jobs per million dollars, while the former generated only twenty-four jobs per million dollars, a mere 39 percent of what the top five generated.[3]

This example illustrates in a dramatic way that the two types of goals—efficiency and equity—are not naturally compatible. Similar conflicts can easily be demonstrated between other potential proxies for goals, including highest average wages and highest expected permanence of created jobs (Garn and Ledebur 1980a, pp. 6-9).

Promotion of Small Enterprises

Recently, there has been interest in targeting at least some assistance to smaller firms. Rationales for doing so reflect the objectives of both industrial policy and locale-based development policy. In terms of equity oriented programs, the basis for this emphasis is the idea that small businesses are the primary generators of employment opportunities in the U.S. economy. This reflects recent estimates that "on average, about 60 percent of all jobs in the United States are generated by firms with twenty or fewer employees, and about 50 percent of all jobs are created by independent small entrepreneurs" (Birch 1979). It is also contended that small firms are responsible for a disproportionate share of new industrial technology, accounting for more than one-half of all industrial innovations (Committee on Small Business 1978; also Garn and Ledebur 1980b). The implication of this second rationale is that industrial policies that encourage innovation

Table 1-1
Economic-Development Performance of Groups of Industries, 1972

Economic-Development Criterion	Top Five Industries by That Criterion[a]	Average Percentage Change in Value Added, 1967–1972	Average Number of Jobs Associated with $1 Million in Invested Capital, 1972
Maximum growth of value added	Lumber and wood Instruments Transportation Tobacco products Electrical machinery	55.1	24
Maximum number of jobs associated with capital investment	Furniture Apparel Leather Miscellaneous Textiles	40.8	61

Source: Adapted from Garn and Ledebur (1980a), p. 29 and Buckrop (1979), p. 9. More detailed data are available in these documents.

[a]Industries are selected from among the twenty manufacturing industries identified by two-digit Standard Industrial Classification (SIC) codes.

and enhance productivity should perhaps be oriented to smaller firms. Might small business enterprises then serve as a point of congruence between the two sets of policies? This would be the case if those smaller firms generating high rates of employment growth were also characterized by high productivity or high rates of increase in productivity.

To test this proposition small firms (those with fewer than 100 employees) in two-digit manufacturing industries were ranked on the basis of economic performance on four criteria: employment associated with capital investment in 1972, average wage level in 1972, value added per employee in 1972, and change in value added per employee between 1967 and 1972. The generation of employment and wage levels are used as measures of locale-based development outcomes; value added and change in value added are used as measures of productivity and hence industrial policy outcomes.[4]

Table 1-2 presents lists of the five industries whose small firms ranked highest by each of these four criteria, along with their ranking on the other three criteria. A propitious outcome in the table would be if a set of industries emerged whose small firms contributed simultaneously to the objectives of both subnational development and industrial policy. However, table 1-2 reveals only a few such coincidences. The petroleum and chemical industries were unique in ranking among the top five industries on four and three criteria, respectively. Much more typical are the nine industries which each ranked among the top five on only one criterion. Correspondingly, the

Table 1-2
For Firms with Fewer than One Hundred Employees, Economic-Development Performance of Groups of Industries, 1972

Economic Development Criterion	Top Five Industries by That Criterion	Subnational Development Goals		Industrial Development Goals	
		Jobs Per Thousand Dollars of Investment, 1972	Average Wage, 1972	Value Added per Production Worker, 1972	Change in Value Added per Production Worker 1967–1972
Maximum number of jobs associated with capital investment	Stone, clay, and glass Apparel Leather Petroleum Furniture	3[a]	12	12	12
Highest average wage	Petroleum Nonelectrical machinery Chemicals Fabricated metals Instruments	10	3	5	9
Highest value added per production worker	Petroleum Chemicals Food Stone, clay, and glass Primary metals	12	6	3	7
Maximum growth of value added per production worker	Lumber and wood Food Petroleum Chemicals Paper	14	8	6	3

Source: Adapted from Garn and Ledebur (1980a), p. 13. More detailed data, including estimates of the magnitude of differences among groups, are reported there.

[a]Rank 1 = best, 20 = worst. Firms with ranks 1 to 5 have an average rank of 3.

average ranks of the industries on criteria other than the single criterion on which they were selected were quite low. For example, the first row of table 1–2 indicates that the five industries selected to maximize the number of jobs associated with capital investment ranked only an average of twelve among twenty industries on all three other criteria. This is even worse than the average rank of ten which would have been achieved were aid spread at random across all twenty industries.

Regional Gains and Losses

The third way in which conflicts between national industrial development and subnational development are revealed is in the patterns of regional distribution of federal resources. As is well known, industry is not distributed uniformly across regions in the United States. Nor does an industry perform identically in different regions (Garn and Ledebur 1980a; Schiller and McCarthy 1980). Nor do all firms within an industry experience growth or decline at the same time (Hall 1980). Therefore, a decision to aid any particular industry (or particular types of firms within that industry) carries within it an implicit decision to distribute federal resources differentially among regions.

To illustrate the complications introduced by such factors, the regional distribution of manufacturing establishments in 1969 and their changes between 1969 and 1975 (as calculated from Dunn and Bradstreet data) are shown in table 1–3. The table indicates that over that six-year period, the south and the west gained larger shares of all U.S. manufacturing establishments, while the shares of the northeast and north central regions declined. These shifts occurred largely through a rate of plant openings in the

Table 1–3
The Regional Distribution of Manufacturing Establishments, 1969–1975

Census Region	Percentage of Manufacturing Establishments, 1969	Percentage of Closures, 1969–1975	Percentage of Starts, 1969–1975	Percentage of Manufacturing Establishments, 1975
Northeast	31.6	32.8	24.1	29.1
North Central	28.1	27.2	24.6	27.4
South	23.6	24.7	26.5	24.1
West	16.7	15.3	24.8	19.5
U.S. total	100.0	100.0	100.0	100.1

Source: Adapted from Garn and Ledebur (1980a), p. 18.

west and the south which were higher than in the other two regions. Plant closures across regions occurred at rates approximately proportional to each regions' shares of all plants at the start of the period.

If past trends hold in the future, these data suggest that an economic development program that prevents plant closures will benefit the northeast and north central regions more than a policy which increases the rate of plant openings. In that case, the west and the south would benefit disproportionately. Political conflict over the geographical distribution of federal aid (sunbelt/frostbelt antagonisms, for example) would therefore arise to complicate an economic development policy selected on efficiency criteria alone.

Political Reactions to Conflicting Objectives

The presence of conflicting objectives and competing uses for government resources, of course, is not unique to economic development policies. The reactions of democratic governments to such conflicts are well-developed and highly predictable. Compromises are struck which disperse resources widely, recruiting more and more persons and organizations into a coalition of program support. One example of this process at work is provided by the history of the Economic Development Administration (EDA). When this agency was created in 1965, its stated purpose was to help seriously distressed local economies move toward the level of prosperity enjoyed by the majority of locales. By 1980, however, 79 percent of the U.S. population lived in areas designated eligible for EDA assistance. It is difficult to imagine that a U.S. industrial development program, no matter how narrowly focused on economic efficiency its original mandate, could resist a similar process. Equity claims of lagging regions; political considerations of putting resources into every senator's and congressman's district; political pressures to prevent the closure of existing plants and the loss of existing jobs, even if redeployment of capital and labor would be more efficient—all are likely to mitigate pure claims of long-term national growth in how resources would be distributed in a government industrial development program.

British experience with public economic development initiatives provides many illustrations of this process. A British economist recently concluded that in more democratic societies, goverment economic intervention is more likely to retard rather than enhance growth. Interest groups, having a more narrow focus than individual citizens, are able to consolidate their members' voices and therefore have more influence than the average citizen. As a result, decisions may be made to appease interest groups, rather than to serve the public interest. One example was the decision of Conservative Premier Harold Macmillan trying to resolve a conflict over the location of a steel mill between Scotland and Wales in the early 1960s. The resolution was to have two smaller, suboptimal mills, one in each area (Brittan 1978, p. 257).

One particular worrisome form which this tendency might take would be that of an industrial policy explicitly geared to *failing* industries. Such is, in fact, the goal of proposals for a so-called "reconstituted Reconstruction Finance Corporation" associated with Senator Edward Kennedy, investment banker Felix Rohatyn, and others. Government assistance to a firm or industry experiencing a *transitory* period of difficulties may be an economically-efficient use of resources. The problem is that it is difficult to distinguish between temporary trouble and permanent decline. Great Britain offers an example of the displacement of government industry-promotion activities toward industries suffering long-term decay. Despite the fact that the stated mission of the British National Industrial Development Board is to channel capital into promising growth sectors, its actual effect has been to divert such capital to nationalized industries—such as steel and shipbuilding—to maintain employment. This misdirection goes far to explain why Great Britain has devoted the same proportion of output to capital formation over recent years as had the United States and yet has achieved far less in productivity gains and market competitiveness from this investment. Between 1958 and 1972, the United Kingdom devoted 13 percent of total manufacturing value added to gross investment, while the United States allocated 12.2 percent. Yet the increase in net output per unit of investment in the United States was 145 percent that of Britain—and in Germany, it was 190 percent that of Britain (Brittan 1978, p. 249).

It would be misleading to imply that *no* government industrial development policies have been well-targeted in terms of economic profitability. The increase in net output per unit of investment between 1958 and 1972 in Japan was 157 percent that of Britain and yet, as mentioned earlier, industrial development capital in Japan goes where government planning decides it should. The majority of experience, however, is not favorable. And the more culturally and politically similar any country is to the United States, the less favorable the experience has been.

While it is possible that the United States could successfully imitate the Japanese model rather than the British one, caution should clearly temper expectations. The most likely prognosis is that channeling substantial industrial development capital through the public sector in the United States might lower, rather than raise, the average return on investment. That the investments might simultaneously promote other important public goals— including *equitable* subnational development—of course, remains true. But these other gains typically do not contribute to the basic objectives of efficiency, growth, and international competitiveness which are the wellsprings of industrial policy.

Pursuing Industrial Policy Goals through Subnational Development Programs

An alternative to expanding the flow of industrial development resources through the public sector would be to leave those resources in private hands through lower taxation. The private corporate and financial sectors are less hampered by political pressure and freer to pursue economic objectives more single-mindedly than is the public sector. To the degree that market competition disciplines private entrepreneurs, this line of reasoning asserts, then maximum economic efficiency is secure.

It would be naive, of course, to assume that such a textbook picture of the market system is a realistic portrait of modern American industrial economy. The vital discipline of market competition works far from perfectly, particularly between large corporations in oligopolistic industries (Galbraith 1971). Furthermore, large corporations, which account for a great proportion of all the jobs and incomes in the United States, are, from the point of view of long-term growth and technological innovation, often poorly managed (Hayes and Abernathy 1980). Nevertheless, it is difficult to imagine, in the empirically portrayed situation of conflicting multiple objectives, that the public sector could perform entrepreneurial functions (such as the identification and promotion of new growth industries) more effectively than the admittedly imperfect private market.

Thus, our conclusions are not supportive of proposals for highly industry-specific forms of national industrial policy.[5] However, our reasoning also suggests, ironically, that an increased emphasis on economic efficiency implies a need for an expanded role for equity-focused economic development programs. The heightened search for efficiency will inevitably increase the number of locales, workers, and firms who find themselves economically dislocated. If the persons and places adversely affected by industrial change are not compensated for their losses and reestablished in alternative economic opportunities, then they will bring political pressure to bear on government to halt the process of economic change. Recent appeals by the American automobile industry and automobile workers for tariff or quota protection against Japanese auto imports is one vivid example. Government action to retrain and reemploy workers, to provide extended unemployment compensation, and to provide inducements to firms to locate in economically distressed locales may thus not only promote equity; they may also be prerequisite to the search for efficiency which will be conducted throughout the 1980s.

Notes

1. These approaches are labeled *industry-neutral* to indicate that the government does not preselect recipient industries. Programs such as tax

incentives for capital formation are obviously not industry-neutral in their effects.

2. These aggregated data are acceptable for heuristic illustration of potential trade-offs; for policymaking, greater levels of industry detail (for example, three of four digit SIC codes) and more recent data would be of great importance.

3. Data on the change in value added is from Buckrop (1979), p. 9. Data on employment changes is from Garn and Ledebur (1980a), p. 29. The job creation estimates represent gross job creation minus estimated job losses due to future plant closures.

4. Of course, we would like to have *marginal* values for each of these measures. Data limitations force us to report *average* values instead.

5. Various *industry-neutral* forms of industrial policy (for example, tax incentives for industrial capital formation or research and development), which are not discussed in this chapter, may also be useful governmental actions.

References

Bendick, Marc, Jr. *A Federal Entrepreneur? Industrial Policy and American Economic Revitalization.* Washington, D.C.: The Urban Institute, 1981.

Birch, David. *The Job Generation Process.* Cambridge, Mass.: MIT Program on Neighborhood and Regional Change, 1979.

Brittan, Samuel. "How British Is the British Sickness?" *Journal of Law and Economics* (October 1978):245–268.

Buckrop, Deborah L. *Classification of Two-Digit Manufacturing Industries on the Basis of Performance Characteristics.* Washington, D.C.: The Urban Institute, 1979.

Burggraf, Shirley. *The Spatial Dimensions of Supply Economics with Energy as an Object Case.* Washington, D.C.: Economic Development Administration, 1980.

Committee on Small Business. *Underutilization of Small Business in the Nation's Effort to Encourage Industrial Innovations.* Washington, D.C.: U.S. House of Representatives, 1978.

Denison, Edward F. "Explanations of Declining Productivity Growth." *Survey of Current Business* 59 (August 1979):1–24.

Galbraith, John Kenneth. *The New Industrial State.* Boston: Houghton Mifflin, 1971.

Garn, Harvey A., and Larry C. Ledebur. *Congruencies and Conflicts in Regional and Industry Policy.* Washington, D.C.: The Urban Institute, 1980a.

———. *The Role of Small Business Enterprise in Economic Development.* Washington, D.C.: The Urban Institute, 1980b.

Hall, William K. "Survival Strategies in a Hostile Environment." *Harvard Business Review* (September-October 1980):75–85.

Hayes, Robert H., and William J. Abernathy. "Managing our Way to Economic Decline." *Harvard Business Review* (July-August 1980):67–77.

Kendrick, J.W. "Productivity Trends and the Recent Slowdown." In *Contemporary Economic Problems,* pp. 17–70. Edited by William Fellner. Washington, D.C.: American Enterprise Institute, 1979.

Norsworthy, J.R.; M.J. Harper; and K. Kunze. "The Slowdown in Productivity Growth: An Analysis of Some Contributing Factors." *Brookings Paper on Economic Activity* 2 (1979):387–421.

Schiller, Bradley R., and Amy A. McCarthy. *Subnational Variations and Industrial Growth.* Washington, D.C.: Economic Development Administration, 1980.

Schwartz, Gail, and Pat Choate. *Being Number One: Rebuilding the U.S. Economy.* Lexington, Mass.: Lexington Books, D.C. Heath and Company, 1980.

Shapiro, Eli, and William L. White, editors. *Capital for Productivity and Jobs.* Englewood Cliffs: Prentice-Hall, 1977.

Tatom, John A. "The Productivity Problem." *Federal Reserve Bank of St. Louis Review* (September 1979):3–16.

Tresize, Philip. "Politics, Government, and Economic Growth in Japan." In *Asia's New Giant: How the Japanese Economy Works,* pp. 753–812. Edited by Hugh Patrick and Henry Rosovsky. Washington, D.C.: The The Brookings Institution, 1976.

Thurow, Lester, C. *The Zero-Sum Society.* New York: Basic Books, 1980.

2

Social-Cost Minimization: A National-Policy Approach to the Problems of Distressed Economic Regions

Elliott D. Sclar

Toward a New Approach to Economic Policy

Gross National Product (GNP) is the total value of all goods and services produced for sale or sold in the economy in some period of time (usually a year). The fundamental assumption which underlies present national economic policy is that the greater the GNP, the greater our ability to provide for the well-being of all members of society. There are two serious drawbacks to this view.

The first pertains to the technique of measurement. The calculation of GNP makes no distinction between goods which make an overall net contribution to our well-being and those which minimize the damage of the ongoing social enterprise. For example, a new automobile rolling off the Detroit assembly line is added into the GNP. If the owner of the new vehicle should drive it out of the showroom into a telephone pole, the medical bills for the injury, the cost of repairing the vehicle, and expense of replacing the telephone pole are also added into GNP. Hence it is only as a first crude approximation that we can say that more GNP is better than less. As a result of such valuation problems many observers have felt it necessary to take a far more disaggregated view of the benefits and costs of the various activities which comprise GNP. This is to determine whether we are the better or the worse for any increase in aggregate output.[1]

This first drawback is not by itself serious enough to undermine the existing approach to economic policy. All that is needed is a more sophisticated and comprehensive measurement technique capable of more clearly valuing the social welfare. A more fundamental difficulty pertains to the

Support for this chapter came from Grant #R01-12H32871 from th · Center for the Study of Metropolitan Problems of the National Institute of Mental Health. The author wishes to acknowledge the help of Thomas Angotti and Peter Marcuse who read and commented on an earlier draft of this paper. Needless to say, any errors that remain are mine.

process by which the output is produced. It is to a discussion of that second drawback that this chapter is devoted.

This chapter argues that many of our most severe social and economic problems are caused by the market's inability to correctly evaluate the benefits and costs to society of various economic undertakings, principally those of a private nature. As a result, present economic policy that heavily emphasizes output maximization, is leading to decreased rather than improved social welfare. If we wish to alleviate this problem, then the emphasis of economic policy must be shifted from one solely concerned with output maximization. The minimization of social cost must be seen as a separate but ultimately equally important factor in policy development. Furthermore, until there are structural changes in the operation of the economy which permit a more positive role for national economic planning, cost minimization must be given far greater weight than output maximization in the decision calculus.

In an ideal neoclassical world, the distinction between output maximization and cost minimization would disappear.[2] For it would be prima facia the case that to efficiently produce maximum output would at the same time minimize the cost of that production. But we are far from such an ideal situation. Those individuals and groups capturing the benefits from increased output and those bearing the costs are more often than not, distinct and separate. As a result more output does not, in and of itself, mean a socially improved situation.

It is frequently argued by defenders of the present output maximizing approach that even this second drawback is not necessarily a fatal flaw. All that need be done is to institute a set of social and economic policies which can be used to effect a redistribution of output from those enjoying the gains to those suffering the losses. Even in the best of political times it was difficult to make any real progress in attaining these goals. This is hardly the best of times.

Implicit in a policy of redistribution is the assumption that real economic growth is occurring. Economic growth is the grease that lubricates and smoothes transactions in our political economy. If the size of the economic pie is expanding it is politically possible to tinker with relative shares because absolute consumption can be left unchanged. On the other hand, when the pie is expanding, the impetus to adjust relative shares is greatly diminished as absolute shares are also rising. However, at present, no significant real economic growth is occurring. As a result, attempts to use policy to adjust the distribution of output are bound to fail. It is essentially the case then that any attempt to redress the balance must focus upon the processes by which we organize ourselves to create economic goods and services. In that sense, social cost minimization is an attempt at making economic policy more supply-side oriented.

Costs and the Private Economy

The need to look at economic activity in terms of the distribution of costs and benefits takes on special importance when we consider the plight of the nation's spatially distinct regions and communities in which economic distress becomes manifest. In them we find unemployment, social and health problems, and the deterioration of both the natural and man-made environment. The key to understanding the spatial effect of the economy's operation is to understand the spatial operation of the microeconomic units that generate economic activity in a private enterprise economy: firms. Firms are the active element through which the actual expansion or contraction of economic activity in a particular time and place is accomplished.

Firms organize production factors for goods and services slated for either further production or final consumption. Private profit is the motivating force that shapes the decision of firms to undertake productive activity as well as guides the selection of products and production techniques. While this motivation has not changed in the more than two centuries since the industrial revolution, the size and scale of firm operations have changed markedly. It is these changed size and scale factors that have important ramifications for the people living in the spatially distinct regions and communities where large firms are active. To illustrate let us consider the process of plant relocation.

The argument for moving economic activity from one plant in one place to another in a different place rests upon the contribution that such a decision will make to the firm's balance sheet. It is plausible to assume that a decision to relocate a plant from region A to region B will be made if it appears to improve profitability. It is also plausible to assume that such a decision will increase output of the firm's product and produce a series of development benefits in region B. However, in light of the potential personal and economic damage left behind in region A, it is not at all apparent that the total benefits of the move (private + social) equal, let alone exceed, the total costs (private + social). In this case it could be argued that less output and profits for a particular firm are preferable to more, when given the larger social context.

If the case for relatively unhampered private control of economic decision making rests upon the assumption that it is in the end, socially beneficial then the preceding example has major implications for altering the role of profits and markets in this process. It is the conventional wisdom that the profit incentive operating through a system of *competitive* markets leads to output and pricing decisions that not only give consumers what they want but also conserve on scarce resources by forcing judicious use. The line of argument developing here strongly implies that this view is not necessarily true.

Let us begin by considering the question of the efficacy of markets as mechanisms for equating costs and benefits of economic activity in a socially desirable manner.[3] For a market to function in such a manner, there are two conditions that it must fulfill; it must be competitive and the externalities that it generates must be, by and large, trivial. According to standard neoclassical theory, for a market to be considered competitive it must be one to which both buyers and sellers have reasonably easy access; it must be comprised of a sufficiently large number of buyers and sellers that none can, by their individual action, appreciably affect the pricing and output decisions of that market; it must be one in which all relevant information about product and price are well known to both buyers and sellers; and it must be a market for a reasonably homogeneous product; that is a product that is interchangeable among different sellers (different brands of soap powder, for example).

The assumption that competitive markets are typical of the American economy is not justified by the available evidence.[4] Competitive markets have effectively disappeared in all but a few isolated instances. These instances are not sufficient to create an effectively competitive market-based economy. The size and scale factors that have caused firm size to grow has meant a decline in the number of sellers in most markets, greater difficulty of entry for potential competitors, loss of relevant product and price information for buyers or high cost to obtain information, and attempts to make easy substitution of similar products more difficult. Taken together these factors have led to the type of market structure characterized as *oligopolistic* and *monopolistic.*

There are three characteristics most typical of such markets: interdependence among sellers, higher prices, and less output than under a competitive market regime. Interdependence is evidenced by the fact that sellers consider other's price and output decisions when calculating their own. This phenomenon typically shows itself in the price leadership characteristic of oligopolistic industries such as steel and automobile manufacturing. In these industries, a price rise is first announced by one firm. Unless there is a severe miscalculation, it is usually followed by comparable price rises among the other sellers in that market. If the price change is too large or too small the move by other sellers will force the price leader to revise his strategy and to bring it into line with the industry-wide wisdom.

Given the ability to act in a concerted manner in pricing and output decisions, oligopolistic and monopolistic firms will use that power to insure the greatest amount of profits possible for the industry and its individual members.[5] This usually means keeping output below that of competitive markets so as to maintain prices higher in relation to costs, the net effect of which will be to keep profit margins high. Once administered prices become the rule, prices can no longer claim the same virtues as part of the social decision making process.

The second condition affecting the operation of markets is the degree to which outcomes resulting from the action of buyers and sellers within a particular market are excluded from effective marketplace consideration. Such outcomes are called external economies (benefits) and diseconomies (costs). Industrial pollution of air and water is the most commonplace example of an external diseconomy. If firms are permitted to dump waste materials in the air and water, they are in effect passing a cost on to the general public that does not show up in the price of the product to the buyer. Similarly, if the result of locating a plant in a particular community is to cause commerce in general to increase, that would be an external economy that is not accounted for in writing.

The ideal of a self-regulating competitive market economy originates with the industrial revolution. The reality, however, of that history is that such a situation has never existed. A principle reason for this can be found in the scale economies which the industrialization process itself created.[6] The key to understanding this argument is to consider the fact that scale economies are generated through increasing division of labor and specialization. Such increased specialization in turn creates increased interdependency among the various members of the population. This situation is further accentuated by the scale economies and specializations added by the concomitant process of urbanization. The results of the higher spatial living densities are such that even lifestyle considerations, such as loud stereos or safety on the streets, affect us.

When external effects are large in number and impact, it is difficult to argue that the marketplace considerations of price and output sufficiently account for all the relevant impacts of economic activity. Furthermore, when those effects are accounted for in markets where administered prices are more reflective of economic power than scarcity considerations, it is that much more difficult to defend a conventional wisdom that argues for the sanctity of market decisions as the measure of social well-being. In terms of distressed communities and individuals, the implication is that more individual well-being may be achieved if less emphasis is placed on the marketplace as decision maker.

This can perhaps be seen more clearly if we consider the role of profits in this economic system, with special regard to their impact upon local communities. Profits play a unique and vital role in a market-oriented economic system. They are the signal that a particular undertaking or activity ought to be done and are also the reward for successfully undertaking that economic activity. To the extent that profits are generated by a market-oriented economy in which the regime of competition, as previously described, is in control and in which externalities are either nonexistent or highly limited, profits can serve to channel activity into socially beneficial paths. This is the case because competition insures that all factors of production are working as efficiently as possible and earning no more than a reasonable rate of return on effort. High profits signal an unexploited opportunity by way of a more efficient production process or new commodity. Resources move to expand use of the new more efficient production process or satisfy the new commodity market. In the process, the high profits dissipate and are reduced to the more general rate of return on effort.

If oligopolistic and monopolistic market power predominates and many externalities abound from marketplace activity, it can no longer be said that profits signal fulfillment of any kind of socially beneficial goal. Rather profits measure the degree to which oligopolistic producers are able to extract a scarcity rent from their activity through the use of economic power. In which case it is no longer possible to prima facia impute social worthiness to activity generated in pursuit of high profits. High profits increasingly come to mean no more than high incomes for their owners, not social progress.

Given the degree to which interdependence abounds in modern society, it is increasingly the case that industry relies on the public sector to provide order for its various undertakings. Consequently, profits increasingly measure the degree to which private interests can manipulate governmental tax, expenditure, and regulatory policy rather than success in marketplace competition. It is frequently the case that profits measure the degree to which any group can through the political process foist costs on other groups. This behavior has a powerful motivation that is rooted in the firm's profit maximizing behavior. In order to increase profit, it is rational for a firm to socialize costs and privately capture gains to the fullest extent possible. The confluence of this behavior within the firm, with the increasingly political nature of profit making, makes the private economic process even more suspect as an allocator of society's precious material resources.

If it is the case that the vital social accounting functions of benefits and costs, once assumed to underlie the private calculus of profits and losses, has all but vanished, then it follows that society must consciously develop new methods for evaluating the implications of economic activity. I would argue that central to any new scheme for deciding upon economic activity must be concern with the quality of life in local communities. Because of the vital connection between employment and well-being, enormous public expenditures for health and social services are functionally related to private decisions about capital investment.[7] Therefore, any attempt to supplant marketplace decisions must include considerations of social cost. This means that it is necessary to go beyond the type of aggregative economic policy characteristic of the 1960s and 1970s that attempted to maximize growth of GNP at stable prices through fiscal and monetary policy.[8] Policy must change in two major ways: a shift of emphasis from output maximization to cost minimization and a shift from aggregative to community specific policies, particularly in the area of investment decisions that affect a community's economic base. A policy of social cost minimization by its very nature takes a more long-term view of social welfare than does output maximization. The argument would be that by conserving and improving our social resources we will, over time, improve individual well-being far more than if we increased short-term output through the market. I would argue that such social cost minimization policy, with its emphasis on community stability, is more likely to produce higher levels of material output over the long-run than the present short-term emphasis on output maximization. Only by such a shift in emphasis will it be possible to have an economy that enriches the material conditions of people without destroying their physical and spiritual well-being.

Social-Cost-Minimizing Economic Development

A healthy interactive economic and social development process is self-sustaining; economic change contributes to social vitality and social vitality enhances economic prospects. The present pattern based on market-oriented critera of profit maximization is *not* that type of process. It is one frequently characterized by serious social and economic losses to communities of people. If these losses are to be relieved, it is necessary that they be recognized in the economic and social development process. Social-cost-minimizing economic development proposes to do that by broadening the criteria by which economic development is evaluated.

First, profitability and output maximization must be devalued as criteria for economic decision making, and social cost minimization must play a larger role. It is not that profits and output should be ignored but they must not be accorded a higher weight than the costs which economic activity also entails. This is especially true when these costs remain external to market-oriented decision processes. That means that the proper social accounting mechanism must be public decision-making bodies that will clearly understand the purpose of economic activity and measures. Then such bodies place all the relevant considerations in perspective.

The goal of economic policy should be to foster a development process in which the community's resource base—people—is continually enhanced. This will mean, for example, that the profit-maximizing decisions of a particular firm must be weighed against their impact upon the various communities so effected. If the gains are outweighed by costs that the enterprise is unwilling or unable to pay, its ability to act must be limited. In the end, it is human development that is the justification for economic development. If such development cannot be assured, or worse, impaired by private investment decisions, there is no good reason to permit them to go forward.

An alternative that can lessen the need for extensive public regulation of the market economy is to create ownership structures that marry the social interests of the community to the economic ones of the enterprise. Such a marriage implies that a self-regulating mechanism exists which cannot only ensure that the economic activity of the enterprise does not harm the community but also guarantees that the profits are available for community use.

There are a number of ways to achieve this, including joint community corporate ventures, community development corporations, and outright public ownership. The criteria for such selections is complex and not germane to this discussion. The point, however, is that such vehicles exist and are a necessary element in any healthy economic development process.

To the extent that human development is the goal, individuals must not only share in the process as members of a community who enjoy more consumer goods, but they must also benefit, as producers, for having made the effort. This means that work must be organized to be mentally and physically safe and it must improve, not diminish, skills. Work must be seen as both a production and a development process for community members. This may mean job rotation or job creating ladders both of which allow workers to continually expand their respective repertoires of skill.

This process is important to the long-term well-being of the community. The more diversified its repertoire of skills the better able it is to adapt to changing economic opportunity over time. Individuals will also be better able to face the future more confident in their ability to accept new situations.

Skill enhancement in operation will also effectively allow for increased worker control over the production process. This is an important complement to the described modified ownership structures. Unless internal work hierarchies are diminished, there is much evidence to demonstrate that altering ownership patterns quickly degenerate into changes of form rather than substance.[9]

The second criterion for healthy development is stable social networks. Such networks are important because they provide a context in which people can live with a sense of their own worth in the world as well as with a source of nurturance and support with which to face life's uncertainties. A major characteristic of output-oriented, profit-maximizing development is that it frequently destroys these networks.[10] In a sense, this second criterion is a derivative of the first. If economic development is such that it creates more community and worker control over the economic process, then, it can be argued, stable social networks will begin to emerge as people settle into more economically secure lives. However, it is the case that creating such networks is also an independent part of a good development policy. This means that economic development must not just create jobs which are intrinsically good but jobs which help the social networks of a community to take root and thrive.

Political Conclusions from Economic Observations

The ideas presented here are not really new. If I make any claim to originality, it is in the juxtaposition of these thoughts and their application to the present plight of local communities. If the reader finds them intrinsically worthy of consideration, that then raises an important political question. If the proposal is clearly reasonable, and has been around in some shape or form for quite a while, why, then, is it the case that it enjoys such little acceptance?[11] The answer is, of course, that ideas, whether good or bad, do not exist in a vacuum devoid of social context. Unless there is a political movement that can give them life, neither their reasonableness nor ability will have any implementation. On the other hand, political movements cannot exist without visions and programs.

It is therefore fitting that this chapter close with a political observation. It is my impression that, in recent years, the degree of regional chauvinism has markedly increased in this country. This should not be surprising given that regionally footloose multinational corporations have been able to exercise effective control over regional resources by threatening to move capital. Regions are vying more and more with one another in a new game of economic mercantilism—each region tries to import jobs and capital from other regions and export its unemployment to those regions. As the economy has increasingly become a no-growth one, this new mercantilism has degenerated into a deadly zero-sum game.[12] No one is prepared to give up anything. One result of this process is manifest in federal legislative and executive inaction in the face of growing unemployment, inflation, and energy problems.[13] Any real change would mean costs to groups unable to impose new policy but strong enough to veto change.

The most hopeful signs that we may develop the effective political will to overcome this inaction also rests at the regional and local level. It can be found in the array of grass roots efforts to thwart plant closings, create worker and community enterprises, develop safe energy, mass transportation, low and moderate income housing and so on. The danger in these efforts are twofold. First, they may fail; a prima facie disaster. Secondly, they may succeed; a more subtle dilemma.

The dilemma of success rests upon the fact that in the absence of a larger political movement that can link local action with national directions, it is easy to envision local groups moving to protect local gains and being coopted by a combination of the new mercantilism and old style regional chauvinism. It is therefore important that as we move ahead with local activity, we also develop a national political movement which creates a vision and program for democratic national economic planning.

Democratic national economic planning strives to create spatial and social equity and balance throughout the process of national economic growth and change. It must also be a type of planning that allows for a broad range of individual initiatives and innovations. While an exact American model of such planning is yet to be created, there are enough lessons and examples from around the world to suggest that such an approach is workable and that we should begin our articulation process. To do less is to jeopardize all the exciting grass roots initiatives.

Notes

1. For a brief discussion of this literature see Heilbroner and Thurow, 1978, p. 340.

2. An ideal neoclassical world is one in which the conditions for perfect competition (discussed below in detail) prevail. In such a world all the important costs and benefits of any economic activity would be almost or completely accounted for in the prices and outputs generated by market transactions. Hence costs and benefits would be as two sides of a single coin. For a complete discussion of this view of economic reality see any standard introductory economics textbook of U.S. origin.

3. The term *socially desirable* as used here refers to the extent to which the observed economic activity fulfills the precepts of neoclassical optimality; namely that resources are being efficiently used and that no one's situation is made worse in the process of another's gain.

4. For a fuller discussion of this point, see Galbraith, 1967.

5. See Baran and Sweezy, 1966.

6. Economies of scale come into being when it is possible to lower the *per unit* cost of production by expanding output. In general, this situation has been obtained in those cases where it is possible to highly mechanize an operation. Such an investment in large fixed plant is economic if the market can absorb a large output. As a result, scale economies have led to a situation in which the benefits of production are shared by consumers and (the fewer) large producers in control of the market. For a more complete discussion of this point see Young, 1928.

7. See for example, Brenner, 1976.

8. The term *aggregative economic policy* refers to the previously described GNP maximizing policy which fails to take into account the crudeness of such a measure as a reflection of social welfare. It is not concerned with shaping the process where gainers and losers are created both interpersonally and interregionally.

9. See Hunnius, Garson, and Case, 1973.

10. I have argued elsewhere (Sclar 1980), that the lack of such networks generates many of the health and social problems which are the social costs of inadequate development. Consequently, measurement of the incidence of those problems, over time, can be an excellent policy-related indicator of the economic development process.

11. The reader should bear in mind that the idea implicit in this chapter is that *more* public role in economic decision-making is preferable to the present situation. On the other hand, the current liberal/conservative debate assumes that *less* is desirable; controversy merely focuses on how to reduce the public role.

12. See Thurow, 1980.

13. *Ibid.*

References

Baran, Paul and Paul Sweezy. *Monopoly Capital.* New York: Monthly Review Press, 1966.

Brenner, M. Harvey. *Estimating the Social Costs of National Economic Policy, Implications for Mental and Physical Health and Criminal Aggression.* Joint Economic Committee, Congress of the United States, 1976.

Galbraith, John Kenneth. *The New Industrial State.* Boston: Houghton Mifflin Co., 1967.

Heilbroner, Robert L. and Lester C. Thurow. *The Economic Problem,* Fifth Edition. Englewood Cliffs, N.J. Prentice-Hall Inc., 1978.

Hunnius, Gerry, G.; David Garson; and John Case, eds. *Workers Control: A Reader on Labor and Social Change.* New York: Wingate Books, 1973.

Sclar, Elliott D. "Community Economic Structure and Individual Well Being." *International Journal of Health Services* 10, no. 14, (October 1980):563–579.

Thurow, Lester C. *The Zero-Sum Society: Distribution and the Possibilities for Economic Change.* New York: Basic Books, 1980.

Young, Allyn A. "Increasing Returns and Economic Progress." *Economic Journal* 38 (December 1928):527–542.

3

The Case against Bailing Out Distressed Areas

Martin T. Katzman

Introduction

Should American society attempt to help distressed areas achieve what are considered decent levels of income and welfare? Such a question can be raised as a matter of philosophical principle or practical politics.

On the philosophical level, the question is one of defining the proper role of the democratic state toward the spatial allocation of resources and distribution of welfare. Ought government have obligations toward places other than to the people who inhabit them? Are places entitled to prosperity, however it is defined?

Economists generally view the welfare of individuals (or families) as the ultimate entity of concern and the welfare of places as mere instruments. Improving individual welfare by targeting policies towards places is seen, at best, as inefficient and, at worst, as parochial pleading for a public subsidy. According to this view, the only proper regional policy should be aimed at correcting distortions in the market created by well-meaning but ill-founded public policy, or by special interest legislation.

Obviously, policy is not made by philosopher/kings in isolation but by the interplay of interest groups, through a process of *partisan mutual adjustment.* In the case of regional policy, coalitions from areas of distress partake of conventional horsetrading. Their success also depends upon first persuading opinion makers, such as the media and intellectuals, and then through them, the electorate that the coalitions' concerns are expressions of the general interest. In pressing for special funding for urban pockets of poverty, big-city mayors have an incentive to create the image that these fiscal and economic problems are caused by forces beyond their control. The mayors may blame the federal government or selfish businessmen, but not their less than wholehearted devotion to the efficient provision of services or policies that encourage business. Furthermore, these public officials must persuade the general electorate that the solution of the particular problem will be of broad benefit.

The author is grateful for the support of the John Solomon Guggenheim Memorial Foundation for a broader study of population change in America. The arguments in this chapter do not reflect the position of the Council for Northeast Economic Action, for whom the author analyzed the cited capital market survey.

This chapter takes the position that while there is a proper role for government in spatial aspects of resource allocation, the political system will not allow government to perform this role with any workable degree of efficiency or equity. Moreover, in an economy plagued by low rates of capital formation and sluggish productivity gains, pressures to rescue unprofitable industries and locations should be resisted vigorously.

The Proper Role for Regional Policy

Economists identify where public intervention in the free market is justified: when individuals or families—not institutions such as municipal or profit-making corporations—benefit.

One legitimate role of government is to improve the distribution of income generated by the private market. This distribution of income, resulting from a complex of structural and individual characteristics, may deviate from what the majority considers decent. Both law and economics hold that equals should be treated equally by the state (although defining who are equals is no simple task), but that unequals may be treated unequally. The progressive income tax, for example, espouses the widely-held belief that households classified by income should be treated unequally, higher-income households being taxed at a higher proportional rate. Other classes of individuals are labeled for special treatment, such as veterans, the elderly, and the handicapped. In the employment arena, particular ethnic minorities and women are so defined for affirmative action purposes. In the arena of school finance, the Supreme Court held that individuals who reside in a common, low-wealth jurisdiction did not constitute a *suspect classification,* meriting redress. Thus, children living in such districts were not entitled to special compensatory measures, even though low wealth resulted in lower levels of public school expenditures. In most states, however, the courts have ruled that children living in poor areas were entitled to such compensation. The winning argument, however, has pressed the claims of people, not places. Indeed, there is evidence that many of the people living in low-wealth districts are advantaged by other criteria, such as race or income, and that many poor, minority children live in high-wealth districts. Property wealth per child is not a totally arbitrary indicator since it influences the collective fate of children in a school district.[1]

The concentration of poor people in a distressed area does not imply that income should be redistributed to that area's governments or industries. For working people in distressed areas, poverty may be a result of employment in relatively low-productive sectors. Perhaps this can be alleviated by encouraging their migration to sectors of higher productivity. Indeed, the spontaneous long-term movement from agriculture to industry in the first half of this century was a spatial movement, from countryside to metropolitan areas. Past public efforts to subsidize agriculture (and forestall such a migration) was at the expense of productivity gains to the overall economy and to the disadvantage of the poor. Education and training is another policy for improving the productivity of the working-age population, who might leave the distressed area. As indicated, most states, as well as the federal government, have enacted programs that reduce the disadvantages poor areas have in funding primary and secondary school education.

For those who are immobilized by age and infirmity, direct income transfers of services (such as food stamps or health care) and income are more effective than area economic development strategies. The non-working population is unlikely to derive much benefit from programs that create jobs.

A somewhat stronger case for area aid is made by the poverty problem of segregated minorities in metropolitan areas. After all, access to jobs is limited by racial discrimination. As discussed, area targeting is likely to miss many of the poor and to include many non-poor in its benefits. Direct aid to poor individuals is, again, more efficient.

Three other arguments in favor of governmental intervention concern the allocation of resources. The first case refers to the production of collective goods, which cannot easily be rationed by the price mechanism. A good example in the regional arena is the Alaska wilderness. It would be difficult to conceive of a workable market mechanism that would enable us to express our preferences for a virgin area that most of us will see only in pictures. The preservation of parts of that area, not unlike the Grand Canyon, are of intangible, but no less real, benefit to all Americans.

Public officials from distressed areas would like to persuade the general public to support distressed-area development in the same way that it would support preservation of areas like the Grand Canyon. Such a case can surely be made for the physical preservation of certain historic buildings or small neighborhoods, which by virtue of their designation, enjoy certain tax exemptions. However, extending such advantages to acres of obsolete or poorly located structures, whose members are engaged in low-productivity enterprises, goes far beyond sensitivity to our historic heritage. It is barely disguised special pleading.

A second case where the government must supersede the unfettered market refers to external economies and diseconomies. Decisions by upstream municipalities and industries to dump effluent in the river affects the health of residents downstream. The sectoral policy of controlling pollution may have regional implications, if industries are driven to parts of this country (or abroad) where the restraints are less severe. An example of an external economy is the provision of basic elementary and secondary education by one state to residents who might emigrate to another, such as the rural blacks in the 1950s and 1960s. The influx of unskilled labor into northern cities has been the source of much of the cities' fiscal distress. Federal aid to education and training improves the human resources of distressed areas in situ. While efficient in targeting the aid to individuals, federal aid to education is not really aimed at aiding distressed areas. Those newly trained as the result of a federal program may leave the distressed area for better employment elsewhere.[2]

Third, distortions in the market caused by monopolies or by government itself may have to be corrected by other interventions. This *theory of the second best* has considerable application to distressed areas. Moes identifies a major reason why the southeast remained impoverished and a source of migrants from the rest of the country: it was restricted in its ability to sell its most abundant commodity—unskilled labor—at a low price. Cheap labor should have attracted an influx of capital that, in the long-run would have resulted in industrialization and higher wages. Moes argues that prior to the 1950s, federal minimum wage laws and nationwide union agreements in well-paying industries discouraged industry from moving south. An auto plant in South Carolina would have to pay the same wages as one in Detroit. Instead of capital moving south, labor moved north and west. Southern states and cities responded by attempting to provide capital and tax subsidies, which, as noted, are not particularly effective. Lack of jobs and capital in distressed areas today may also result from similar rigidities in the labor market.[3]

Policymakers in the United States have generally not found these justifications compelling enough to enact a systematic area-development strategy. Among the industrial nations of the world, the United States pursues area development with the least clarity of purpose and level of funding. Although policies of consequence were pursued when the railroads were built, in the twentieth century the federal government has done little, outside the Tennessee Valley Authority, to consciously promote area development. This is not to say that regional interests in the pursuit of the pork-barrel have been insignificant or that sectoral policies have not had regional consequences. Indeed, many of the problems of distressed areas can be traced to inadequate sectoral policies. There are many examples of sectoral policies that have effected regions unevenly.

> Irrigation projects of the Bureau of Reclamation in the west have accelerated the decline of agriculture in the humid southeast, and hence the rural immigration to northern cities in the 1960s.

> Regulated railroad rates that discriminate in favor of raw materials and against processed materials encourage mining in rural areas, and discourage recycling in urban areas.

Minimum wage laws have historically slowed down the industrial expansion of the southeast and currently reduce the employment opportunities of minority youth, who are disproportionately concentrated in cities.

Poorly funded elementary and secondary education for blacks in the south prior to the 1960s resulted in relatively low levels of marketable skills among migrants and their children to northern cities.

The pursuit of policies by distressed areas have played no small role in their problems. Distressed cities in the northeast have traditionally provided a wider range of services than sunbelt cities. The difference between the two groups of cities is attributed to greater efforts at income redistribution in favor of the poor. Partially reflecting the income-redistributive motives, more employees are required to perform given tasks in northern rather than in sunbelt municipalities. Effective income redistribution is difficult in northern cities because unsympathetic legislatures prohibit them from annexing growing areas on the suburban fringe. While most of the northeastern and midwestern cities have been frozen in their turn-of-the-century boundaries, most sunbelt cities have been able to incorporate the growing tax base on the fringe. Under the circumstances, income redistribution on the part of confined northern cities is self-defeating. It merely attracts more poor and repels the middle class.[4]

The Near-Impossibility of Accurate Targeting

What would an efficient regional policy look like? Under the ideal state of affairs, Congress would establish the goal of improving the average income in areas with a disproportion of deprived individuals. It would establish criteria that would enable the bureaucracy to unambiguously rank areas by magnitude of distress and allocate the available subsidies in that order. These subsidies might take the form of direct federal expenditures on public works, business or homeowner loans, loan guarantees, or intergovernmental transfers. These programs would be targeted so that as many distressed individuals as possible would be direct or indirect beneficiaries of the policy, with a minimal number of undeserving individuals benefiting.

There is little reason to believe that such a well-honed regional policy could be legislated, much less implemented. In fact, there is too much experience to the contrary. Since the criteria for defining distress determine each congressional district's eligibility for aid, such a process becomes highly politicized. The pressures to expand the charmed circle of *privileged misery* are great. For example, the original intention of President Kennedy to revitalize the depressed mining areas of West Virginia was diluted by the concept of an Appalachia extending from New York State to Alabama. As the Area Development Agency was superseded by the Economic Development Administration, the pressures to change the criteria for distress resulted in including about half the population in eligible areas. President Carter's urban and regional policy proposals of 1978 make areas with about 50 percent of the population eligible for aid. Attempts in the 1960s to concentrate Federal aid in a few *model cities* with extreme distress were followed by the dilution of the program when it extended to more than 100 cities.

A second reason that targeting is diluted is the inability and unwillingness of policymakers to articulate clear-cut criteria for selecting projects within eligible areas and evaluating their success. This is because pork-barrel-cum-redistributive ends are intertwined with trying to make better use of human and capital resources. Usually, an incredible potpourri of factors are considered in project selection, such as minority entrepreneurship, application of high technology, and creation of employment. Projects that are economically unprofitable are generally excluded from consideration. However, projects with the greatest economic profitability are not automatically selected. In other words, economic profitability is a constraint not the maxima in project selection. Additional banking criteria, such as adequate security for debt or low debt-equity ratios of the project, are often rejected out of hand in federal credit programs. Banking criteria are viewed as placing undue attention on profitability, to the neglect of *social goals,* although trade-offs between social and economic goals are rarely specified. More to the point, the complexity of competing objectives and selection criteria makes accurate targeting nearly impossible. One consequence of these vague or competing criteria is the vulnerability of program administrators to favoritism and corruption. How could it be otherwise?

A third reason why effective spatial targeting for income distribution purposes is rarely possible is that the poor are not sufficiently segregated from the remainder of the population. If one drew a circle around the deepest pockets of poverty in a metropolitan area, one would discover that a large number of residents within the circle were not poor and that many of the poor lived outside the circle. While enlarging the circle increases the coverage of the poor, more non-poor are also included. Indeed the higher percentage of poor captured in the charmed circle, the higher the percent of non-poor of the total population of the distressed area. As a numerical example, the Community Development Block Grant area in Dallas includes about 30 percent of the total population, 50 percent of the Hispanics, and 80 percent of the blacks. Only about one-sixth of the households has an income half the city median, while most are of moderate income. Nearly a quarter of the households have incomes above the city median. The potential for errors of omission and commission is glaring.[5]

Finally, projects in the distressed area do not necessarily benefit residents of that area. Experience indicates that return migrants are usually the beneficiaries of new job openings in distressed areas. These return migrants often have aquired on-the-job training and formal schooling superior to nonmigrant residents.[6] Conceivably, this problem could be counteracted by packaging manpower training for area residents with capital assistance. The Department of Labor and the Department of Housing and Urban Development are experimenting with such an approach by linking the CETA and UDAG programs.

The Mystique of the Financial Fix

The major instrument of regional policy has been the capital subsidy. There are several reasons why this is an ineffective instrument.

First, capital is not as important a determinant of business location and expansion decisions as labor costs/productivity and market access.[7] This is because only about one-quarter the average firm's value added is contributed by capital and because interregional capital transfers are fairly efficient.[8]

Second, firms in distressed areas are not necessarily plagued by capital access problems. A recent survey undertaken for the U.S. Economic Development Administration asked 2,000 firms about their difficulties in obtaining a wide range of capital instruments, from line of credit to common equity. Predictably, firms with higher debt-equity ratios had a more difficult time than firms with lower debt-equity ratios. With firm size measured by employment, smaller firms had a more difficult time than larger firms. The highly leveraged and smaller firms were obviously greater risks to potential creditors. Interestingly, central city firms were no more likely to be highly leveraged or smaller than suburban or rural firms. When debt-equity ratio and firm size are held constant, rural firms appear to have the greatest difficulty. This problem may stem from the lack of competition in rural banking, partly maintained by prohibitions against branching in many states. When firms were classified by region (northeast, midwest, Rocky mountains), there were few discernible differences in difficulties in obtaining capital. These results suggest not regionally targeted financial subsidies, but policies to improve the access of small and rural firms to capital.[9]

While capital market subsidies are the most commonly used tool for area development in the United States, they are not the only possible instrument. Tax incentives, frequently offered in Europe, such as deductions or credits, may be offered to firms locating in distressed areas. [10] Although U.S. states and municipalities have offered tax inducements to industries locating anywhere within their jurisdiction, these benefits have not been used as a targeting device.

Another concept under consideration is the creation of *free enterprise* zones within distressed areas. Such zones would be free of many regulations, such as the minimum wage. How effective such an approach would be in inducing the expansion of business in, for example, inner cities depends upon how costly these regulations really are. A relaxation of the minimum wage may indeed be an important relocation inducement to unskilled-labor-intensive industry. Whether or not it were spatially targeted, a relaxation of the minimum wage might have positive effects in alleviating youth unemployment.

The relaxation of regulations is likely to be debated on its own merits, not as a policy for alleviating pockets of distress. Whether many other regulations, controls on toxic substances or air pollution, could be waived within narrowly targeted areas is doubtful. This is because areas adjacent to or downstream from the distressed area would be affected by such *external diseconomies.* The relaxation of sulfur emissions standards in Bedford-Stuyvesant might increase the acid rain in Scarsdale.

The Proliferation of Entitlements

A larger role for the federal government in alleviating area distress extends the new political economy of entitlements, that would permit institutions to survive whether or not they were successful. Bailing out Lockheed was perhaps the first step in creating this new entitlement, although there were extenuating circumstances. When New York City (as well as banks that invested in the city's bonds) was bailed out the entitlement to poorly managed municipalities was extended. Chrysler is perhaps the ultimate expression of this no-fault philosophy. With these precedents, it is becoming more difficult for the federal government to refuse requests from any business or government in a distressed area. The number of areas potentially entitled to federal aid are almost limitless. Examples include: (1) semi-arid farming counties stretching from Kansas to Texas above the Oglalla aquifer, which is rapidly being pumped dry by excessive irrigation; (2) *energy towns* which are likely to boom as mining sites, until the coal or shale plays out; or (3) cities dominated by major industries, like automobiles or steel, which have declined as a result of errors in corporate strategy. Pouring capital into unproductive institutions, like poorly managed municipalities or firms is dangerous for an economy plagued by low productivity and is unlikely to help the poor in the long run. It effectively slows down the growth of economic wealth, which can be more effectively redistributed by direct transfer payments to individuals and families.

Conclusions

What then are the solutions to the problems of distressed urban areas? Targeting subsidies to areas is likely to be ineffective and inefficient in raising individual levels of well-being. Income maintenance is better handled by measures that deliver income directly, such as a negative income tax, than by indirect measures such as subsidies for job creation in the areas in which the poor live. The purely fiscal problems of these areas can be alleviated by abandoning income-redistribution programs from federal and state governments and by intergovernmental transfers that vary inversely with area income, like some state educational aid formulas.

Finally, it may be more practical and efficient to remove as many as possible of the sectoral distortions causing area distress. To return to the cited examples, a reduction in subsidies for irrigation in the arid and semi-arid west would revitalize agriculture in the humid southeast. The impending deregulation of railroad rates is likely to eliminate the favored position of shippers of raw materials and encourage recycling in urban areas. The potential of inner-city areas as recycling locations is promising. The federal takeover of welfare would discourage the movement of dependent populations into areas which merely provide superior benefits.[11]

Notes

1. *San Antonio Independent School District* v. *Rodriguez,* 411 U.S. 1, 93 S.Ct. 1278; see also Lawyer's Committee for Civil Rights Under Law, "Update on State-Wide School Finance Cases," Washington, D.C. (February 1978). In legal parlance, a suspect classification is one which serves no rational public purpose, but which may be used to discriminate invidiously against the classified group. Prior to the rise of affirmative action, racial or ethnic classifications were suspect.

2. Edward, F. Denison. *Accounting for U.S. Economic Growth, 1929–1969.* (Washington, D.C.: Brookings Institution, 1974).

3. John E. Moes, *Local Subsidies for Industry* (Chapel Hill: University of North Carolina Press, 1962). For references on the theory of the second best, see John F. Due and Ann F. Friedlaender, Government Finance (Homewood, Ill.: Richard D. Irwin, 1977, 6th ed.), pp. 93–94.

4. Thomas Muller, "Growing and Declining Urban Areas: A Fiscal Comparison," (Urban Institute, Paper 0001-2, March 1976).

5. Martin T. Katzman et al., "Pockets of Poverty in Southwestern Cities: Implications for Targeting Community Development Block Grants," University of Texas at Dallas, prepared for the U.S. Dept. of Housing and Urban Development, March 1979.

6. William H. Miernyk, "Local Labor Market Effects of New Plant Locations," in *Essays in Regional Economics,* pp. 161–185. Edited by John F. Kain and John R. Meyer. (Cambridge, Mass.: Harvard University Press, 1971).

7. Council for Northeast Economic Action, "An Analysis of Gaps in the Capital Market," First National Bank of Boston, prepared for the U.S. Economic Development Administration, 1981.

8. William J. Stober and Lawrence H. Falk, "Industrial Development Bonds as a Subsidy to Industry," *National Tax Journal,* 22 (June 1969), pp. 232–244.

9. Council for Northeast Economic Action, "An Analysis of Gaps."

10. James L. Sundquist, *Dispersing Population: What American Can Learn from Europe* (Washington, D.C.: Brookings Institution, 1975).

11. While this chapter was under revision, a similar recommendation was published by the Panel on Policies and Prospects for Metropolitan and Nonmetropolitan America, President's Commission for a National Agenda for the Eighties, *Urban America in the Eighties: Perspectives and Prospects.* (Washington, D.C.: GPO, 1980).

Part II
Rural Development

4

U.S. Economic Development Policy: The Urban-Rural Dimension

Russel L. Barsh and
Jeffrey Gale

Introduction

Current business literature abounds with analyses of the potential for a *reindustrialization* of America. Little did Professor Etzioni, who coined the term, anticipate its ultimate impact. From *Business Week* to *Forbes* and beyond, the agenda for U.S. revitalization is debated heatedly. Reindustrialization is the latest twist in the continuing puzzle of economic development policy, and its contemporary popularity sheds light on some unyielding biases in the formulation of government programs.

In the pages that follow we will review economic development from the federal level, with particular emphasis on the urban-rural dimension. We will not describe specific programs but rather try to reveal a pattern of biases we believe have become endemic to U.S. policy and to identify the accompanying problems. We begin with a brief theoretical discussion of economic development, then suggest several alternative conceptual schemes to structure the disparate bits and pieces of U.S. economic policy history. We offer several sociopolitical scenarios to explain recurrent patterns in federal programs as the product of systems that defy classical economics. Last, we investigate whether there are differences in practice or theory between *urban* and *rural* economic development in current U.S. policy, and whether there should be.

What Is Economic Development?—An Expansive View

Speakers of one language often think they share the meaning of a word until a precise definition is required. *Economic development* is an example. Like *basic education* or *equal opportunity*, it is an ideal that no one has the temerity to disclaim—or to define. Ambiguity is actually helpful in politics, which may explain why sweeping generalities have become an art form in national legislation. Even if well-intentioned, however, an ambiguous goal is meaningless because progress towards it cannot be measured or validated.

Perhaps we can agree that *economic development* has something to do with economics and with development, and that it is a good thing. But how broadly will we define *economics*? Early utilitarians identified economics with anything that increased human happiness. Their standards of value and wealth were candidly subjective and universal. The monetarist and quantitative emphasis of this century has diverted economics from its original humanistic breadth and bred an implicit bias of the form: "If it cannot be counted it isn't economics." It may be that twentieth-century North Americans have evolved economic preferences so strongly favoring durable goods that an economic science entirely based on cash values is a very near approximation to reality. If so, contemporary western economics is merely a special case of the original utilitarian model. It cannot be applied with equal validity to nonwestern societies, or to western subsocieties that derive a significant proportion of their aggregate utility from non-tradeable features of their social, political, and physical environment.[1]

Like *evolution*, *development* connotes progress from less adaptive to more adaptive and successful forms of organization. This connotation bears a great deal of prejudicial conceptual baggage. Development towards what future state of perfection? Beginning with the Roman Lucretius, social evolutionists have supposed that western civilization was the inevitable goal of history. On the contrary, biological evolution is replete with examples of turnoffs, parallel paths, reversals and "hopeful monsters"—sudden, qualitatively new forms that violate Darwinian assumptions of gradual progress and either vanish in a blaze of glory or forge unforeseeably successful paths to survival. If, in addressing the relatively concrete goals of fecundity and biomass accumulation biological adaptation cannot, in a changing universe, achieve *perfection* by any one direct path, it appears hopelessly simplistic to conceive that the vastly greater task of increasing human happiness can proceed by some unique and direct route.

If it is to have universal validity, then, a definition of economic development must eschew either a narrow view of economics or a simplistic notion of development. Economic development is any change in the use or distribution of societal resources that increases happiness. The corollary is that happiness is subjective and must be measured by the people experiencing the change. External, objective standards, such as dollar product or dollar income, are imprecise depending upon the society's relative priority of durable or tradeable goods. Since individual preferences change and the physical world changes, at any one instant an economy may be said to be developing if it changes direction promptly in response to societal changes. In other words, economic development is a gun pointed at a moving target.

Justifying Intervention

If we purport to operate within a free market framework, the only legitimate justification for intervention is evidence that free market conditions have been violated. A market defect acts as an obstacle to normal economic evolution by misallocating resources. It may accelerate or decelerate investment in a sector by distorting capital requirements, shifting resource endowments, or changing transactions costs. A defect may be as generalized and intrinsic as buyers' lack of perfect information about prices, or as specific and tractable as law taxing or otherwise discouraging the use of a particular resource. A missing definition of a property right can be a market defect.[2] Without patent or copyright laws, for example, it would be relatively risky to invest in the creation of new ideas. Putting solar energy to work depends first on defining rights of access and use.

Not all defects deserve a cure, however. Defects that exist because of law (or the absence of law) may be resolved by rulemaking, but subsidizing defective sectors necessitates taxing relatively more efficient ones. Net benefit does not automatically result. Many apparent defects may be time-related and not truly defects at all. Lack of information may be temporary, as may be lack of capital. Accelerating the accumulation of information or capital in such instances does not perfect the market. It simply redistributes wealth from fast-evolving to slowly-evolving sectors of the economy. There is a temporal transfer of wealth without net increase. Hence the fact that an economy is developing slowly does not, in itself, justify intervention. In a theoretical free market, each sector develops at a unique rate reflecting its attractiveness relative to all other sectors. A time subsidy alters individual sector rates of change up or down without improving the net velocity of the system.

The Unit of Analysis

A geographic area, industrial sector, economic or social class, or subculture may be the beneficiary of a public policy. If other geographic, industrial, class, or subcultural groups experience decreased welfare as a result, there may be little or no aggregate net gain. The social and geographical unit of policy analysis therefore affects the apparent rate, magnitude, and direction of economic change. When formulating a development strategy for a limited geographic area, limiting analysis to its immediate environs often conceals regional redistribution of wealth. In the United States, each jurisdictional level (local, state, regional, and national) judges policy against the standard of internal gains, ignoring externalized costs. The smaller the unit, the greater the spillover of costs and benefits and the less precise the analysis. On the other hand, political freedom is increased by decentralizing economic regulation. The price we pay for government decentralization is living with neighboring communities' costs.

If the city is separated from its rural environs, analysts miss regional transfers of benefits and costs. Strategies increasing the velocity and scale of urban economies often do so at rural expense. The city may have the legal right to do this within our framework of hierarchical government, but it would be wrong to justify doing so on the scientific basis that the city is developing as a result. The only bias-free geographic unit of analysis is the whole, universal economy, transcending all political boundaries. When any smaller unit is chosen, we must be candid about the biases implied.

Analytical units are customarily, and almost always uncritically defined in time as well as space. This, too, results in bias. For capital markets, the long-run may be a year or two. For consumer behavior, time horizons may be fifteen or twenty years. The lifetime of a policy altering the physical or chemical environment such as construction, paving highways, or committing land to agriculture or mining, may be centuries. Just as a precise geographic frame of analysis must reach the farthest ripple in economic space, it must extend to the most distant ripple in economic time. Any narrower scope underestimates both benefits and costs, not necessarily in equal proportion. Once again, the precision of analysis is directly proportional to its breadth in space-time.

The persuasive demands of politics, practicality, and information costs tend to limit most economic development analyses to very narrow space and time. It is vastly simpler to say something about the impact of a public policy on a single industry in one city within a generation's time, than to assess its full impact. Such a limited analysis may approximate reality if the contemplated policy has low spillover, a very short lifetime, and no residuals. These are not conditions lightly to be assumed, however. Free market capitalism assumes that capital and, to a lesser extent, labor are highly mobile. If true, the spillover effects of economic change are geographically pervasive. We must conclude that policy studies limited in space, time, or sector often select policies that appear efficient, but in actuality are merely regional, temporal, or sectoral redistributions of wealth.

U.S. Economic Development Thinking and Its Biases

U.S. Economic development policy appears to favor (1) building infrastructure, (2) inducing investment, and (3) reinvestment. Infrastructure building can be thought of as providing what are perceived as the basic capital improvements necessary to make a community attractive for investors and labor. Typical examples are direct public financing of schools, roads, power generation and transmission, water supply and water treatment. Infrastructure is an "investment in future development."

Investment-inducing activities divert public and private capital to favored nascent industries. Donation of federal lands in the west to nineteenth-century railroads is a classic example. Reinvestment programs by contrast involve trying to keep afloat sinking ships, such as obsolete industries or communities that have lost their locational advantages. They capitalize sectors when private sources of capital no longer are willing to bear the risk, such as with Chrysler. Although periodic disinvestment is inherent in capitalism, it often proves politically difficult in a democracy.

Economic development arguments characteristically are made and political battles fought in the United States on the issue of economic growth. Growth in recent years has come to mean increase in the real GNP. But GNP merely captures the dollar sum of goods and services in trade, and reducing all economic evaluation to cash transactions elevates the national over the local and the quantitative over the qualitative. The result is economic policy biased toward industrialization, urbanization, structural and cultural homogenization, and acculturation. Because the success or failure of programs is measured in flows of dollars, barter and self-sufficiency are excluded from consideration. A GNP-based economic policy is like a gross sales or market share objective in business, blindly equating big with rewarding.

Urban society is most likely to benefit from this export orientation in which maximizing trade is more important than efficiency. For example, the costs of shipping raw materials from rural areas to cities and then back as finished goods are counted as benefits in a GNP-based model. Additionally, this bias in favor of maximizing trade restructures the economy in ways that make it virtually impossible for communities to survive in relative isolation, and limit the decentralized development of cultures. Since U.S. rural areas are at a disadvantage in terms of population and thus representation, political forces naturally tend to build rural development policies upon urban perceptions of need. This momentum is enhanced by the tendency of bureaucracies charged with policy implementation to judge programs in terms of cost or effort rather than result. Rural systems based on renewable resources such as soil and water are labor-intensive, highly decentralized to the individual or family level. As such, they lack the scale and visibility cities and agencies associate with growth. Government prefers rural industrialization.

The Tools of U.S. Economic Policy

Economic development studies tend to define policy too narrowly, missing most of what government does to affect the rate and direction of economic

change. We define *economic policy* as anything government does to change
the capital endowment or cost of capital for a locality, group, or sector.
This includes policies affecting information availability (as form of capital)
and risk (a factor in the cost of capital). We assume that capital and labor
are relatively but not completely mobile, such that a policy change will influence location initially, and eventually will affect everyone whether its
original target is a locality, sector, group, or general capital markets. An
economic policy may directly favor a target group or industry, or favor it by
favoring a support sector, or by disfavoring a competing sector, or by disfavoring a competing sector.

U.S. economic policy is far more complex than capital subsidies and
building infrastructure through public works. Table 4–1 summarizes activities listed in the Catalog of Federal Domestic Assistance that affect relative
development. The scale of most of these activities is unknown since, unlike
explicit transfer payments, their dollar cost to the Treasury may bear little
relationship to benefits they confer on the national economy. Tax relief and
price supports together involve a direct fiscal cost at least ten times greater
than all nominally developmental federal programs combined. It is impossible to discuss U.S. development policy meaningfully to the exclusion of
such powerful economic factors.

Most of the activities summarized in table 4–1 are explicitly or implicitly regional in scope. A public housing project affects the level of investment in the local construction sector, for example, and then by increasing
housing supply influences the regional supply of labor. Transportation
development, energy and water supply, and flood insurance have similar
regional effects. Many nominally sectoral strategies also tend to have limited geographic scope. Price supports subsidize rural products such as eggs,
milk, grains, and vegetable fibers. Most public lands are rural and, when
leased at a discount amounting to a sectoral subsidy, affect rural communities in the first instance. Product regulations and procurement contracts
tend to affect urban areas, while trade relief and tax relief affect parts of
both urban and rural economies. Some economic policies have changed
their role and scope over the years. A century ago limited liability was
directed chiefly at railroads and subsidized agricultural expansion. Today
the most familiar example of limited liability is the Price-Anderson Act,
which shelters nuclear power generation from full liability for accidents.
Although many nuclear parks are located in rural areas so that the cost of
accidents would have a rural scope, the benefits of increased power supply
are primarily urban and industrial.

Another useful way to conceptualize the redistributive aspects of U.S.
economic policies is shown in figure 4–1. All governmental programs allocate either fund or risk, either directly (through government mechanisms) or
indirectly (through private mechanisms responding to government pro-

grams). Allocation of funds and risk may be positive (subsidy) or negative (tax). Using this scheme helps identify additional activities rarely associated with economic development. For example, the FBI crime lab indirectly reallocates risk by assisting crime detection and deterrence in predominantly urban, high-crime areas. Increased urban safety lowers local insurance rates and business costs—an indirect subsidy to urban investors. When economic development is examined in this broad framework, the conclusion is unavoidable that the current U.S. policies which affect development are in scope and interaction, beyond comprehension or rational coordination.

Agencies and Constituencies

Table 4-2 identifies explicitly developmental U.S. programs with their bureaucracies and emphasis.[3] Many of these programs have a natural constituency and are so distributed among federal departments. If the *agency capture* model of administrative politics is valid,[4] each local or sectoral group commands its own part of the national economic policy arsenal in its own self-interest. We observed in the last section that an integrated national economic policy is chimerical in light of the multitude of programs, their range and complexity. The fragmentation of responsibility and constituencies work to keep things that way. There can be no other result since programs continue to be added to the system on a piecemeal, crisis-response basis.

Structurally and intellectually, U.S. urban and rural policies remain ill-defined and in a state of flux. The Housing and Community Development Act of 1977 mandated development of a National Urban Policy to supersede the earlier goal of a National Urban *Growth* Policy. The change for the first time suggested a concern for quality rather than quantity. In March 1978 the Carter Administration responded by announcing seven governing principles, four broad goals and ten major policies. As former U.S. Department of Housing and Urban Development (HUD) Assistant Secretary Orlebeke observed at the time, however, the Carter Administration's plan contained little more than platitudes.[5] Given the Cabinet-level warfare among HUD, HHS and Commerce described by Robert Freilich as one in which pleasing all three departments creates a "diffuse and directionless web," the Carter plan was doomed to perpetuate the subsidy grabbag problem.[6] First indications suggest the Reagan approach will emphasize disinvestment in declining cities, a significant redirection but one that already is drawing howls from the northern industrial cities. Reinvestment may be irreversibly entrenched.

Urban programs have a relatively diffuse organizational base, dispersed among the Department of Commerce (Economic Development Administra-

Table 4-1
Federal Activities Affecting Capital Costs and Endowments

Economic Factors Affected (in the first instance)	Primary Scope of Activity		
	Regional	Sectoral	General
Real (financial capital)	Public Works Disaster relief Fuel allocation Flood insurance	Public lands lease Procurement contracts Stimulus grants Low-interest loans Guaranteed loans Tax advantages exemptions/shelter tax deferral investment credits accelerated depreciation	Capital markets regulation federal reserve system SEC regulation banking and lending Insurance market regulation Law enforcement
Labor (human capital)	Housing projects Highway systems Urban mass transit	Vocational/technical education grants Higher education fellowships Direct training	Primary education grants Public assistance Unemployment insurance Health insurance Wage and hour regulations Occupational safety Labor relations regulation Civil rights enforcement Veteran's benefits

Information

Public research
Grant/contract research
Clearinghouses
Technical assistance
Demonstration projects

Patent, copyright, trademark

Competition

Licensing
Product regulation
design control
advertising
marketing assistance
demarketing
product grading
Limited liability
Trade relief (tariffs, quotas)
Price supports
Futures markets regulation

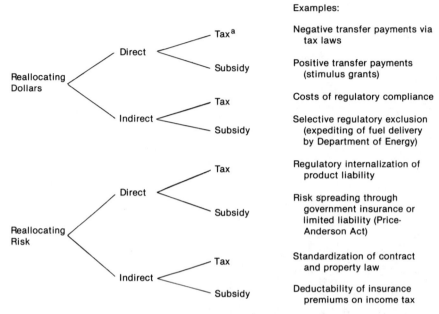

[a]The term *tax* here is used in its economic sense (anything that increases costs) rather than its narrower fiscal sense (a government collection of wealth).

Figure 4-1. Dollar/Risk Structure of Federal Developmental Activities

tion), HUD, Interior, Transportation, the Employment and Training Division of the Department of Labor, and the Community Services Administration. Rural development politics enjoys a tighter organization focus in the Departments of Agriculture and Interior, and domination by a relatively homogeneous interest group—farmers—with historically strong, albeit declining influence. Rural-oriented programs nevertheless reflect urban bias toward building capital infrastructure. Depression-era programs such as Rural Electrification supported both agricultural and industrial opportunities.[7] In 1972 the Rural Development Act shifted emphasis to industrialization and urbanization of rural areas,[8] recreating within the Department of Agriculture a program parallel to urban reinvestment and reindustrialization agencies.

From our review of current programs, we have concluded:

1. programs have evolved around a large number of constituencies with different and often incompatible agendas;
2. given this conflict of agendas and the dispersal of programs among competing agencies, together with the near-impossibility of assessing

Table 4–2
Major Current Federal Economic Development Programs

Agency, Program, and Major Constituency	Applicant	Form of Aid	Demographic Limits	Emphasis
Department of Agriculture, Farmers Home Administration (agricultural interests)				
Business and Industrial development loans and grants	Private	Grants, loans, loan guarantees	Non-urban < 50,000	Investment
Water and waste disposal systems for rural communities	Public	Grants, guaranteed and insured loans	Rural < 10,000	Infrastructure
Community facility loans	Public	Insured loans	Rural < 10,000	Infrastructure
Department of Commerce, Economic Development Administration (large business/commercial)				
Title I: Public works and development facilities	Public	Grants, loans	Designation as an economic development district or as a redevelopment area	Infrastructure/Reinvestment
Title II: Business development loans	Private	Loans, guaranteed loans		Reinvestment
Title III: Technical assistance, research and planning	Public	Grants		Reinvestment
Title IX: Special economic development and assistance	Public	Grants		Reinvestment
Trade adjustment assistance	Private	Loans, guaranteed loans	None (based on evidence of distress)	Reinvestment

Table 4-2 continued

Agency, Program, and Major Constituency	Applicant	Form of Aid	Demographic Limits	Emphasis
Community Services Administration (social action/poverty interests)				
Community action	Public/private	Grants	Distressed urban/rural	Reinvestment
Community economic development	Community development corporation	Grants	Distressed special impact areas	Investment/reinvestment
Department of Housing and Urban Development (large cities, urban poor)				
Community development block grants (large cities)	Public	Formula grants	Cities > 50,000 in SMSAs	Investment/reinvestment
Community development block grants (small cities)	Public	Grants	Urban counties < 200,000, cities/towns < 50,000	Infrastructure reinvestment
Urban development action grants	Public	Grants	Distressed cities/urban counties	Reinvestment
Section 312 rehabilitation loans	Private	Loans	Distressed urban areas	Reinvestment
Department of Labor, Employment and Training Administration (organized labor)				
Title II: Comprehensive employment and training service	Public	Grants	State, local government > 100,000, consortia	Infrastructure[a]
Title VI: Countercyclical employment programs	Public	Formula grants	State, local government > 100,000, consortia	Reinvestment[a]
Title VII: Private sector initiative program	Public	Grants (to be refunded)	State, local government > 100,000 consortia	Investment[a]

Small Business Administration (small businesses)				
Section 7(a): Regular business loans	Private	Loans, guaranteed loans	None	Investment
Sections 501, 502: State and local development company loans	Public/ private	Loans, guaranteed and insured loans	None	Investment
Small business investment companies	Private	Loans	None	Investment
Air and water pollution control loans	Private	Loans, guaranteed and insured loans	None	Investment
Department of Transportation (highway, mass transit interests)				
Section 3: Capital improvement loans and grants	Public/ private	Grants, loans	None	Infrastructure, reinvestment
Section 5: Capital and operating assistance formula grants	Public	Formula grants	None	Infrastructure

aStimulating employment here is treated as a step in forming human capital infrastructure, or attracting investment or reinvestment in a local market.

many kinds of programs' true costs and benefits precisely, little possibility of coordination currently exists;
3. no overall framework is in place nor is the urban/rural dimension de-
    fined in more than nominal terms;
4. programs nevertheless have distinctively regional effects which may
    work at cross-purposes; and
5. whether labeled urban or rural, most nominally developmental pro-
    grams are devoted to building infrastructure and inducing investment
    or reinvestment for industrialization.

The Policy Shell Game

Most of the activities summarized in table 4–1 and figure 4–1 are essentially
redistributive rather than allocative. Purely redistributive policies are not
inherently undesirable or *false* in some empirical sense. A redistribution of
wealth may increase one group's material comfort, for instance, and simultaneously increase donor group's sense of equity. That would be developmental, as we have defined the term.[9] In other cases, redistributions are
developmental only in the short-run or within a narrow geographical framework, when the analysis excludes distant or future donors from consideration. Politics is no stranger to the art of making a zero-sum game look like a
free lunch. We will draw several examples from contemporary U.S. energy
policy.

Grants and low-interest loans for oil shale and tar sands demonstration
projects combine a direct capital subsidy with reducing the cost of private
capital formation. If private capital markets functioned well, private investment in oil shale and tar sands recovery research would increase as the
demand for secondary domestic oil supplies grew, that is, as the nation
approached exhaustion of primary oil supplies. The price of primary oil
would increase gradually until it met the declining price of secondary oil, at
which point there would be substitution. Subsidizing the development of
secondary oil technology simply accelerates the time of substitution. There
is no net social benefit because the cost of research and development is paid
as taxes rather than at the pump.

The proposed oil pipeline from Washington's Puget Sound to the Great
Lakes would involve both temporal and regional redistributions. Oils tran-
shipment would increase supplies in the midwest at the expense of increasing environmental risks and (arguably) reducing fisheries supplies in the
Pacific northwest into the future. Field gas pricing, a target of the new
Administration, is another regional transfer. Price controls reduce the cost
of natural gas to pipeline destination states, artificially reducing gas supplies in producing states. In each of these cases, the long-run effect is to

lower factor costs and increase investment in a place, as well as an industry, in which energy is a major input or product. Net economic gain does not necessarily follow.

The classic example of temporal transfer of wealth is the disposal of nuclear reactor by-products. By externalizing this cost of nuclear power generation in time, operating costs are reduced, investment is attracted, and supply increased. In the short-run energy becomes relatively inexpensive and plentiful. The long-run effect is uncertain and depends upon a race between the deterioration of current disposal and containment systems and the discovery of better ones. Future generations may be forced to bear the costs of present energy consumption. Even national highway policies have regional and temporal effects. Building and improving roads in an area accelerate migration and industrialization, with the effect of taxing existing cities to create new cities as if it were settled that, on the whole, more cities are better. In the extreme this accelerates the decline of existing cities and thereby becomes a policy that creates its own justification.

Overall, U.S. economic development policy mixes accelerating tendencies for growth (taxing existing sectors to encourage new ones) and stemming tendencies for decline (taxing healthy sectors to save sickly ones). But if weak market forces are augmented and negative market forces resisted at the expense of strong, positive market forces, there can be no net gain other than a reduction in the volatility of the economy as a whole. In other words, this policy pattern is countercyclical and stabilizing. It reduces risk in some sectors by punishing successful risk-taking in others. It institutes a process of temporary regional and sectoral fixes that cancel one another out, but in the short run appear to offer competing interest groups *wins* and *losses.*

The Market Design Alternative

Market design is the only economic policy that is primarily allocative within the assumptions of a competitive free market system. We define market design as any policy that reduces transactions costs by increasing certainty and information generally, bringing the real market closer to the ideal. Market design addresses the rules of the game rather than the initial endowments of the players or the substantive results of play. By reducing uncertainty about the rules and the nature of the game, design, in principle, increases the number and velocity of transactions and brings more players and resources into action. Risk and uncertainty inherent in the game remain, hence the outcome depends on the skill and luck of the players. Design is indifferent to geography, time, or sector.

The U.S. economy already is designed by federal and state laws governing property rights, contracts, business organization and competition.

Largely common law rather than statutory, these rules define who may play, who owns what, what may be done with property, to what extent property expectations can be enforced, and how property rights may be transferred. To the extent that these rules are universal, unambiguous, notorious, and enforceable, the market game can be played with a minimum of intrinsic risk. Transactions need bear little or no premium for procedural disagreements among the players, or for the risk of theft. The collective or public cost of the system is limited to rule enforcement.

Because time works change in all things markets require continuous redesign. Light and air were important goods in Enlightenment England, for instance. It was appurtenant to ownership of a dwelling. More than a century ago U.S. courts redefined real property to include light and air on the grounds that urban developers' cost of buying up this right was retarding the growth of cities.[10] Now that passive solar heating has become feasible and desirable in residential construction, local laws protecting light and air are reappearing. The market is being redesigned to accommodate a "new" good, but any redesign is costly because it upsets prior economic expectations. Changing the rules in mid-play taxes players at random. An effective design policy, therefore, must consider the benefits and costs of each change.

Perhaps no market can be designed efficiently. After all, promulgating a rule has costs. Getting people to know about it is costly (and rarely attempted). The most benign form of rule enforcement is costly. Can any market rule justify its cost? Consider the economics of universality. A theoretical free market is wholly individualized. Each transaction is unique and there are, by definition, no compulsory rules. None are needed because information is perfect and market forces automatically discipline cheaters and welchers. In a real market, in the absence of perfect knowledge, rules create information and secure expectations but at the cost of standardizing transactions. The less homogeneous the players and their preferences the greater the disadvantages of standardization. The more people you have, the greater the diversity and the more likely it is that a general rule will fit no one well. In large democratic jurisdictions general rules will reflect the preferences of the majority and misallocate the resources of minorities as surely as explicit taxes and subsidies.

Cynical Scenarios of the Role of Development

If it is so difficult to justify economic development policies on objective grounds, why do we engage in so many of them? We will suggest several possible roles economic development programs play in the U.S. economy, none of which has anything to do with economic development. We assume that democracy, to some extent, permits localities to compete for national transfer payments, and that, to some extent, national institutions and agencies operate independent of regional politics.

Welfare Cost Avoidance. Since the Depression-era evolution of social insurance programs government has borne directly the costs of job creation and of unemployment. Investment in job creation, if successful, reduces social insurance payouts. If there is a strong popular preference for reducing welfare costs on ideological grounds ("make 'em work for their welfare"), government will spend more than a dollar in job-creation costs just to avoid a dollar of unemployment compensation. Under these circumstances, subsidies creating otherwise non-viable jobs may be pursued because they reduce welfare costs and purchase the *appearance* of private sector health.

Subsidizing non-viable jobs may save direct government outlays by sharing costs with the subsidized industries. On the other hand, it is more detrimental to economic efficiency than outright transfer payments to the unemployed because it diverts capital from healthy sectors to subsidized ones. To that extent, the government's direct saving is offset by a misallocation of national capital and decrease in overall efficiency. Once it has invested in an industry, the government may be tempted to protect its investment through increased subsidy and protective regulation. This further misallocates resources and stimulates other sectors to demand comparable favors. A feedback loop develops and leads to more subsidies, greater inefficiency, and hence, ironically, to more welfare.

Amortized over the lifetime of an industry, the capital cost of creating a permanent job is less than the cost of annually subsidizing a marginal job. Over the lifetime of a political administration (four to eight years), it is cheaper to contribute small annual subsidies to maintain a marginal job than to bear the total cost of capitalizing a permanent position. For this reason, government always tends to ward continuous operating subsidies over one-time capital grants, which decrease economic efficiency and increase the total long-run public cost of subsidization.

The Insurance State. Classical capitalism assumes that people are risk-takers. True free markets reward risks that are successful and punish unsuccessful gambles. In the optimistic America of the last century, rich in undeveloped natural resources and surplus skills and labor, free market capitalism offered a practical dream. Immigrants had little to lose and everything to gain. It was an era still committed to the maxim of Elizabethan adventurers: "Who would not trade tolerable certainties for excellent uncertainties? Fortunes won and lost by ambitious perseverers and stellar rises to wealth and power were a real part of the American experience.

What happens when a capitalist society matures? Its resource endowments have largely been committed, many irreversibly. Some are exhausted. Its population has grown to fill its economic carrying capacity. A majority of citizens are relatively rich in material possessions and no longer lack essential comforts. Under these conditions citizens are more concerned about losing ground than about becoming wealthier. The everyday reality of rags-to-riches fades into a belief that individual fortunes no longer can be made, that new opportunities are so costly and complex that they can be tackled only by great corporate engines, that we are (in the phrase of Justice Brandeis) a nation of clerks. Conspicuous government spending and regulation, corporate and labor oligopoly politics, and interdependence with world markets leads to a conviction that the economy is volatile, fickle, and insecure. Risk becomes an enemy rather than an opportunity.

Government responds by using its resources to insure industries and communities against economic failure. This insulates existing sectors from market forces, perpetuating existing inefficiency and, as world economic conditions and technologies change, causing continuously increasing inefficiency. Market discipline—risk of failure—no longer operates to stimulate innovation. Industries are permitted to externalize their techological disadvantage, and cities their locational disadvantages. As inefficiency accumulates a greater share of public investment is required to prevent widespread unemployment—another feedback loop spiral. Protective regulation also reduces market risk, increases inefficiency, accelerates demand for countervailing economic subsidies, and causes more inefficiency.[11] Any productive net output of industry is consumed by insurance costs to maintain the existing structural and income status quo.

This is not a welfare state in which citizens are assured of some minimum level of economic condition. A welfare state is dynamic above the lower income limit established by subsidies and the upper limit resulting from redistributive taxation. Although the guarantee of minimum security chills risk taking, it does not completely discourage or prevent upward mobility. On the contrary, an insurance state is inherently static. Existing class structure and relative income levels are preserved at public expense. A welfare state taxes the top of the income pyramid to support the bottom, while an insurance state taxes everyone to keep everything exactly where it is. An insurance state, then, is "welfare for all."

The Pie Game. There is no evidence that national subsidies are distributed on objective grounds. Many federal spending programs, such as defense procurement, are notoriously political. Others, like urban mass transit and housing aid, have become factors in winning endorsements for presidential campaigns, and still others, like the 1980 Alaska Lands Act, have stimulated overt interstate power rivalries. In fact, all federal spending is frankly redistributive and part of a game in which cities, states, and regions form transitory coalitions to raid the public purse—and one another's natural resources—through the medium of Congress. This is inevitable within the republican design of our government, which permits a majority to rule minorities. In this context, what is good for the ruling coalition is developmental and is subsidized. Development is a euphemism for the pie game.

This explains conflicting and uncoordinated development programs. Each, in its turn, benefited a regional or sectoral game winner. Since regions and sectors differ in resources and objectives, no national objective economic goals are possible and we are condemned to compete perpetually for funds to achieve varying and inconsistent local short-term goals. A rational society would accommodate economic and cultural diversity by permitting each subculture sufficient fiscal and regulatory autonomy to define and achieve its own version of development. That, we suggest, was the original plan of the Constitution. Congress was to be the referee, not the principal player. Once the constitutionality of federally mandated geographic redistributions of wealth had been established, however, regions realized there was more to be gained by taxing one another's economies than by policing their own.

The pie game pits rural areas against cities in competition for pie share. Urban and rural objectives do not always conflict and broad regional coalitions sometimes form joining cities and their environs. The only certainty is that no stable pattern emerges. Each new coalition adds another program to the system without eliminating existing ones. In the short-run communities experience apparent gains or losses in real welfare, but the aggregate national effect is simply a permanent drain on all economic resources. Taxes and regulations swell to accommodate each newly won program.

Avoiding welfare cost and maintaining the insurance state keeps people in the same place by neutralizing catastrophic, cyclical, and long-term declines in communities' economies. In the pie game, however, communities experience real (albeit temporary) bursts of artificial prosperity, stimulating migration. Migration increases winners' social costs and drains losers' labor supply, offsetting the benefits of winning and deepening the economic blow of losing. This triggers new game alignments and coalitions and further misallocations of national labor resources. When dying cities win at the pie game, outmigration slows and possibly reverses, discouraging growth of new cities that are better located. Returnees dilute salvaged cities' subsidized prosperity and generating fresh demands for external aid—another feedback loop.

Government, Inc. In the most cynical view, the objective of national economic development policy is to maximize the consumption of government-produced goods and services. There is no incentive or discipline to increase public welfare, the effect being simply to maximize the public cost of accomplishing nothing. Economic development is a bureaucratic institution with a growing appetite and the political capability to feed itself. Since the profit of government is tax revenue, the economic development policies of Government, Inc. will favor tax-generating activities. Capital-intensive, large-scale production of durable, exportable goods will be given priority because it involves lengthy chains of distribution and hence a multitude of taxable loci. Subsistence activities and barter markets will be discouraged because they produce no taxable cash transactions, regardless of their capacity to generate real economic welfare.

U.S. Development Policy and Federalism

The United States at first conceived of itself as an essentially rural distribution of undeveloped western land. Newly ceded Indian territories were resold to settlers for as little as twelve and a half cents per acre, or about one-tenth of market value. After the war, rural subsidies extended to free grants of homestead tracts and two-mile-wide railroad corridors. Early in this century attention shifted to regional infrastructure such as roads, electric power and irrigation systems. Since the Depression, however, U.S. rural economic programs have lost their emphasis on expansion and power-intensity, with most investment going to preserve existing entry at a steady state through price supports and the farm parity concept.

During the nation's first century the federal role in the cities was subdued. Until the direct income tax was authorized by the Sixteenth Amendment in 1913 the federal government's greatest fiscal resource was undeveloped public land, most of which was rural. Federal economic programs favored rural sectors simply because Congress had few direct means to subsidize cities. At the same time, however, the eastern state governments actively subsidized manufacturing by means of pump-priming capital grants, land grants, monopoly charters, limitations on liability for debt and accidents, and criminal prosecution of labor organizers.[12] State legislatures directly financed the construction of roads, bridges, and power dams, and also gave monopoly charters to private investors who undertook urban improvements. Thus, while Congress tried to draw the population westward with the promise of cheap or free land, the eastern states struggled to hold on to their population by industrializing at public expense.

These two countervailing and uncoordinated demographic strategies merged quite by accident during the Depression. Strapped by financial failures and fiscal overruns, state governments turned to Congress to assume the costs of local programs. The price states paid for this was federal direction and standardization. Beginning with the National Industrial Recovery

Act, Congress successively assumed all of the industrial developmental activities formerly administered (in one form or another) by state legislatures. Federalization soon included business organization and financing (Securities and Exchange Act of 1934), power generation (Public Utility Act of 1935), and urban housing (Housing Act of 1937). Specialized federal agencies for new-entry financing (Small Business Administration, Economic Development Administration) and direct public enterprise (Tennessee Valley Authority, Bonneville Power Administration, Amtrak) now round out the federal industrialization arsenal.

Perhaps Congress' original rural perspective and its recently absorbed urban responsibilities never have been completely reconciled. Urban and rural programs are administratively independent and constitute competing power centers within the Executive. The only evidence of coordination we can find—and it is not altogether positive—is a recent shift in federal urban programs away from real growth in favor of the same kind of steady-state thinking that has dominated federal rural programs for the past fifty years. Since 1960 an increasing share of federal urban investment has gone into the regeneration or rehabilitation of dying urban areas without candidly assessing the underlying causes of urban decay. Keeping old cities alive regardless of the revealed locational disadvantages is a kind of urban parity concept. It may prolong urban poverty by discouraging the evolution of economically healthy new cities. The birth, growth, and death of cities may be as inevitable as the birth, growth, and collapse of individual industries as economic conditions change.[13] Contemporary programs assume that these cycles can be suspended.

What Is Rural Development?

It is difficult to answer this question without reference to widespread assumptions about urban development. A developed city generally is taken to be one in which there is high employment and high median income, with an economic foundation in the manufacture and distribution of goods. A developing city should be growing in physical and population size; although, paradoxically, size and density also are characteristic problems of urban areas. Popular notions of urban development tend to include what John Kenneth Galbraith calls "symbolic development," that is, physical symbols of wealth, power, and change such as vast modern buildings, parks and public monuments.[14] Growing attention to quality of life factors in urban studies has forced some awareness of the extent to which this ideal of intense, accelerated urbanization and industrialization may work temporal redistributions of wealth. The early generations of master builders profit, and future generations of urban denizens pay.

What, then, does a developed rural economy look like? To judge from the contemporary federal programs administered by HUD, Labor and Commerce, it seems Congress thinks developed rural economies look like urban economies. Federal rural intervention tends to promote industrial infrastructure, industrial relocation, and wage-labor employment programs. Undoubtedly, building factories and industrial parks is more impressive, at Congressional appropriations time, than buying some cattle or helping with tractor repairs. To survive budget hearings, administrators must be able to call upon a rich supply of symbolic successes—the bigger and costlier the better. The problem also reflects an underlying confusion of manufacturing with growth. Rural economies are land-extensive and in many areas still involve a high rate of small, family ownership. Analysts steeped in the prejudice that modern growth must be corporate, capital-intensive and large-scale must find it difficult to urge spending public treasure to keep rural lands rural.

If cities are rational locational phenomena, are rural areas simply places that happen not to be cities, or do they have locational advantages of another kind? Just as cities take advantage of the location of transportation, labor, and often of nonrenewable resources such as minerals, rural areas take advantage of the location of renewable resources such as soils, climate, fisheries, and timber. A perfectly stable city would enjoy a unique logistical location immune to the vicissitudes of international economic change. The perfectly stable rural area would enjoy a unique or uniquely accessible primary renewable resource, relatively immune from long-term fluctuations in supply and demand. Perfect stability obviously is as illusory as infinite growth, either for urban or rural areas, but the most competitive economies may be those that approach these theoretical conditions. Cities may be inherently more vulnerable to decay because their chief advantages tend to be transitory (location) or mobile (labor).

Although their individual lifetimes may be limited by independent forces, cities and rural areas cannot exist without one another. In an age of high-speed transportation, this coexistence no longer need imply close proximity but, as yet, no city can survive without a supply of animal and vegetable food, water, or fiber. For the city to prosper these requirements must be supplied efficiently. This implies that a developed city cannot exist without a developed rural economy. Development as a whole, requires a synergy of urban and rural areas. At some point, radical urbanization begins to divert needed capital from rural economies, increasing primary factor prices to cities and decelerating urban growth. In an unregulated market the distribution of land area, population, and capital between urban and rural areas will fluctuate in dynamic equilibrium as the relative demand for urban and rural outputs changes. Any intervention that subsidizes urbanization—or that reindustrializes areas that are tending naturally to reruralize—misallocates factors and underdevelops the whole economy.

Closing Thoughts: Development Policy and Freedom

In a heterogeneous, cosmopolitan, or culturally pluralistic state, there are important additional reasons for avoiding overindustrialization. The population of such a state is likely to reflect both urban and rural quality-of-life preferences. *Rurality* is a good purchasable at the cost of relocation, and it is optimal when people may move freely between urban and rural environments. In this age of reaction to materialism, what we call rurality may be one of our society's most valued goods. For government to subsidize (and therefore perpetuate) the expansion of cities and the development, in rural areas, of new urban centers is to regulate the supply, price, and consumption of both ruralty and its counterpart, urbanity. In a free economy, government ought not manipulate demography any more than it ought to control the production of durable goods.

There is no categorical distinction, then, between urban and rural development. Urban and rural areas both should be permitted to take advantage of their locational endowments which, over time, may shift enough to make cities out of farms, and farms out of cities. Thus far we have been cynical about the potential for genuine economic development policy, arguing that U.S. federalism historically and structurally has worked against stability and encouraged redistributive games. We have suggested that the U.S. economy has assumed a mature state in which avoiding risk and loss is more important than generating new wealth. It is inappropriate, however, to leave this topic with a feeling of helplessness. Rather, we hope we have demonstrated through a little license and hyperbole that economic development is a truly wicked intellectual problem about which policymakers know little and assume much. Reconceptualization of the problem within the kind of systems perspective we have used here in which political structure, implementation politics, demography, and social goods all play significant roles may suggest the new paths we need to take.

Notes

1. E.F. Schumacher, *Small Is Beautiful,* (New York: Harper and Row, 1973) has popularized this position.

2. A case study of problems arising from undefined and consequently insecure property rights is R.L. Barsh, *The Washington Fishing Rights Controversy* (rev. ed.), (Seattle, University of Washington Business Administration, 1979).

3. The programs are those identified as developmental in *Guide to Federal Resources for Economic Development,* (Washington, D.C.: Northeast-Midwest Institute, 1979). The Institute represents the interests of industrial eastern states.

4. Orlebeke, "Carter Renews the Romance With a National Urban Policy," *Planning,* August 1978, p. 11.

5. R.A. Posner, "Theories of Economic Regulation," *Bell Journal of Economics,* Autumn 1974, p. 335.

6. G. Wright, "Perspectives on National Growth and Development," paper prepared for the President's Biennial Report on Development, February 1976, nicely reviews the history of U.S. urban programs.

7. See generally, T.R. Ford, (ed.), *Rural America: Persistence and Change,* (Ames, Iowa: Iowa State University Press, 1978.)

8. North Central Regional Center for Rural Development, *Communities Left Behind—Alternatives for Development,* (Ames, Iowa: Iowa State University Press, 1974); Maddox, *Toward a Rural Development Policy,* (Washington, D.C.: National Planning Association, 1973).

9. We assume the perceived equity is a good and that individuals in society have preferences for the amount of equity or social justice they hope to "buy" through charity, taxes, and other collective programs.

10. See M.J. Horwitz, *The Transformation of American Law 1780–1860* (Cambridge, Mass.: Harvard University Press, 1977, p. 46). It is interesting to speculate whether relieving urban developers from this cost accelerated the growth of American cities relative to English cities. If so, urban immigrants were ultimately donees of prior urban dwellers' property: a zero-sum game.

11. A wonderful example of this is the Small Business Administration's program of hardship payments for businesses affected by everything from competitive imports to the costs of complying with federal and state environmental and product safety regulations.

12. L. Hartz, *Economic Policy and Democratic Thought: Pennsylvania, 1776–1860,* (Chicago: Quadrangle, 1968).

13. We are indebted to Professor Jack Lessinger, University of Washington, for a preview of his manuscript, "Cycles of Urban Development and Obsolescence," which affords some persuasive historical statistical evidence on this point.

14. *Economic Development,* (Boston: Houghton Mifflin, 1964).

5

The Decline of California's North Coast Redwood Region

Dudley J. Burton and
Irvine Alpert

While most of the contemporary concern about economic decline is in urban industrial areas, the phenomenon also occurs in other locations. Decline occurs in different ways within natural resource-based economies, as well as in industrial ones, and within renewable resource systems as well as non-renewable ones. In other words, both secular (long-term) and cyclical decline can be a problem in agricultural and mineral-based production communities, the dust bowl and Appalachian mining regions, for example, as well as in industrial areas, such as the northeast.

The following discussion examines a variety of analytical and policy issues that emerge in the dynamic of a timber-based economy under the influence of a strong environmental advocacy. What patterns of distress do we have? How was that distress created? What policies, if any, can moderate it? What issues are raised by such policies? How can such distress be prevented?

The case under consideration is the north coast redwoods region of California. Timber production in this region peaked in 1959 with the rapid liquidation of old-growth, essentially non-renewable, redwood stands. The speed and destructiveness of this process generated a reaction by environmentalists and others to force the creation, in 1968, and the expansion, in 1978, of a Redwood National Park (RNP). Virtually everyone agrees that Park efforts hastened and intensified the short-term decline of the region but was not the cause. At the same time, concern expressed by environmentalists and their friends in government encouraged—and sometimes forced—changes in resource management that would be beneficial in the long-term. However, the cultural and social changes (including policies) necessary to achieve such environmental transition in the long-term and to ameliorate the efforts of rapid regional decline in the short-term, raise a variety of complex analytic and policy issues.

This example is a useful lesson for policy dealing with energy and mineral boom towns in environmentally sensitive areas like Alaska, for the economic situation in western Oregon and Washington and, even on an international scale, for emerging timber economies in Brazil and southeast Asia.[1]

Regional Characteristics

The north coast refers to Humboldt and Del Norte counties, which are at the most northerly end of California's redwood range. This is the only place in the world with any significant stands of virgin coastal redwood (*Sequoia semper virens*), most of which are preserved in the federal and state parks. The area is sparsely populated (120,000), about 80 percent forested, and accounts for about 4 percent of national softwood production. Approximately 25 percent of employment and about one-third of value added are directly attributed to the wood products industry. Fisheries, tourism, and growing marijuana are the main secondary activities. The federal presence in the area and in resouce management looms large, since roughly one-half the region's acreage is in the national and state parks, National Forest, and BLM-managed lands.

Unemployment in the north coast is a continuing and severe problem, and many people have dropped out of the job market completely. While there are some relatively high-paying jobs in the timber industry, aggregate median income for the region is significantly less than for the state of California as a whole. The State Employment Development Commission targets the two-county area as a distressed region. There are seasonal, cyclical, and secular trends that exacerbate the unemployment problem. First, the logging industry is all but closed in the winter months of heavy rains; second, the redwood industry as a whole (though less than other wood products industries) is responsive to cyclical characteristics of the housing market, and the entire region is in a secular decline due to the unavailability of timber supply. Even in the best of times, unemployment is higher than the California average, and it will go still higher as policies to mitigate the Park expansion terminate.

The north coast reflects in an intensified way the general policy problem characteristic of the entire Pacific Northwest coastal strip. This is the management of decline in forest output and the transition to a viable second-growth timber industry. The trends evident in western Washington and western Oregon are exacerbated here because of the removal of over 30,000 acres of old-growth redwoods from production through the creation of RNP. Because of prior mismanagement, present annual production of 1.2 billion board feet will drop to 700 MBF or less by the year 2000.[2] The primary aim of public policy here has been, and should continue to be, the strengthening of the timber economy. There is general consensus on this point.[3]

The decline of timber resources on private land has intensified interest in the adjacent Six Rivers National Forest, which has generally been better managed. This, too, is a dynamic repeated throughout the nation. But the National Forest is legally mandated to cut at or less than sustained yield. Local timbermen want the forest to adopt a *departure* schedule (cutting rates higher than sustained yield) because of severe economic conditions in the region. Wilderness advocates are seeking more wilderness designations under the RARE II process, and conservationists, particularly the professional foresters, are worried about both alternatives. Lawsuits and rhetoric abound.

While there is not much danger that the major timber corporations will move away from the north coast, a variety of tough policy problems arise. These all focus on how to maintain high employment levels in an economy where there is both less output and more capital intensity. In particular, these refer to alternative methods for forest rehabilitation, forms of economic diversification, and the creation of secondary wood-products markets.

History of the Region

The story of the north coast encapsulates the history of America's frontier. In aboriginal times, several peaceful, settled tribes of Indians lived in the area, making use primarily of abundant fish and wildlife. The lure of gold brought the first major waves of outsiders to the area, but is soon became apparent that timber would be the basis for its wealth.

The development of timber production was slow for several reasons. First, the huge old-growth redwood trees were too large for existing technology. Second, the terrain was so rough that many areas were virtually inaccessible. And finally, the distance to markets made transportation costs prohibitive. With increasing demand from San Francisco and the development of steam shipping and steam technology in the woods, the area experienced an economic boom which lasted—along with its seasonal and business cycle fluctuations—until its peak in 1959. Whereas in 1890, 200 million board feet of timber were milled in the region, in 1959 the figure was 1.2 billion board feet. In good times, hundreds of mills were in operation and anyone who wanted a job could get one. During economic downturns, the regional economy would virtually stop. Little or no attention was paid to the resources base during much of this period, as conservation legislation came only in 1945. Because of nonexistent or poor forest regulation, much of the once productive redwood and fir timber lands now grows only brush or scrub oak. In 1930, the timber sector provided half of all jobs in basic industry; by 1950, it provided 70 percent; by 1980, this figure was down to 25 percent.[4]

History of Park Creation

For a long time, environmentalist interest in the redwoods was represented by the Save the Redwoods League (SRL). This organization helped to create California's state parks policy and has worked with the state to acquire thousands of acres of redwood parkland. Due to its generally conservative philosophy, its necessarily close-working relationship with redwood timberland owners, and its desire to protect its tax-exempt philanthropic status, the SRL did not concentrate on developing good conservation policies for the region. When the Sierra Club became concerned about the rapid and destructive liquidation of the region's remaining old-growth redwoods, it began to focus on both preservation and improved resource management. By the mid-1960s, the Sierra Club's preservation approach was the advocacy of an RNP. The Sierra Club and the SRL disagreed over where this park should be, its appropriate size, and what effect it would have on the region. Soon after Congress voted to create RNP in 1968 it became clear to the Sierra Club and other environmental groups that the park represented an unworkable compromise. It could not be protected from activities on adjoining commercial timberland. Consequently, there were both renewed efforts to enlarge the park and increased interest in forest management policies. In 1978 the Park was expanded, taking 10,600 acres of prime old-growth timber out of production and laying off approximately 1,000 people. However, in the intermediate term, several hundred new jobs will be created from the increased tourism associated with the Park.[5]

Overall the preservationist assertion that America was soon to see its last redwoods was clearly a case of public relations hype, putting symbolic value on protecting the world's tallest trees. Redwood is a most hardy species and has never been close to extinction. Much of the national park battle concerned the old-growth redwood—how much should be saved and who should control it. The RNP battle was one of the most highly publicized and virulent environmental battles of the 1960s and 1970s. Local opposition to the park expansion did result, however, in some economic mitigation efforts, described below.

Although they were not cutting down the last redwoods, local timber firms were rapidly liquidating their old-growth timber, according to the precepts of good forestry economics. They fueled the controversy by mismanaging their stands, overcutting, and over the years, damaging much of the productive forest land. The transition from an old-growth (non-renewable) to a second-growth (renewable) forest was poorly planned and executed. The lack of good forest regulations made this transition far more economically and ecologically destructive than necessary.

Timber-Management Policy

When timber operations started in the mid-1890s up through 1945, there was essentially a free market in wood production on the north coast. This was a period of frenetic exploitation with almost no public involvement in forest production, except through minimal fire prevention regulations. In 1945, when industry fear of and public pressure for federal land use and forestry regulations was highly visible, California passed its first Forest Practices Act (FPA). The composition of the rule-making Board of Forestry—with all its members from the timber industry or forestry education—and its procedures for rule making, enforcement, and evaluation of timber cutting demonstrate that the regulations were conducted by and for the industry.[6]

The purpose of the regulations was for short-term industrial self-governance. The regulations did not adequately anticipate and deal with the transition from old-growth forests to second-growth stands. Little attention was paid to restocking requirements, erosion control, wildlife habitat and water quality, and none at all to the social impact of timber production. In short, the regulations failed to deal with the problems in the north coast.[7]

The 1945 Forest Practices Act was eventually ruled unconstitutional in 1971. It was found that an industry dominated rule-making board was a violation of constitutionally mandated due process.[8] In 1973, the California legislature passed a new Forest Practices Act that was heavily influenced by environmental pressures. Under the new legislation there are significant changes in the composition of the governing Board and in the review process for timber harvesting. The new regulations, by including values beyond mere short-term timber output, are more oriented towards the long-term health of the state's private forest lands.[9] In conjunction with the Federal Clean Water Act and with the California Environmental Quality Act, the new forest regulations are a vast improvement.[10] The combination of a mature, stable, well-organized redwood timber industry and improved timber regulation assures that the environmental abuses which, in part, created the present situation will not recur.

Contemporary Policy Options

The main problems in the north coast today, for which policies ought to be developed, are the following: unemployment, a lack of economic diversification, wasted and unregenerated resources, and inadequate inter/intra-regional transportation systems. The area is isolated, provincial, and not well-suited for non-resource based industrial development. Essentially, all studies of the area agree on these problems and on the main types of appropriate policy responses. These are: (1) improvement in the scope and quality of the natural resource production base, (2) economic diversification, and (3) infrastructural developments. The first refers primarily to timber and fisheries resources. The second includes better utilization of timber (as in chips, pulp, and wood energy), the improvement of operating plant, the use of previously wasted timber resources (oak and other scrub timber), and the general acceptance—or tacit encouragement—of the recently burgeoning cottage industry in growing marijuana. The third includes harbor, airport, highway, and timber access road improvements.[11] The disagreements are on alternative strategies, the costs and benefits associated with each, the speed with which results can be achieved, and the likelihood of success.

A variety of state, federal, and local programs and agencies are now in place to implement these various policy goals. Even before, and in anticipation of, the RNP expansion in 1978, Humboldt County created the Redwood Regional Economic Development Commission (RREDC) to study development problems and to seek federal and state grants for development projects. The Economic Development Administration of the Department of Commerce has provided $5.5 million to the area, primarily for marina development and airport improvements. This funding is intended to aid commercial and sport fishing and tourism, respectively. The Park expansion legislation included a Redwood Employees Protection Program (REPP), to protect timber industry workers laid off due to the park expansion, and a program which provides up to $33 million for forest rehabilitation in and around the Park. The State of California has created a Forest Resources Improvement Program (FRIP) to provide direct grants-in-aid for small timberland owners to rehabilitate their lands, and the RREDC has proposed a timberland loan program. The adjacent Six-Rivers National Forest is mandated to create a management plan which takes into account regional problems and the specific implications of the RNP expansion. Finally, both state and local law enforcement agencies have been trying variously to regulate, evaluate, and act on the growth of marijuana. The chief concerns regarding these activities are whether they are adequately funded and sufficiently coordinated to work effectively together.[12]

Rather than to describe and comment directly on each of these agencies and programs, it is more important to articulate the analytic and political dilemmas that they collectively raise.

Market Imperfection. As with all boom-bust processes, and perhaps all development problems, the north coast case illustrates how the market has failed to produce a stable, broadly efficient, and equitable system. For a long time, redwood, like many other natural resource commodities, was underpriced, with inadequate accounts of reproduction costs. These unpaid costs of waste, overproduction, and ruin of the resource base are expensive and must now be paid. The policy question is how, and to what extent, can or should such problems be prevented?

A lesson to be learned from this case is that natural resource economies require supervision. Current antiregulatory sentiment notwithstanding, it is evident that the social costs of well-planned use of resources are less than the costs of social and environmental distress associated with laissez-faire management. Such planning must take place not only at the local and multi-regional level, but also at the national level if booms and busts in supply and demand are to be moderated.

Cost-Benefit Analysis. The familiar problems of accounting costs, benefits, and time preferences are evident in these policy disputes. They are exacerbated, however, by the role of aesthetic and environmental values— the beauty of redwoods or the value of forests in filtering air and water—in addition to economic values. Much of the dispute about the park, particularly the relative costs of jobs lost, dealt with these issues. More recently, as the next discussion shows, the issue of risk has become prominent. In general, there is groping for a working definition of *ecological efficiency* or overall balance of society and nature; this in contrast to narrower conceptions of economic efficiency or a romantic reverence for natural processes.

Labor-intense vs. Capital-intense Development Strategies. Some studies show that, whereas manual forest rehabilitation can cost $300-$900 per acre, aerial spraying of 2,4-D costs about $40-$60 per acre.[13] How is the social value of employment to be weighed against the environmental and health risks of widespread spraying? Further, the capital-intense method does not utilize the fiber or energy resources destroyed, so there is another loss in addition to that of jobs. Small-scale, self-organized work cooperatives argue that they can clear land for about $75 per acre rather than the $300-$900 figure (presumably for skilled loggers) because they have less overhead and more incentive.[14] While there is no single solution, it does seem that public policy analysts must look carefully at both alternatives. In order to accomplish vegetation management objectives, cost effectiveness is an essential criterion. However, there is presently insufficient information for detailed cost effectiveness comparisons between pesticide and manual techniques, especially ones that take into account environmental side-effects. The social benefit of work experience, self-organization, and employment lead some observers to conclude that the traditional capital-intensive methods should be used sparingly and under carefully controlled conditions.[15]

Management Concerns. The history of California Forest Practice Regulation shows that large-scale, stable, capital-intensive corporations are usually better land managers than small-scale land owners or independent woodsmen.[16] Indeed, they are now spending a great deal of money to improve their timber productivity. Yet there is real concern in an economy like that of the north coast that "the tail will wag the dog," or that corporate interest will become the regional interest. Both traditional and novel forms of economic organization seem necessary to countervail against such corporate power. These include support and technical assistance for small land owners, and the encouragement of competitive businesses as well as cooperatives and employee managed firms. Economic distress has made these alternatives more viable and politically tolerable, particularly in forest rehabilitation. Thus, policies should futher encourage these social goals as strongly as the environmental and resource goals.

Public Monies on Private and Public Lands. Regional recovery can happen only if large amounts of money are available for private landowners to improve their resources. This includes tax incentives, grants, loans, and technical support. However, some of these landowners have profited from prior abuses of their lands. What, then, is the connection between public and private costs and benefits? These questions suggest that, while public investment on private lands is necessary, every effort should be made to distribute as widely as possible—that is, through employment and training— the direct rewards of resource development investment.

Conversely, the choices that public land managers make about forest management techniques and goals will have great impact on how private landowners choose to invest in capital and labor. New general questions are thus raised about the management of public lands. How should the goals of production, reserves, recreation, environmental buffers, wilderness, and other values be met? What is to be done when some of these goals are clearly contradictory? These questions will require far more sophisticated technical, as well as political analysis, than they have yet received.

Employment Policy and Work Organization. The pacific woods have a history of radical unionism. But now, many of the area's workers are nonunionized, the unions are docile, and the unions have even sided with industry to oppose conservation and regulatory reforms. These workers can learn from others in Maine, Oregon, and Washington about organizing around conservation issues.[17] Workers will face difficult choices and some radical opportunities as job prospects decline and shift from highly paid logging jobs toward lower status, lower paying rehabilitation work.

These rehabilitation and alternative development projects provide opportunities for new small businesses, worker cooperatives, and workers assuming responsibility of existing firms, such as small sawmills. These alternatives have the added benefit of complementing, and sometimes confronting, the dynamics of corporate centralization and exaggerated community influences previously described. For example, the Hoedads in the forests of Washington and Oregon are a collectively owned and operated labor-intensive, politically active enterprise which works with corporations and public forest managers to carry out rehabilitation projects.

Illegal Economy. The growing and selling of sensimilla marijuana is now the region's second largest industry, surpassing tourism but still behind timber in revenues generated.[18] Yet there are peculiar political, moral, legal, and economic ambiguities. The profitability of the industry depends upon its illegality; its revenues are untaxed; it breeds at least some crime and violence. At the same time, the industry supports many people, some of whom are also publicly supported. It is *the* economic base in the region's poorer areas. Some of this marijuana grows on land that could be growing timber. While the Drug Enforcement Administration is putting pressure on local law enforcement agencies, at this point a policy of benign neglect seems to be politically the most sound and developmentally the most advantageous. There is a clear need for more research to determine the actual size and significance of this activity.[19]

Conclusions

The problems of the redwood region derive from a rapid decline in its natural resource base combined with intensified conflict over the resources that remain. This will be a generalized pattern as we move into what Schnaiberg calls "environmental scarcity" or what Richard Barnet calls "the lean years".[20] If redwoods were more geographically dispersed and if this were an earlier phase of our history when we had an open frontier, we might see the region left to ruin as logging and lumber mills moved elsewhere.[21]

This case shows that while environmental regulation is expensive and imperfect, weak regulation is even more expensive and imperfect. The historic failure of regulation is at the heart of the current ecological and social problems in the region. The appropriate relationship between ecological capability and economic demand cannot be resolved once and for all, but this relationship must be at the heart of anticipatory planning for regions like the north coast.[22]

Drastic changes are underway in the north coast, and they have not all been adequately understood. These include changes in the kind of work available, the degrees of work organization, alterations in status hierarchies, and levels of government involvement in the economy. These transitions, complex and paradoxical, are producing a cultural schizophrenia. The culture of the frontier—individualist, independent, entrepreneurial, destructive, and short-sighted—is inexorably giving way to one of conservation, management, and socioecological planning. While the north coast presently offers few achievements, (and will not for many years) it does illustrate some underlying policy issues, such as market imperfections, the allocation of costs and benefits, and the role of underground economies, which arise in many cases of economic decline and redevelopment.

Notes

1. A survey of these patterns of relevance includes Ann Markusen and Jerry Fastrup, "The Regional Way for Federal Aid," *The Public Interest,* Fall, 1980, pp. 87–99; Michael Rogers, "The Great Alaska Raid," *New West,* July 16, 1979, pp. 23–30; James Agee, "Issues and Impacts of Redwood National Park Expansion," *Environmental Management,* vol. 4, no. 5, 1980, p. 412; and Spencer Reiss et al., "Vanishing Forests," *Newsweek,* November 24, 1980.

2. These findings are attributable to: John G. Miles, "Humboldt County Timber Trends, 1970-2000," Report of John G. Miles Co., Inc., Eureka, California, 1970; William McKillop, "Economic Losses Associated With Reduction in Timber Output Due to Expansion of the Redwood National Park," California Resources Agency, Department of Forestry, Sacramento, California, 1977; Daniel Oswald, "Prospects for Sawtimber Output in California's North Coast: 1975-2000," USDA Forest Service Bulletin PNW-26, Pacific Northwest Forest and Range Experiment Station, Portland, Oregon, 1978.

3. Greenacres Consulting Corporation, "Redwood National Park Proposed 48,000 Acre Expansion: Data Review and Analysis," U.S. Department of Commerce, Economic Development Administration Technical Assistance Project, 1977; QRC Research Corporation, "An Economic Development Action Plan and Strategy for Humboldt County, California, prepared for Humboldt County Board of Supervisors, EDA Title IX Project No. 07-09-01916, 1978.

4. There has been a gradual process of concentration in the industry so that now four large scale and stable firms control the bulk of milling and processing. The large firms presently control or own about 50 percent of the

region's private lands. Henry J. Vaux, "Timber in Humboldt County," University of California, Agricultural Experiment Station, Bulletin 748, 1955, p. 7; State of California, "Projection of Employment by Industry and Occupation, 1980:1985, Humboldt/Del Norte Counties," 1979.

5. U.S. Department of Interior, "Report for the Congress Mandated by Section 102(a) of Public Law 95-250: Appropriate Federal Actions to Mitigate Economic Impacts Due to Expansion of Redwood National Park," prepared in consultation with U.S. Department of Commerce and Department of Labor, January 1, 1979.

6. T. F. Arvola, *The Regulation of Logging in California:* 1945-1975, State Resources Agency, State of California, Division of Forestry, 1976.

7. For example, as early as 1955, Vaux ("Timber in Humboldt County," pp. 21-26) showed the resource base was being poorly managed and that without changes in policy the region would eventually face a drastic economic decline.

8. See *Bayside Timber* v. *Board of Supervisors of San Mateo County.* App. 97 Cal. Reported 431, September 6, 1979.

9. For a discussion of the legal and environmental issues in this problem, see Thomas Lundmark, "Regulation of Private Logging in California," *Ecology Law Quarterly,* vol. 5 1975, pp. 139-188.

10. Robert N. Coates et al., *Assessing Cumulative Effects of Silvicultural Activities,* John Muir Institute, 1979, G. W. Dean et al. "Structure and Projections of the Humboldt County Economy: Economic Growth Versus Environmental Quality," University of California, Giannini Foundation Research Report 318, 1973; Greenacres Redwood National Park.: QRC, "An Economic Development Action Plan."

11. *Ibid.*

12. See, for example, QRC "An Economic Development Action Plan;" and General Accounting Office, "Congress Should Scale Down Redwood Employee Program Benefits," HRD-80-63, July 3, 1980.

13. QRC, "An Economic Development Action Plan," pp. 67-69.

14. Northwest Coalition for Alternatives To Pesticides "Manual Release of Conifers," 1979.

15. For an excellent overview of this topic see Jan M. Newton, "An Economic Analysis of Herbicide Use for Intensive Forestry Management," parts 1 and 2, Northwest Coalition for Alternatives to Pesticides, Eugene, Oregon, 1979.

16. Henry Vaux et al., "Socioeconomic Impact Data For Redwood National Park: A Report to the Denver Service Center of the National Park Service," University of California, Berkeley School of Forestry, 1973.

17. Phyllis Austin, "Meet the Men Who Are Organizing the Maine Woods," *Maine Times.* August 8, 1975; Myron W. Levin, "Frustration in

the Maine Woods Has Erupted in Violence," *Maine Times,* Sept. 16, 1977, Diane Lefer, "The Maine Woodcutters: Nothing to Show But Dead Man's Hands," *Maine Times,* August 1, 1975 and "Maine's Forgotten Wood-cutters II, *Maine Times,* August 8, 1975.

18. James Finefrock, "Raiding California's Marijuana Farmers," *San Francisco Chronicle* October 7, 1979 p. 1; David Nooran, "American Weed...It Satisfies," *Esquire,* January 1980; and *Wall Street Journal* articles on July 15, July 22, July 29, August 4, and August 9, 1980.

19. Dudley Burton and Irvine Alpert, "A Socioeconomic Analysis of the Marijuana Industry of the North Coast of California," forthcoming.

20. Alan Schnaiberg, *The Environment: From Surplus to Scarcity* (New York: Oxford University Press 1980), and Richard Barnet, *The Lean Years* (New York: Simon and Schuster 1980).

21. This pattern happened in the Southeast, but a new timber and pulp industry is emerging to utilize trees planted during the Depression by the Civilian Conservation Corps. Many of the North Coast programs are more sophisticated versions of this basic policy direction.

22. For a theoretical discussion of this problem, see Andre Gorz, *Ecology as Politics* (Boston: South End Press 1980).

**Part III
Urban Development**

Development for Whom: A Critique of Federal Development Policy

Roger J. Vaughan and
June A. Sekera

The ability of distressed urban communities to withstand the federal government's best-intentioned and financed efforts is one of the few constants during the past two decades of federal development policy. And where improvement has occurred, it has often been at the expense of the original residents: communities have succumbed to the federal bulldozer or to the inroads of gentrification. However, most neighborhoods that were distressed fifteen years ago remain distressed today. There are very few examples of successful development in distressed communities that have improved the economic well-being of the poor residents. Our targeted programs have been more concerned with *where* publicly subsidized development occurs, and insufficiently concerned with *for whom* the development occurs.

Yet the opportunity for successful development of distressed areas remains a challenging alternative to massive capital projects or reliance on transfer payments. The purpose of this chapter is to explore some of the issues that must be addressed if we are to develop a consistent and effective strategy for encouraging development in distressed neighborhoods. These efforts must emphasize developing and exploiting the entrepreneurial skills of local residents to start and manage enterprises that meet local needs. This is very different from the traditional approach of providing property tax exemptions and abatements and other fiscal incentives to companies prepared to locate in or open a branch in a distressed community.

Community-based economic development (CED) is an elusive concept to define. Although some proponents have attempted to define CED in terms of *outcomes*—increased income or improved job opportunities—these measures miss the central point: community-based development is concerned with the *process* of development. A community economic-development strategy is concerned with harnessing the community's human, physical, and financial resources to improve the environment, the quality of services, and the economic prospects of low-income residents. It is a strategy that enhances the capacity of a community to address its own social and economic problems.

The long-run goal is to enhance the ability of the community to undertake development that results in sustained growth. *Development* is a qualitative change which entails changes in the structure of the community including innovations in institutions, behavior, and technology. *Growth* is a quantitative change in the scale of the community—measured in terms of investment, output, consumption, and income.

The first section of this chapter briefly examines the causes of neighborhood decline, because the purpose of public policy must be to address the underlying causes. Too often, policies have addressed the symptoms—repainting deteriorating store fronts, providing loan guarantees to failing businesses, or income transfers to poor residents. The analysis of the cause enables us to define the goals of a community-based strategy.

The second section reviews past federal programs that have attempted to resolve the economic and social problems of urban neighborhoods. The reasons for their failure help define a more appropriate strategy for the 1980s.

The third section discusses the policies that should be pursued in order to encourage a development process that builds upon and enhances community-level resources.

The Roots of Community Decline

The transition of an urban community from one of cohesion and economic viability to one of fragmentation and despair is the result of many forces, both internal and external. It is important to develop at least a rudimentary understanding of the causes, otherwise public programs will persist in being mere palliatives—cosmetically addressing the symptoms of the problems, not the problem itself.

Community decline is more than merely the loss of population. It is the *selective* outmigration of middle-income households, educated and skilled labor, and other vital components that reduce the viability of the community as a place to do business. This is a process that is compounded by the withdrawal of private investment. It is not the presence of low-income households that is the cause of the decline. There are many low-income neighborhoods that remain stable, viable communties with access to private capital and job opportunities. The causes of decline lay beyond the income status or the behavior of the residents.

From the perspective of public policy toward community economic distress, we should distinguish three types of causes of decline: first, natural market forces; second, the failure of markets to allocate resources efficiently and equitably; and, third, the impact, often inadvertent, of public policies on the geographic distribution of residential and economic activity.

Certain market forces have been important in the selective outmigration of households and firms from urban communities. First, the growing importance of world trade for urban and rural communities in the United States undermined the economic vitality of areas specializing in low-skilled labor-intensive activities such as apparel, textiles, and fabricated metals. As tariffs have been progressively reduced, those areas whose comparative advantage most closely paralleled that of our trading partners found themselves in competition with cheap foreign imports. Industries that had traditionally received urban immigrants from abroad and from rural areas faltered, and the first rung on the economic ladder was removed.

Second, technological change led to a shift in the location of economic activity away from urban centers. Manufacturing no longer relied upon railcenters, but upon trucking, and single-story, linear-flow plants that required more land than the city could reasonably offer. The growing service sector has created many marginal jobs offering low pay and few opportunities for career advancement. Finally, those benefiting from economic growth used their growing real incomes to purchase more residential space in sprawling suburbs—residential clubs whose minimum entrance fee included ownership of an automobile.

But while market forces explain change and problems faced by certain communities, they cannot explain the persistence of those problems. Transitory misery has been the unwitting lot of many sectors of society. The rapid mechanization of agriculture during the 1930s through 1950s drove many small farmers and farm laborers into cities, where the vast majority found employment. Yet the poor residents in urban communities, devastated by the decline of manufacturing, have not been able to adjust as rapidly.

Why have not declining prices for land and structures and reduced wage rates stimulated the development of alternative economic activities for unemployed residents in declining communities? The reason is that markets do not always work efficiently. There are barriers to effective market operation that result, in part, from the innate operation of markets themselves and, in part, from the effects of public intervention in the development process.

First, markets operate through flows of information. As jobs have become more complex, the amount of information that an employer requires about an employee's skills and experience has multiplied; the information an employee must have about a potential opening has multiplied exponentially. At the same time, affirmative action requirements, minimum wage laws, safety and health regulations, and other hiring requirements have greatly complicated the operation of the labor market. So, employers seek to use cheap, informal, information networks, a move that favors established employees and their families and friends. At the same time, the tax structure has worked against hiring the unskilled. The unemployment insurance premium—that in most states is levied on the first $6,000 of wages—has become a head tax that discriminates disproportionately against low-income workers.

The complexity of manufacturing operations has also increased the amount of information that an investor—a bank loan-officer or a venture capitalist—must collect before determining the viability of a project. Again, there are short cuts that can be used to screen loan applicants such as the location of the project or even the race of the applicant. This process is weighted, too, by financial institutions whose regulations actively discourage investors from taking risks. As a result, startups depend on an entrepreneur's circle of family and friends for initial funds and naturally discriminate against those with limited resources. The wealth of the potential founder has become a more important factor than the viability of the actual business. At the same time, a business wishing to borrow capital has no choice between a loan at two or three percentage points above the prime rate from a bank and a loan at four or five times the prime rate from a loan shark. A community in transition requires risk capital, yet risk capital is not available. The result is that the community does not transform. It is pushed into a downward spiral that market forces cannot retard or even ease.

But the harm from public policies does not end with the impairment of labor and capital markets. Federal policies have systematically, if inadvertently, encouraged urban disinvestment and therefore exacerbated the problem of core communities. The federal highway system, the tax benefit of home-ownership, and federal grants for water and sewer systems encouraged the growth of sprawling suburbs for middle-income households. Business depreciation allowances and the overall business tax structure subsidized new construction at the expense of rehabilitation and repair. Assistance to the poor was provided only if they remained in the central city where two-thirds of public housing was erected.

The result is that poor communities have been left without the institutional, human, and physical resources to preserve or sustain their role as viable economic areas. The expertise necessary to provide development assistance, the resources to maintain infrastructure, the education necessary to offer a balanced workforce, and the private capital necessary for project development have all been siphoned by the pattern of suburbanization.

Paradigm Lost

By mid 1960s, the intransigence of the urban poor in the face of sustained national growth was apparent. Clearly, additional federal assistance was required.

The federal government had experimented with geographic targeting through the Area Redevelopment Administration (later to become the Economic Development Administration) that attempted to aid development in rural Appalachia. Urban Renewal had been used to clear slum areas on the belief that the problem lay in the quality and design of the physical environment. Model Cities attempted to fuse both these programs and direct aid to those urban areas with the greatest concentration of poor, rural immigrants. The Urban Development Action Grant program has provided funds for major commercial projects in urban cores.

The paradigm applied to the design of this program was the same as that used to aid less-developed countries—that the problem of poverty stemmed from the lack of physical and financial capital. The response, both abroad and at home, was massive infusions of money for large-scale projects. The programs ignored the need to also develop institutional capacity and human capital for locally controlled development and long-run growth. The new capital projects to rebuild the decaying community effectively bypassed the local residents.

The nation's foreign aid program gradually changed from one that focused on physical capital to one focused on institutional capacity building and on investing in human capital. Instead of building massive hydroelectric dams, aides worked in rural villages to improve local irrigation and soil conservation techniques. It was a much more labor-intensive form of assistance, and led to fewer photogenic projects. But it was a broader-based development strategy that involved a much larger segment of the developing society.

We have not made the same transitions in our domestic assistance to less-developed communities. We still provide transfer payments on terms that further weaken the already frail family and social fabric. We retain our faith in large capital projects as the basis for alleviating economic distress. Our training programs teach skills needed by large manufacturers, not the skills needed to enhance the economic viability of poor communities.

The community development paradigm is flawed by two basic errors that have led to a waste of the dollars spent under these programs and to a further weakening of the entrepreneurial energies and abilities in the assisted communities. First, the programs were predicated on the belief that a concentrated infusion of capital alone would improve the local economy. Second, federal, state and local governments have distributed resources among communities based on abstract indices of economic distress without considering the prospects for successful investment. Communities are encouraged to export data proving their plight in exchange for development handouts. These precepts are not the appropriate basis for the development of an effective program. If anything, they guaranteed not only program failure, but also an exacerbation of the original problems.

The capital-intensive approach to local economic distress has a long and well-documented history. Governments have provided large capital grants much more freely than they have provided other forms of assistance that would have been less visible but ultimately, more effective. Declining industrial areas have been converted into vacant industrial parks. Tax incentives have been offered to private corporations willing to open branches in distressed communities. Public office buildings have been erected in target areas. Grants have been awarded to developers as bribes to build in distressed areas.

Major capital projects offer several political and administrative advantages. They are highly visible: groundbreaking and completion offer attractive media opportunities. The building itself offers tangible evidence of the commitment by federal, state, and local governments to resolve urban problems. The structures offer the symbol of hope without hope itself.

The *flagship project* approach to development does not work. Public subsidies do not necessarily lead to increased investment. Jobs, except those requiring low or no skills, created do not necessarily go to community residents. To a large extent, the public funds displace private funds. UDAG grants reduce the private capital needed for each project. During the delay, necessitated by the complex procedures surrounding grant applications and awards, land prices rise and construction costs become inflated. As a result of public intervention, the project may be shifted a few blocks to better serve the needs of the poor community. But these subsidies do not create new projects. They rarely increase the number of jobs in the community or change who gets the jobs.

Second, the residents of the distressed neighborhood are not considered during the design and execution of the project, although it is their economic and social misery that made the project eligible for federal assistance. There are few provisions that allow the local poor to secure jobs in the new structure, and many of the vacancies may be filled by recent (foreign) immigrants.

The project does nothing to change the capacity of the community to address its economic and social problems. If anything, its strength has been eroded by the destruction of housing to build the structure and by the inflation of a new workforce whose consumption patterns spur the growth of new shops and restaurants that do little to meet the community's needs.

Finally, targeting these projects to needy communities creates the illusion that progressive steps have been taken to alleviate community distress. We have confused *expenditure* in a community with *investment* in a community. The latter should be measured in terms of the increased well-being of the original residents, and of their increased capacity to respond to local economic and social problems. Spending money in the geographic areas of a distressed community does not necessarily "trickle down" and benefit the low-income residents. To the extent that an investment is successful and enhances the land values in a neighborhood, it may spur gentrification, driving out the very people it was, ostensibly, designed to assist. Community residents have neither learned new skills nor been given the opportunity to exploit their entrepreneurial potential. They have been passive observers to a building project.

The tendency to attempt to solve problems by large-scale spending extends to many federal programs. The energy crisis has not been addressed by removing the barriers to the development of alternative energy sources. Instead we have created the Synfuels Corporation, which is projected to spend more during the next decade than will be spent on welfare and community assistance combined. It will fund huge projects that private financial institutions have had the good sense to avoid. The Synfuels Corporation is ignoring appropriate technology in the same way that our urban assistance has ignored appropriate infrastructure. Distressed communities do not need convention centers, sports stadia, or huge commercial developments. They need improved public services, better housing, and entrepreneurial opportunities. They do not need projects imposed from the outside. They need the opportunity to control and manage their own environment and economic future.

Even where we have attempted to target federal assistance toward communities, we have done so in a perverse and counterproductive way. In an attempt to help those in need we have directed resources not toward opportunities but toward symptoms of despair. The formulas through which grants are allocated include such largely irrelevant statistics as the percent of the housing stock built before 1940—a boon for gentrification—and the overall level of population—a boon for statisticians and census adjusters. We have faced the embarrassing prospect of communities, indeed, whole cities, seeking to establish, statistically, the depth of their problems rather than seeking opportunities for development.

Because community economic development has, too frequently, focused on social factors, it has not devoted adequate attention to appropriate capital and investment needs. Federal community development policies often assume that the causes of decline are the disintegration of a community's *social* fabric and therefore have failed to restore the economic, technical, and physical resources, as well as the human capital that the community needs. Bradford (1978) suggests that public efforts are mistargeted because they focus on assisting affected individuals and programs in declining neighborhoods without supporting the larger economic framework on which these individuals may depend. (For example, housing rehabilitation programs are directly related to the local housing market.) We have measured the success of federal aid to distressed neighborhoods not in terms of improved skills, local institutional capacity, or jobs for local residents. Instead, success is measured by correlating, across the country, per capita expenditures with indicators of economic distress such as per capita income, the incidence of poverty, the rate of unemployment, or some arbitrary index of all of them.

Not only have we created a set of incentives that, if anything, undermine entrepreneurship, we have also taught communities to develop plans that primarily meet the needs of federal program administrators rather than their own.

We must stop emphasizing the direction of federal spending to distressed areas. Instead, we must consider the programs as investments. This means that the performance standards by which we judge programs must be radically changed. That success (in encouraging community-based development) enjoyed by the Ford Foundation, and other not-for-profit groups, has resulted from their willingness to provide a long-term commitment and not to demand an immediate return. Venture capitalists do not demand a return from their investments at the end of the first year. They are willing to wait and to nurture the fledging company with adequate funding, management advice, and technical assistance. Even if the returns on such high-risk investments are low, they are higher than the return earned on income transfers. Investments in community development must be made in the same way. The following section outlines an improved public sector strategy directed at encouraging economic development in and by distressed neighborhoods.

Paradigm Regained

As we develop alternative programs as a response to our past failures, we must recognize that there is no single policy that will unlock the potential of our distressed communities. Not only are the causes of community decline both far-reaching and complex, but the programs of past decades have further eroded the social and physical infrastructure in the very areas they were intended to help. Further, although our focus is upon public policies, it is evident that successful community development will require both public and private sector initiatives.

Public policies must explicitly recognize that the motivation for revitalizing our distressed communities exists most strongly in the communities themselves. Unemployed workers, welfare recipients, and victims of ghetto crime have more to gain from improved economic conditions than the bureaucrats in city hall, the state capitol, or Washington. Similarly, the motivation for the private sector—from major banks to mom and pop grocery stores—is obvious: profit. We must find ways to harness these incentives for creative change.

The answers are not simple. In the remainder of this chapter we outline policies that respond to the complexity of the problems. Our recommendations are directed to actions at all levels of government and at the community level. Some are short-term and can be undertaken relatively quickly;

others would require long-term regulatory or statutory change. But simple solutions to complex problems will turn out no better than past attempts.

Greenlining an urban neighborhood by declaring it an enterprise zone is no more likely to lead to community-based development that benefits the zone's residents than was the 1950s' Urban Renewal designation or a Model Cities designation more than a decade ago. Neither would a rapid expansion of the grants to Local Development Corporations guarantee that these groups would be able to manage development within their communities.

Public policies must address three broad but related issues if they are to establish the foundation for sustained economic development in distressed areas:

To remove the barriers and disincentives that now obstruct economic improvement in poor communities.

To make available the managerial, technical, and legal talents needed for sustained growth.

To construct a community-based development strategy that fosters a bottom-up rather than top-down process for revitalization.

Our premise is that successful economic improvement of impoverished communities rests on expanding the local *private* economy. The national hallmarks of local poverty—high unemployment rates and welfare rolls— are not indications of poor places but of poor people. Merely throwing money at places will not remedy the problems; it must get into the hands of the people who live there. The most promising potential lies in giving poor people better access to business ownership. Secondly, job creation through new business development, regardless of who the owner is, will provide new jobs. But creating only low-wage, secondary labor market jobs, or strategies such as a subminimum wage for youth, will not provide the basis for long-term, sustained growth. Expansion of the local private economy must occur through expansion of individual economies.

Removing Barriers to Community-Based Development. In the long-run, sustained economic growth will depend on federal and state initiatives to remove the regulatory and tax barriers that have discouraged capital investment and job development in distressed communities. For example, there is evidence that capital markets fail to provide capital to risky projects. Banks do not price risk, they ration their funds to avoid risk. A small business that cannot get a bank loan at three or four points over the prime rate must turn to a loanshark for three or four *times* the prime rate. The combination of regulation, taxation, and institutional inertia has denied funds to projects that, while risky, are worthwhile.

This means, first, that we need to review the way loans are classified by bank regulation, the tax treatment of bad loans, and innovative risk-pricing devices such as equity kickers. It also means that some type of direct public involvement in providing both debt and equity capital for enterprise development in distressed neighborhoods will be essential. But it does not mean that the public development finance agency must consistently back losers. The paradigm is not that of a charitable organization making grants to worthy causes, but that of a venture capitalist recovering from the successful projects what is lost on the unsuccessful.

The human capital market also works inefficiently, particularly for low-income and unskilled individuals. They are not able to borrow to finance training and education programs. They lack information concerning the availability of programs and job openings. Publicly subsidized programs often fail to impart skills that are needed by the private sector. Labor market information networks that work relatively efficiently for the skilled and highly educated do not work well for the economically disadvantaged. A long-run strategy for community-based development must include measures that build and strengthen these networks. Community-based organizations (as will be discussed) can play a vital role in this task.

Finally, many communities lack necessary public infrastructure for sustained growth, such as transportation access, cleared land, buildings and structures. As development begins, federal and state commitments of public investment will be necessary. However, the approach should not be to build and hope development ensues, or to impose a master plan of public projects. It should be to work with local groups to respond to mutually agreed development needs. Speculative industrial parks rarely induce development. Public backing for projects that have some private sector commitment can work.

Inducing Investment. In addition to these long-run, market perfecting mechanisms, there are several initiatives that can be targeted toward encouraging enterprise development in distressed areas. These initiatives would be based on the expertise and technical talents of a community-based organization (CBO). How these can be developed is discussed in the following section.

The types of local enterprises encouraged in distressed neighborhoods determine whether development will occur for the residents or at the expense of the residents. The key elements are *control* of the development process and *ownership* of the enterprises. The typical response has been to offer property tax exemptions and abatements, subsidized loans, direct grants, labor training subsidies, and other inducements for companies that move into or threaten to move out of a distressed community.

These types of bribes rarely affect location decisions, and even if they did, it is doubtful whether local community residents would benefit. Those who do find employment in the publicly subsidized firm are likely to also find unattractive, low-paying jobs that offer little opportunity for advancement. The concept of enterprise zones, advanced by Representatives Kemp and Garcia, provides extensive tax incentives to businesses within designated areas, and would be the reductio ad absurdum of this approach.

The recent emphasis on small businesses following the much-quoted research result by David Birch of MIT that showed that small business is a primary source of new jobs, does not represent a fundamental change in this policy. Tax incentives designed to foster small business development in distressed areas are more likely to find their way into the pockets of land developers and designers of IRS-proof tax shelters than to seriously influence the growth or location of small businesses. These businesses lack both the accounting expertise to manipulate tax incentives to their advantage and the taxable income to make incentives worthwhile.

Of course, sustained and successful community growth will involve the immigration of some enterprises. However, community control of the overall process and of key elements of the local economy is essential. The types and extent of community control will vary among areas, and there are many means through which it can be achieved. There are four important roles that a CBO can play that allow it to shape local development and to ensure that a large part of the development occurs *for* the community:

Land Use Control. Rezoning is a critical element in redevelopment and changing zoning ordinances will determine where development occurs within the community. In some cities, land use decisions have been decentralized to community planning boards. Unless these boards act efficiently this can discourage private capital. But conducted efficiently it can ensure the compatibility of development with local needs.

Alternative Enterprise Ownership. Cooperatives and employee ownership plans are both useful tools in encouraging new types of enterprise that can provide jobs for local residents and also develop new enterprises in nontraditional areas. For example, alternative energy development, rental housing rehabilitation, rail branch lines, and decayed commercial strips, could be revitalized through community cooperatives. A threatened plant closing can be averted through employee ownership. However, many financial institutions are unwilling to finance what they regard as nontraditional business organizations. A CBO with a well-established business reputation would be useful in securing capital and perhaps even be a source of equity capital.

Redevelopment Tax. The redevelopment of an area necessarily means the relocation of some existing businesses. Some will be unable to pay for relocation and will close down. A small tax levied on any developer upgrading or converting a building can be used to fund relocation within the community. A tax may seem perverse in a community that is seeking the infusion of private capital, but it, in fact, may be beneficial. First, many deteriorating structures and sites in distressed communities are owned by real estate speculators, waiting for the community to take-off. The tax would discourage this. Second, the tax would fall upon the owners of the site of the taxed structure, not upon the new developers, and therefore be largely neutral with respect to investment decisions.

Perhaps the critical function for ensuring that development occurs for the community is to develop entrepreneurs within the community. They do not have to be graduates of a fashionable business school or be daily readers of the *Wall Street Journal*. However, they will have to be aggressively sought out and provided with assistance. There is no simple key to helping someone start his own business, and it is no easy undertaking. But many fail due to lack of basic types of expertise that can be taught through relatively unsophisticated and inexpensive methods. There are several steps that can be taken to foster business development by local would-be businessmen. These include:

elementary courses in business and business management. (A surprising number of area residents will probably have some informal experience in business. Most businesses fail in their early years through elementary management mistakes.)

assistance to existing local businesses, such as bookkeeping to loan packaging.

loaned executives from private corporations.

internships by business school graduates with CBOs, either during their graduate studies or in exchange for a grant to defray school fees.

We will also need to experiment with nontraditional forms of ownership such as cooperatives, employee stock ownership plans, joint public/private ventures, and other programs that provide both nontraditional sources of capital and also a measure of community control.

Community-Based Development. Fostering a community-based organization (an institution that may be anything from a mini-Chamber of Commerce to a full-fledged Community Development Corporation) is a central component of neighborhood revitalization. However, identifying a CBO and assisting it in ways that develop its capacity is easier to write about than to undertake. CBOs range from highly professional organizations that own and manage enterprises, to small groups meeting in church basements eager to clean local commercial strips, to fly-by-night grant writers able to commit to paper the rhetoric that public officials like to read but with little interest beyond that.

We should distinguish two types of public support that are necessary for CBOs: first, seed money to enable the CBO to reach critical mass; and second, operational support to enable the CBO to continue as a functioning unit. Both of these activities require different financing.

Public seed money run the very real risk of subsidizing the wrong group or the wrong activity. It is difficult to ascertain that the CBO: (1) represents the local community; (2) communicates with the local community; (3) has plans that are consistent with the community as a whole; or (4) has the energy and talent to carry out its proposals. To minimize these potential problems, public money should only be available if certain conditions are met.

Perhaps the simplest and most effective approach is to provide matching funds. Grants would be available only for those CBOs that have already been able to raise money locally through membership fees from residents, merchants, and local businesses. The process of raising funds will put the group in direct contact with the community and also ensure that activities are responsive to local needs. The most frequently raised objection to this approach is that it penalizes low-income communities. However, even the poorest communities often have extensive resources that can be augmented by drawing upon voluntary contributions in kind and in cash from the private sector. The matching rate could be adjusted to take account of local resources thereby providing a higher rate for poverty areas. Without demonstrating the resourcefulness to raise money, and without subjecting itself to the discipline of approaching community members, a CBO may never gain the influence and ability to help meet local problems. If we are to create an effective system of CBOs we must be prepared to accept a rigorous process of selection.

The rigors of the selection process can be mitigated by the provision of what is mystically referred to by the federal bureaucrats as technical assistance. Few incipient CBOs understand the requirements for accounting and the basic mechanisms of business finance. Under the Reagan Administration, it is unlikely that much direct federal assistance for local business development will be forthcoming. In any case, the business skill of many bureaucrats is often limited to balancing their own checkbooks. However, states and local governments can fill the gap. Technical assistance does not have to be expensive. Many corporations are willing to loan executives, trade associations can put CBOs in contact with retired business people, and universities have an abundant supply of faculty and students with necessary skills. State governments may be able to increase the supply of private sector assistance in several rather low-cost ways:

a tax credit for corporate contributions (cash and in kind) to CBOs (Pennsylvania has passed appropriate legislation).

business fellowships that pay a low-income MBA's tuition fees in return for which, after graduation, the student works for one year with a CBO.

extending the curricula in universities and community colleges to include how-to courses on entrepreneurship and local development.

The purpose of public policies is not to persuade the private sector to do something to which it is fundamentally opposed. Most corporations are aware of the benefits of vital and healthy neighborhoods. They are rightly suspicious of being drawn into yet another ill-conceived public private partnership, and are unfamiliar with many public policy issues. The overall public strategy must be to create efficient information networks so that CBOs, corporations, and public officials work together rather than in ignorance of or in conflict with each other.

The guiding principle for the provision of operating support to CBOs must be to reward successful local initiatives. Our tendency in the past has been to subsidize needy rather than effective local initiatives. CBOs should have en equity interest in the outcomes of their projects. There are a variety of mechanisms that can be adopted to provide this incentive. First, if the CBO has assisted in packaging a project that is financed through Industrial Revenue Bonds, it should be rewarded through a service fee of either two or three points paid when the financing is completed or through a fee that adds, say, one quarter of one percent to the interest rate. This is below the fee typically charged by private consultants for the same services. In return, the CBO would work with the business that has received the financing and assist it in finding and training appropriate labor, applying for zoning waivers, and other bureaucratic tasks that many small businesses are ill-equipped to perform. A similar type of service fee could apply to local lending undertaken by federal, state, and local development finance agencies. For example, a state agency that has financed an industrial or commercial project on a lease back arrangement could require that the leasees enter into a contract with the CBO which might provide development services to the project. Those CBOs that can establish a sound, businesslike reputation may eventually work directly with private financial institutions, assisting in loan packaging and loan servicing. They may also be able to charge for finding and training skilled labor. These type of returns have the dual advantage of (1) avoiding the political and institutional barriers that plague attempts to help CBOs through direct public appropriation and of (2) rewarding those CBOs that *do* projects rather than merely plan them.

A second source of operating funds is through charging fees for the direct provision of services. Imaginative CBOs have proved capable of delivering such services as neighborhood security patrols, para-transit social and health service delivery, day care centers, housing rehabilitation and weatherization, and housing maintenance. In almost all cases, the city or state is the contractor, but there is no reason why the private sector should not find such services sufficiently valuable to pay for them.

The activities listed in the preceding paragraphs are traditional areas for CBO involvement—either directly or through a not-for-profit subsidiary. But there are other, less traditional, types of activity that could be profitably undertaken by a CBO. Without discussing the complex economics of these new industries, we can identify areas that merit consideration by an active and innovative CBO.

Cable Television: As an increasing number of communities are "wired," usually with surplus public access channels, a CBO could operate programs providing both economic and cultural fare as well as local public information announcements (job openings, sources of small business lending, etc.).

Alternative Energy Development: Soaring energy prices have made many alternative energy sources—district heating, co-generation, small-head hydro, passive solar, and windmills—economically viable. A CBO could act as a mini-public utility or cooperative in developing these sources.

Waste Recovery: Although many types of waste recycling and recovery are economically viable, clumsy and centralized urban bureaucracies and fragmented rural bureaucracies have often failed to take advantage of the opportunities. A CBO may be able to operate efficiently where local government has failed.

Privatization of Public Services: Property tax cuts, rising public service costs, and prospective reductions in federal intergovernmental aid will necessitate the privatization of certain types of public service delivery. CBOs would be able to operate special transportation services, garbage disposal, and even recreation programs.

The successful development of these community-based activities will not be easy. The federal, state, and local regulatory environment will have to change, public service commissions will have to modify their pricing and franchising policies, local government will have to learn to live with CBOs, and CBOs will have to learn the business of business. But none of these changes is impossible. Indeed, most are inevitable.

The third source of operating funds is through direct grants, either from not-for-profit organizations or from public agencies. Just as in the case of seed money, a strong case can be made for providing direct grants as a match to funds raised through the two sources just outlined. We will not foster imaginative and effective CBOs unless we reward effective behavior. Needy areas are probably best assisted by example.

Conclusion

The failure of federal, state, and local programs to provide effective development in distressed communities can be traced to a fundamental confusion of expenditure within a community to investment in a community. Large-scale public works projects or massive tax incentives to private business *do not* lead to the type of development that benefits community residents. In addition, we have not offered the appropriate incentives to foster development of the capacity within community-based organizations to control and stimulate community-based organizations.

Instead of dismantling community aid programs, as the Reagan Administration is threatening, we should retarget the assistance to reward successful CBOs and to emphasize enterprise development at the local level. There should also be broad-based changes in tax and regulatory policies to encourage investment in risky projects, and to improve skill training and education. There is no single, simple cure for neighborhood distress, but there are a number of policies that offer much more promise than our present, confused nostrums.

Reference

Bradford, Calvin, et al. "Community Development Policy Paper: Structural Disinvestment: A Problem in Search of a Policy" Northwestern University, Evanston, Illinois, 1978, unpublished manuscript.

7

Capital and the Economic Development of Distressed Communities: The Role of Federal Development Financial Programs

Steven D. Davidson and
Paul L. Pryde

Introduction: The Concept of Economic Development

The period following the Second World War and ending in the early 1970s marked an era of unparalleled economic growth in the United States. During this time, the American economy served as a catalyst for improved standards of living and rising expectations in this country and throughout the world. Real output growth, as measured by the Gross National Product, consistently exceeded 3 percent reaching its apex in the late 1960s when real annual growth rates surpassed 4 percent with prices remaining relatively stable. By contrast, the national economy has experienced a perceptible decline in growth during the last decade. The average rate of real economic growth was nearly half of the preceding years. By the beginning of the 1980s, stagflation had become established. As a result, pessimism has colored the outlook on the immediate future.

Various factors have contributed to the present condition. They include: high rates of inflation; low levels of capital formation and savings; inadequate long-term capital investment; uncertainty within the capital market accompanied by gyrating interest rates; unacceptable rates of unemployment, particularly among the young and minorities; cost and availability of conventional energy supplies; a decline in productivity; and mounting trade deficits. The marginal impact that recent monetary and fiscal policies have had on recent economic events suggest that traditional macroeconomic policies may be insufficient to stabilize long-term economic growth. The fact that some sectors, such as health, housing, and energy, are subject to particularly acute price rises and that traditional manufacturing sectors, such as the steel and automobile industries, are becoming less competitive in the world market suggests that structural changes are occuring within the economy. To generate long-term growth, the efficiency of specific product and factor markets must be considered along with the macroeconomic issues of general price, production, and employment levels.

The burden of this uncertain economy, however, is not being shared equally. Communities sensitive to economic fluctuations or dependent on a single industry tend to suffer disproportionately when sectors of the economy stagnate, because they have greater difficulty adjusting to change. The decreased economic activity and increased unemployment experienced by the traditional industrial centers of the northeast and midwest and their attendant fiscal crises are examples of the uneven distributional impact of recent events. The special problems of many urban areas were brought to public attention by the plant closings and displacement of workers in Michigan and Ohio.

In addition to the economic problems, there are social and personal costs associated with local economic decline. The resulting unemployment encourages instability within the community. The civil disturbances in Miami last year serve as a haunting reminder of what might happen if economic conditions worsen and local residents perceive a lack of opportunity. The effects on the individual are equally harmful and they often take the form of alcoholism, crime and family deterioration.

The growing amount of magazine and newspaper space devoted to the issue of reindustrialization is perhaps the best evidence of what appears to be a clear national consensus on the need to do something about the country's economic ills—unemployment, inflation, bankrupt multi-nationals, deteriorating frostbelt cities, and declining productivity.

Unfortunately, there is not an equally clear consensus on exactly what government should do. As Roger Vaughan and Peter Bearse point out in a recent report on federal development policy, failure to identify basic objectives of economic policy accounts for much of the confusion that surrounds national development strategy.[1] Strategies become hopelessly contradictory when consensus is not achieved because objectives have not been defined.

To eliminate the confusion to which Vaughan and Bearse refer—to understand what an effective development policy should be—it is first necessary to understand what economic development is. One of the most useful definitions of the elusive term has been provided by Charles Kindleberger, a well-respected development economist.

According to Kindleberger, economic development means more than economic growth. It implies changes in "the technical and institutional arrangements by which output is produced."[2] Vaughan and Bearse used the same idea to develop their theory that differentiates between *qualitative* and *quantitative* changes.[3] The first includes changes that occur outside the economic structure; that is, innovations or transmutations in institutions, behavior, or technology. the automobile, and now the computer, have played major roles in shaping America's economy and institutions.

Quantitative change reflects internal characteristics of the scale of the economy. It is here that we think in terms of investment, output, consumption, and income. Shifts in income, price and population may affect the location of jobs and significant economic activity. Regardless of whether these changes are aided by government action, they demand modifications in economic relations, structures, and institutions.

Development, in short, is the continuing process of adjustment to events, and as such, is essential to continual and healthy economic growth.

If it is true that development is largely the process of adjustment to change, then the goal of development policy should not be to help people resist change but to enable them and their enterprises to respond successfully. In terms of employment, such policy should help people cope with national and regional shifts "in *levels* of employment, *locations* of employment, *who* gets jobs and the *types of jobs created*."[4]

Most economists agree that the development process depends largely on a continuing occurrence of what Albert Shapiro, former professor of management at the University of Texas, calls "entrepreneurial events," that is, the creation and expansion of new enterprises. According to Shapiro, development strategies that are designed to support the process of business formation have four advantages that generally are not derived from other approaches to development such as the relocation of branch plants:

1. *An increased ability of the community to make appropriate responses to changes in the market place.* Effective programs for enterprise formation provide a "response capability" to predicted and unpredicted events; new firms can be created or expanded faster than changes can be made in major corporations.

2. *An actuarial approach to events.* A large number of independent companies (as contrasted with a small number of corporate plants) provides a community with a variety of independent decision-making units, each appraising the environment from its own vantage point. There is an extremely low probability that all of these independent units will make the same, perhaps incorrect response to the same event. On the other hand, the corporate monolith must unify all views into one, perhaps erroneous, action.

3. *Greater innovation.* Almost all of the available evidence shows that small firms are more innovative than large, more mature companies.

4. *Low political and economic risks.* The potential benefits in successfully forming an enterprise are great. Another Xerox could be created. The potential negative consequences of failure are not nearly as dramatic. At the very worst, the failing enterprise will be traumatic for its founders and backers. It will rarely represent a net loss for the community.

The remainder of this chapter examines in detail the role of capital in the economic development process. We are particularly interested in the problems confronting urban areas that have experienced employment and population losses and severe economic deterioration. The following sections

(1) look at the available information on economic development and its implications for the use of capital and financial incentives in economic development; (2) examine the logic and rationale for appropriate intervention in the capital markets; (3) discuss federal economic development in distressed communities; and (4) summarize the recent performance of public credit or development finance programs.

Economic Development and Capital: Myths and Realities of Job Creation and Economic Development

The overriding goal of any realistic economic development strategy must be to create private sector jobs; it is the most productive method to increase and equitably distribute real income growth, especially in distressed areas. Harold Hovey has estimated that an annual expenditure of $1 million for twenty years of income maintenance payments or public service jobs adds $1 million to the local economy and an additional $430,000. By contrast, spending $1 million each year for twenty years on capitalizing private jobs (that otherwise would not exist) provides a continuous income stream, secondary employment, and ever-growing investment. Hovey estimated that, by the twentieth year, the $1 million dollar investment will result in an annual income of five million dollars to local residents. Furthermore, unlike income maintenance payments or public service jobs, private sector employment generates a continuous stream of benefits from the export of goods and services.[5] Public sector jobs programs are also subject to uncertain tenure because they are sensitive to political machination. In addition, some subsidized job programs may lack incentives for employee performance and production. As a result, workers may not develop appropriate attitudes or derive any feelings of accomplishment. Finally, the opportunity for advancement is considered greater in the private sector since successful firms grow rapidly.

The relationship between creating employment, deciding on a location, and economic development is frequently misunderstood. It is generally assumed that corporate branches leave areas which are in economic decline for those which are growing. In reality, it appears that the celebrated movement of some branch plants and corporate headquarters from the northeast and midwest to the south and west is exaggerated and provides an incomplete view of the development process. Wolman, for example, found that corporate relocation accounted for less than 1 percent of all employment.[6] Most businesses that relocate tend to move relatively small distances and they rarely move outside the metropolitan area. These well-documented moves are, in fact, due to differences in the rate of business births and deaths.

In his recent analysis of Dun and Bradstreet data, David Birch of the Massachusetts Institute of Technology found that the creation and disappearance of independent business and branch plants explain most employment changes.[7] He also found the job loss rate to be roughly the same throughout the country. According to Birch, fast growing and dynamic areas actually *lose* jobs at a (slightly) more rapid rate than declining areas. Houston, for example, loses more jobs than Buffalo or New Haven. The high rate of job loss is consistent among regions and metropolitan areas with communities, on the average, losing about 50 percent of the employment base every five years and with only a 1 percent variance within business cycles. Birch concludes, therefore, that the key to economic growth is the rate at which businesses are formed and expanded; in other words, the rate of occurrence of entrepreneurial events.

In earlier research, Birch found that (1) business expansion and births accounted for virtually all new employment with 40 percent birth-generated employment and 60 percent expansions produced by independent entrepreneurial establishments; (2) independent businesses with separately located branches each account for half of all employment; branch plants tend to be more important to employment in the south/rural areas; independent businesses are more important in the north/urban areas; and (3) the most fascinating and interesting results, from a public policy perspective, however, is firm size vis-à-vis employment creation. Businesses with less than twenty employees generated two-thirds of all jobs and small independent firms created slightly more than half of all jobs.[8]

Birch's work has been criticized for two reasons. First, that there has been a shift from manufacturing to service industries that may have skewed the results in favor of smaller firms. Second, that the period under study, 1969–1975, may not be typical enough from which to draw conclusions. However, his conclusions have not been generally disputed. According to Birch, small businesses generated all net new jobs in the northeast and provided the national average in the midwest. As Vaughan and Bearse conclude, "small firms have been a significant force in the job creation process."[9]

Support for the proposition that small businesses have been significant generators of employment is also provided in a study by the National Federation of Independent Business (NFIB).[10] Businesses that employ less than 100 people increased 13.2 percent between 1967–1972 compared with 8.9 percent for firms with more than 1,000 employees. NFIB data indicate that this represents a reversal of trends from the prior decade.

In addition to creating jobs, small businesses are generally more responsive and adaptive to local conditions. They are more likely to produce goods and services appropriate to the locale and they can be aware and sensitive to local community needs. A strong small business sector provides a more diverse and resilient economy than one that is dependent on fewer large businesses. The former is less vulnerable to external shocks. One analyst supports this view apropos inner cities by stating "the problem of inner cities is not so much due to the loss of jobs but rather the poor rate at which they are being replaced.[11] If the economy of the inner cities is to be revived, Birch's findings would suggest that an urban development strategy must be based on conditions favorable to entrepreneurial risks.

Economic Development and the Cost of Capital. Another widely held belief is that companies locate where they do because of tax and financial incentives offered by local, state, or federal grants. Financial costs are assumed to be of great importance when a firm is selecting a location. Unfortunately, research and experience find this view to be erroneous.

Traditionally, states have attempted to foster economic growth by offering tax holdings and capital subsidies. The evidence shows, however, that reducing the cost of capital or taxes only influences the location decision when alternative sites are equally appealing. This is logical since tax and capital costs represent a small percentage of total expenses and interest rates do not differ significantly between regions. For example, a Federal Reserve Bank of Boston study concluded that state and federal taxes comprise about 4.4 percent of total costs.[12] Another study, based on IRS data, concluded that capital costs are ten percent of total business costs. By contrast, according to a study by Cornia and Testa, labor costs are about $.66 of each dollar value added.[13] Access to growing markets and the availability and cost of skilled labor are more important determinants of location. Population shifts, therefore, have a greater effect on location than capital costs.

In addition to their deductable impact on location decisions, tax and financial incentives may also be wasteful. The investment tax credit, for example, is taken by all firms that invest in fixed assets whether or not they did so because of the credit. In other words, a tax credit enacted to encourage investment in plant and equipment goes to firms who would have made the investment *without the credit* as well as those for whom the availability of the incentive was the decisive factor. Similarly, it is unclear how sensitivity of the capital expenditure and expenditure decisions are to accelerated depreciation allowances and corporate taxes. Econometric models demonstrate that the decision to invest is based principally on plant capacity, expected sales, productivity, and profitability. Consequently, it has been postulated that tax incentives—even those geographically targeted—may influence the timing of investment but not the decision to invest. This issue undoubtedly will continue to be debated.

Although financial and tax incentives are unlikely to be influential in attracting industry, high taxes can be a deterrent. If taxes in one jurisdiction are substantially higher than those in a neighboring one, then its attraction may be diminished. This implies that favorable local tax policy is unlikely to significantly enhance an area's attractiveness but a relatively heavy tax burden can reduce it.

The Importance of Capital in Economic Development: A Summary. It must be concluded that economic development is inextricably related to business formation and expansion. The movement of corporations from one locality to another is an insignificant factor in this process. However, especially young and small enterprises do play an important role. Business or enterprise development is strongly influenced by market access, land, and labor cost and availability. However, the cost of capital is unlikely to significantly affect economic activity. It is appropriate, then, to ask whether public intervention in the capital markets, through various tools at the disposal of public policymakers (direct loans, guarantees, subsidies) is proper. If the private financial markets do not allocate funds to credit-worthy firms who also have the capacity to generate income and employment, then intervention is proper. In other words, policy should endeavor to mitigate capital gaps created by imperfections in the capital markets. Although reducing the cost of capital through subsidy will have only a marginal impact on business decisions, the inability to obtain appropriate capital can debilitate an otherwise successful business venture, handicap economic development, and remove opportunities for employment. Public capital or development finance policies should emphasize the availability rather than the cost of capital.

Attacking Capital Market Failures

Although capital markets generally work well, evidence reveals that imperfections restrict the availability of capital to expanding young and small firms that, as we have seen, are important as potential employers and contributors to local economic development. These market failures also hinder mature firms, on the verge of closing, who have the potential to become profitable again through new management or reorganization. Such failures also deter employees and communities from acquiring those branch plants and subsidiaries that parent corporations have deemed expendable. However, given the demonstrated importance to and value of expanding new and small businesses, their capital availability problems are a greater constraint to economic development.

The view of capital markets from the perspective of the major corporation, for example, Fortune 500 companies, differs significantly. The large corporation has a wide array of sources of capital at its disposal. It has easy access to regional and money center banks who vigorously compete for the corporate account. Corporations are also able to participate in the many new financial markets, including the commercial paper and eurocurrency markets. They are able to raise long-term debt and equity in the public markets through insurance companies and investment bankers.

For the younger and smaller enterprises, the search is generally limited to local sources of credit who are hesitant to provide funds to them, especially during the start-up phase. The predominant sources of capital are not the financial institution or formal market but the entrepreneur's family, friends, and personal savings. When capital is provided through institutional sources, it is available in an inappropriate form, relatively short-term bank debt. Long-term debt and equity, the patient money crucial to the success of new and small businesses in the early years of operation, is frequently not available. Such financing is valuable to these firms because it does not require immediate repayment and makes internal reinvestment of revenue possible.

Unlike established corporations, new and small firms also lack substantial retained earnings or sufficient cash flow to meet working capital requirements. With less flexibility in the timing of their external financing decisions, new and small businesses do not have the luxury of delaying the search for this capital until market conditions are optimal.

Because young and small firms do not have access to the national financial markets, the characteristics of local sources of capital become important. Once again, we find that it is the availability rather than the cost of capital that is important since studies indicate that interest rates do not vary widely among regions.[14]

Research and experience have documented the following as the factors that have contributed to existing capital gaps:[15]

Risk. Although, on the average, small firms are as profitable as major corporations, their rates of return are subject to greater variation. Greater risk and uncertainty, therefore, are associated with investment in small firms. Unless risk can be reduced, pooled or spread, a financial institution is less likely to invest in such enterprises. This is especially true of commercial banks where the interest income on loans between small and large businesses does not differ significantly. Hence, there is little incentive to accept the inherent risk of young and small businesses when the more certain income from larger companies is available.

Transaction and Information Costs. Evaluating a financial transaction is time consuming and expensive. On-site inspection of the project, analysis of financial statements and discussions with the management team are required. These costs are generally fixed and do not vary with the size of the loan. Therefore, the costs associated with relatively small transactions discourage such transactions. Financial institutions are also reluctant to invest in firms about whom information is not readily available. Obtaining such information is not always easy and can be costly while information about publicly held corporations is available through annual reports and other documents.

Prejudice. Lenders and investors tend to be skeptical about products, processes, locations, management forms (for example, cooperatives), and people they do not know. They are reluctant to finance new production techniques, products, and firms. Financiers carefully scrutinize backgrounds of new borrowers and enterprises with unconventional organizational structures. This is an especially difficult barrier to overcome for minorities and women and for firms located in communities perceived to be economically distressed.

Government Regulations. The regulation of securities markets and financial institutions occasionally have had the unintended effect of increasing the cost and decreasing the availability of seed money and venture capital. The Securities and Exchange Commission, for example, requires a registration fee, an annual report, and multiple copies of several financial statements which make the cost of marketing a small issue in the public markets prohibitive. These expenses can be as high as 15 percent of the capital raised.[16] The regulation and examination of financial institutions encourage conservatism. The regulation of financial institutions also restrict competition by creating barriers to market entry. Receiving a charter for a new bank has become very difficult. The Glass-Steagal Act which prohibits commercial banks from engaging in investment banking activities, such as equity investment, further decreases competition between financial institutions.

Conclusions

Recent events have had an unsettling effect on many urban areas, particularly those in the northeast and midwest, that have become dependent on the traditional manufacturing industries. These communities confront severe economic distress and rising unemployment. They must face the challenge of developing or creating a different and more diverse economy. The engine of this process must be young and small, expanding firms. Research, principally by David Birch, has shown that it is the *rate* at which businesses expand and contract rather than corporate branch plant relocation that determines employment, which is the most important measure of development.

Although the cost of capital as a factor in business location and expansion has been exaggerated, the availability of capital is important to business formation and expansion. Imperfections in the financial markets restrict access to external capital for young and small firms.

The importance of small and young business to the development process combined with their difficulty in obtaining sufficient capital suggests that federal development finance programs must play an important but limited role in stimulating distressed areas. A sharp reduction in federal financial resources would be harmful. However, it should not be inferred that existing programs cannot be improved. For example, the criticism that public business financing efforts can and sometimes do displace private capital is not without merit. Development finance programs must be more carefully tailored to eliminate imperfections in the financial markets.

A review of existing federal economic development programs indicates the following improvements should be considered:

Direct the Public Financial Resources to Deserving Firms in the Most Distressed Communities. In comparison to the capital available in the financial markets, public development finance resources are miniscule. In order to use these funds most efficiently, they should be targeted to communities where unemployment and economic distress are most severe. A good model might be the regional development policies of European countries in which less than a third of the population is eligible. This is in sharp contrast to practices of the Economic Development Administration. Testimony during reauthorization hearings for the Economic Development Administration in 1979 revealed that over 80 percent of the country was eligible for assistance.

Place Greater Emphasis on Long-Term Equity Financing. For reasons stated earlier equity capital is the most appropriate and rarest form of financing for young and small firms. Yet most federal assistance takes the form of debt. Several states provide models upon which equity financing programs could be based. The Alaska Renewable Resources Corporation, Massachusetts Technology Development Corporation and the Massachusetts Development Finance Corporation all make equity investments.[17] The third organization is particularly relevant because it makes investments in distressed communities. A fourth model is the Connecticut Products Development Corporation which received a royalty payment (that is, percentage of revenues rather than profits) as compensation for its investments.

Develop Risk-Pooling and Risk-Spreading Devices. A reason that financial institutions are hesitant to invest in young and small businesses is that such investments are perceived to be risky. If the risk could be pooled among several institutions, the reluctance presumably would diminish. Models already exist at the state level. Several insurance companies provided the capitalization for Massachusetts Capital Resource Corporation (MCRC) in exchange for state tax abatements. The companies receive tax reductions as long as MCRC invests a specified amount of its funds in expanding, high-risk companies. Another example are the so-called bankers' banks that have been created in several primarily agricultural states. Small banks have invested in a financial institution that serves as a captive whole-sale bank. Although their objective is to assess funds for loan, they could evolve into a risk-spreading institution.

Encourage Financial Institution Participation in Guarantee Programs. Guarantee programs intended to reduce risk to financial institutions have been constrained by the concern about the expenses and time associated with participation in such programs. Bankers frequently complain that government regulations and excessive turnaround time discourage their participation. To be most effective, the guarantee programs should be more simply designed. One reform might be to issue financial institutions lines of guarantee credit which would reduce the need for supervision of each proposed loan. Under another approach proposed in California, the bank, borrower, and government would contribute reserves to a loan loss fund. The reserve fund would be used to purchase defaulted loans, thus reducing the delay and bureaucracy characteristic of many existing programs.

Reduce Transaction and Information Costs. An element often overlooked in federal development finance programs is the importance of providing management and financial packaging services. Although such services are available in some agencies, efforts are frequently inadequate and underfinanced. Yet many deals are not undertaken because of prohibitive transactions and information costs. This problem could be ameliorated if more emphasis were placed on the technical assistance aspects of development finance. An idea that periodically has been forwarded is to pay the development organization a finder's fee for originating and/or packaging a deal.

Review Financial Institution and Capital Market Regulations. Development finance policies have concentrated on direct expenditure and guarantee programs. The impact of harmful regulation frequently has been overlooked when examining capital market operations vis-á-vis economic development. Reform of financial institutions and securities laws can increase the capital available to young and small firms with only minimum public expenditures. Changing regulations that stifle competition among financial institutions, discourage risks, and encourage financial market concentration would create greater efficiency and capital availability to all creditworthy firms.

Notes

1. Roger Vaughan and Peter Bearse, "Federal Economic Development Programs: Framework for Design and Evaluation," p. 1.
2. Belden Hull Daniels, Nancy Barbe and Beth Siegel, "Building Capacity for Development and Innovative Issues for CETA Funds," p. 8.

3. Vaughan and Bearse, "Federal Economic Development Programs," p.5.

4. Vaughan and Bearse, "Federal Economic Development Programs," p. ii.

5. Larry Litvak, "Commercial Bank Financing for Small Business Enterprise in Arkansas," p. 21. He cites work by Harold Hovey.

6. Belden Hull Daniels and Michael Kieschnick *Development Finance: A Primer for Policymakers, Part 1: What Government Finance Programs Can—and Cannot—Do,* p. 61. Harold Wolman, "Components of Employment Change in Local Economies: A Literature Review, was cited.

7. David L. Birch, *Choosing a Place to Grow: Location Decisions in the 1970s.*

8. David L. Birch, *The Job Generation Process.*

9. Vaughan and Bearse, "Federal Economic Development Programs," p. 26.

10. National Federation of Independent Business, *Factbook on Small Business.*

11. Stewart Butler, *Critical Issues: Enterprise Zones: Pioneering in the Inner City,* p. 16.

12. Lawrence Litvak and Belden Hull Daniels, *Innovation in Development Finance,* p. 28.

13. Belden Hull Daniels and Michael Kieschnick, p.8: they cite Cornia, Testa and Stocker "Local Fiscal Incentives and Economic Development."

14. Paul A. Mayer, "Price, Discrimination, Regional Loan Rates and the Structure of the Banking Industry" in *Journal of Finance,* pp. 37–45.

15. For an in-depth discussion, see Belden Hull Daniels and Michael Kieschnick's *The Theory and Practice in the Design of Development Finance Innovations* and Steven Davidson's "Rural Development Finance: The State of Our Knowledge."

16. Belden Hull Daniels and Michael Kieschnick, *The Theory and Practice in the Design of Development Finance Innovations.*

17. More comprehensive descriptions of federal programs are available in Gail Kendall's *A Primer on Development Finance in New England* and Northeast-Midwest Institute's *Guide to Federal Resources for Economic Development.*

18. Lawrence Litvak and Belden Hull Daniels *Innovations in Development Finance.*

References

David L. Birch. *The Job Generation Process.* Cambridge, Mass.: MIT. Program on Neighborhood and Regional Change, 1979.

David L. Birch. *Choosing a Place to Grow in the 1970's.* Cambridge, Mass.: MIT Program on Neighborhood and Regional Change, 1981,

Stewart Butler. *Critical Issues: Enterprise Zones: Pioneering in the City.* Washington, D.C.: Heritage Foundation, 1980.

Belden Hull Daniels and Michael Kieschnick. *The Theory and Practice in the Design of Development Finance Innovations.* Cambridge, Mass.: Harvard University Department of Urban and Regional Planning, 1978.

Belden Hull Daniels and Michael Kieschnick. *Development Finance: A Primer for Policymakers,* 3 vols. Washington, D.C.: National Rural Center, 1979.

Belden Hull Daniels, Nancy Barbe, and Beth Siegel. "Building Capacity for Development: Innovative Uses for CETA Funds." *Commentary.* Published by the National Council for Urban Economic Development, October 1980.

Steven Davidson, "Rural Development Finance: The State of Our Knowledge." *The State of Rural Economic Development.* Washington, D.C.: National Rural Center, 1981.

Derek Hausen, "Banking and the Finance of Small Business." *Working Papers.* Washington, D.C.: Council of State Planning Agencies, 1979.

Gail Kendall, *A Primer for Development Finance in New England.* Boston, Mass.: New England Regional Council, 1981.

Larry Litvak, "Commercial Bank Financing for Small Business Enterprise in Arkansas. *Working Papers.* Washington, D.C.: Council of State Planning Agencies, 1979.

Lawrence Litvak and Belden Hull Daniels. *Innovations in Development Finance.* Washington, D.C.: Council of State Planning Agencies, 1979.

Paul A. Meyer, "Price Discrimination, Regional Loan Rates and the Structure of the Banking Industry." *Journal of Finance* 22 (March 1967): 37–45.

National Federation of Independent Businesses. *Factbook on Small Business.* Washington, D.C.: National Federation of Independent Businesses, 1978.

Northeast-Midwest Institute. *Guide to Federal Resources for Economic Development.* Washington, D.C.: Northeast-Midwest Institute, 1979.

Roger Vaughan and Peter Bearse. "Federal Economic Development Programs: A Framework for Design and Evaluation." Prepared for the Commission on Employment Policy, October 1980.

8

The Industrial Restructuring of South Wales: The Career of a State-Managed Region

Philip Cooke and
Gareth Rees

Introduction: The Structure of Dependence

"Notwithstanding the actions taken by Government, there exists in Wales not a jobs gap but a jobs chasm into which the economic and social structures of large parts of Wales are in danger of falling" (House of Commons 1980). With these words, the all-party House of Commons Committee on Welsh Affairs concluded its recent report on the economic problems of Wales. For a century and a half, the industrial South has been the dominant economic and population focus of the country. This region now faces a crisis of unprecedented proportions, brought on by the effects of the recession on its traditional industries which produces coal and steel, as well as other major employment sectors. Moreover, as the Committee makes clear, government policies have failed to provide adequate responses to this crisis. Indeed, state interventions both currently and in the past have actually contributed to the vulnerability of the communities of South Wales.

The essential context here is set by the historical development of the region's economy in a markedly *dependent* form. The absence within Wales of the preconditions of capitalist growth meant that the nineteenth century exploitation of metal and coal reserves in the South was financed overwhelmingly by merchant capital originating outside the region (Daunton 1978). Moreover, the continuing orientation of the two basic industries toward the export of commodities for use in other parts of Britain or abroad ensured that merchant interests maintained their dominance over the development of South Wales. As a result, technological innovation (especially in the coal industry) was stunted and there was a relative absence of diversification into other related industrial sectors, such as engineering (Holmes 1976). And, of course, the economic and social catastrophe of the 1920s and 1930s tragically highlighted the weaknesses of this industrial structure.

107

The Development of a State-Managed Region

The response to the crisis of the inter-war period was the massive increase in the state's involvement in the management of the economy and the general organization of social life. The state accepted commitments to economic growth and full employment, which were to be achieved by Keynesian fiscal and budgetary measures, as well as the nationalization of key sectors (coal, steel, railways, and public utilities). In addition, the creation of a welfare state involved the development of an enlarged system of welfare and social service provisions, most of them on a nonmarket, decommodified basis (Miliband 1978).

This settlement of 1945 marked, then, a major victory in the struggle for improved lifeconditions for the working class; it marked the creation of major spheres in which the form of operation of the traditional capitalist market ceased to be dominant. However, it is important to recognize the essentially *negotiated* character of the settlement: it also conferred significant benefits on the controllers of capital as a condition of its acceptance. Hence, the welfare state removed from the private arena the responsibility for the reproduction of labor-power. Keynesian demand management was used to maintain levels of domestic demand and, in an often contradictory way, to protect the interests of an internationally oriented finance capital through balance-of-payments and, hence, sterling manipulations. Equally, nationalization has been used as a means of organizing essential industries to supply cheap inputs to private industrial capital. In short, the dramatic increase in the functions of the state was the basis of capitalist restabilization. Nevertheless, the post-war British state has reflected the potential that governments have had to implement policies that operate in the interests of workers, *in spite of* the constraints set by the necessity of maintaining the conditions of capital accumulation: this ambiguity is central to any *theoretical* understanding of the state.

Nowhere has this been more apparent than in South Wales, dominated by state-controlled industries (coal and steel) and the recipient of special aid under regional policy to attract new manufacturing industry and thus diversify the employment base (Morgan 1979). Hence, for example, the development of (then) cheaper sources of energy during the 1950s precipitated a state-managed conversion to a multi-fuel economy in Britain, designed to supply industrial capital at lowest cost (Carney 1980). The effects in South Wales, historically a high-quality but high-cost coalfield, were calamitous. The 1960s saw a severe contraction, with the closure of over eighty of the region's pits. Inevitably, the speed of this run-down resulted in the creation of a large labor-reserve (despite considerable net emigration) (Rees and Rees, forthcoming) and the removal of employment opportunities from extensive areas of the region. In steel, it is true that defensive pressure from workers' organizations was important in preserving the traditional geographical focus of sheet-steel and tinplate production in South Wales, to avoid the social distress that would have resulted from relocation to other technically suitable sites (Warren 1970). However, this pressure coincided with the owners' desire to minimize disruption of production at a time when private industry was desperately short of metal supplies. The increase in the importance of steel-making to the regional economy, which resulted from the investments made in new plants during the 1950s did nothing to alter South Wales's role as a *primary producer.* Even by the late 1960s very little of the increased output was actually processed for finished products within Wales (Buchanan 1968).

Even regional policy, which was strongly supported by both the labor unions and sections of capital, especially during the classic period of modernization of the British economy during the 1960s, had highly ambiguous effects (Rees and Lambert, forthcoming). Hence, to characterize the acceleration in the growth of manufacturing jobs and new establishments in South Wales during this period as a straightforward success for regional policy (Moore and Rhodes 1975) is an oversimplification. It is to ignore, for example, the attractions of the region as a site for industrial platforms for the penetration of new markets (for instance in the European Economic Community) by transnational corporations (Davies and Thomas 1976). Moreover, for certain manufacturing sectors, the availability of a pool of (mostly) female labor—low cost and non-unionized—has been an important determinant of locational decisions (Massey 1979). Most critically, however, the types of jobs that have been created have been limited largely to those low-skill routinized functions typical of a secondary labor market (Lovering 1978; McNabb 1980). Much the same applies to the service industries, where by far the greatest employment growth has occurred (and which, of course, is only indirectly affected by regional policy).

In summary, then, the experience of South Wales during the twenty-five years after 1945 is prototypical of what the settlement implied for such regions. Capital was able to shift its use of the resources of the region (and in particular labor-power) without altering the essential vulnerability that derives from dependence. Moreover, it was precisely the thorough-going intervention of the state that enabled this shift to occur: the state directly facilitated the processes of restructuring through its policies. But also, the involvement of organized labor in the formulation of state strategy, while enabling significant advances for working people, also had the effect of deflecting more fundamental conflicts. All these circumstances have set major preconditions for the current crisis in South Wales.

The Current Crisis

These characteristics of the settlement of 1945 became accentuated with the deepening of the economic crisis during the 1970s. After a series of spectacular confrontations with labor unions, coinciding with the Conservative administration of 1970 to 1974, the close *incorporation* of the unions and, to a lesser extent, the employer's organizations, into the process of state policy-formation came to be seen as essential. This was necessary to combat the inflationary pressures generated by labor's ability to win wage increases, which was inherent in the strategy developed after 1945. Such incorporation was similarly valuable in restructing British industry in the face of intensifying international competition, through, for example, the national industrial strategy and National Enterprise Board (NEB) (Cameron 1979). At the British level, the results of such corporalist policies (Winkler 1977) was to restrict the growth of real wages, without improving economic competitiveness (Glyn and Harrison 1980).

In South Wales, the dominant trends in capital restructuring continued. Hence, the Welsh Development Agency (WDA), a state-financed body, with both labor unions and employers involved in its management, was established in 1976 to promote industrial efficiency, further economic development and safeguard jobs in Wales. This marked a move away from the direct subsidy of creating jobs (expressed most clearly in the abolition of the Regional Employment Premium in 1977) toward the subsidy of individual firms, by providing loan and equity finance, and building advance factories. Whatever its potential, the WDA has made little impact on the underlying problems of South Wales. Its financing programs have been excessively conservative, constrained by strict, state-imposed criteria, irrespective of some expensive investment failures. More generally, it has failed to pursue a strategy of integrated economic development and has not provided quality jobs where needed. The WDA has merely responded ad hoc to preexisting trends in industrial change (Cooke 1980).

In coal and steel, however, the strengths of organized labor were much more apparent. The prospects of the British coal industry had been transformed by changes in the world fuel economy and, more locally, two successful strikes in 1972 and 1974, the latter of which brought down the Conservative administration. Even in South Wales, beset by problems over production costs, the working parties (comprising government, unions, and the National Coal Board (NCB) considering the development of the industry in the region, made commitments to major new investments in 1974 and again in 1979. However, the fragility of such corporatist commitments became apparent with the 1979 election of a Conservative administration firmly committed to the disciplines of the monetarist free market.

The steel industry has been the victim of even sharper policy switchbacks. The British Steel Corporation (BSC) responded in the early 1970s to changes in the world steel market by new investment in two of the South Wales plants and the proposal to close the other older ones, with the loss of some 9,000 jobs (BSC 1973). However, the defensive strength of labor during the period of corporatism was sufficient to postpone these closures: a decision that in 1980 was used by government to justify further run-downs. The accelerating contraction of the steel-consuming sectors of domestic industry in the face of international recession and growing import penetration has wholly undermined the attempt to achieve internationally competitive productivity and pricing levels within the BSC, producing an enormous overcapacity and operating losses.

The failure of corporatist strategies to cope with the worsening economic crisis presaged the most radical break in the development of state policy during the post-war period, marked most clearly by the election of the Thatcher administration. The absence of popular support for corporatism laid the foundations for the current attempts to roll back the frontiers of state intervention, as the necessary condition of controlling inflation, restoring individual incentives and thereby promoting ultimate economic recovery (Jessop 1980).

In South Wales, the disastrous effects of these policies merely serve to underscore the continuing vulnerability of its economic structure. In the private sector, redundancies are running at record levels; a trend which may be accentuated by cuts in regional policy. The 1980 Coal Industry Bill severely limits investment in the region. Most importantly, the BSC has been set limits on its borrowing capacity, as well as the requirement to be profit making in the medium term. The panic response has been to mount a further massive demanning program, involving the loss of some 11,500 jobs in South Wales by the end of 1980. At present, BSC's losses continue to mount (there was a pre-tax deficit of £279 million for April to September 1980) and a management proposal to shed over 4,000 further jobs in the region during 1981 was unveiled in December 1980.

Given these problems—and their inevitable multiplier effects—it is not surprising that unemployment in Wales as a whole has been predicted to reach 15 percent by 1983, without taking account of any further steel cuts (Cambridge Economic Policy Group 1980). It would appear, then, that following a long period of attempted *reconstruction* of the South Wales economy, we have now entered a period of economic *destruction*. And it is to this that the Welsh Affairs Committee drew attention in the quoted passage.

Toward an Alternative Strategy

The severity of the crisis confronting the communities of South Wales demands some evaluation of alternative development strategies. Three are currently being canvassed: continued monetarism; a return to Keynesian corporalist policies; and the radical restructuring demanded by the Alternative Economic Strategy (AES). The debate over these has focused on their merits in terms of regenerating the economy as a whole (Glyn and Harrison 1980). Less attention has been paid to their regional effects. In part, of course, British economic health is necessary for the recovery of regions such as South Wales. However, the foregoing analysis demonstrates that it is not a *sufficient* condition of ensuring good quality jobs—and consequent living standards—for those men and women in the region who want them.

Against this, any continuation of monetarist policies will be disastrous in the short-term. However, the proponents of such policies clearly base their case upon longer-term prospects. Hence, it is argued that by driving out of business less efficient firms and curbing the powers of unions, the foundation is being laid for the emergence of an internationally competitive core of British industry. The central difficulty, however, is that it is impossible to predict the levels of bankruptcy and unemployment that will be necessary. Moreover, even if the strategy were successful in British terms, there is nothing to suggest that the problems of South Wales would be eradicated. The operation of this kind of free market is likely to generate a distribution of economic activity that implies only extensive emigration from the region (as the Prime Minister has already indicated: *Hansard* July 24, 1980). Accordingly, commentators have urged the necessity of relief measures for the region (Griffiths et al. 1980; Welsh Affairs Committee 1980) which in effect imply an ad hoc resumption of Keynesian/corporatist policies—strong regional policy, subsidies to industry, etc. Clearly, these are most unlikely to be implemented in isolation from a general adoption of such a program. In short, a return to the Labor administration's program of the later 1970s. There is no doubt that, *in the short-term,* this strategy would relieve the intense unemployment problems of regions like South Wales. For example, even the subsidy of international levels of the fuel inputs to the BSC would preserve many thousands of jobs (in steel and coal) which, at a minimum, would enable a socially responsible reorganization program. The expenditure of public funds in this way would be preferable to spending on unemployment compensation and other welfare benefits (Rowthorn and Ward 1979).

However, there is no recognition here of the *fundamental* changes required in the British economy. Hence, to use the steel example again, it is unlikely that demand for British crude steel will rise significantly in the long-term. The development of production capacity in less-developed countries, the Soviet bloc, and the reduced demand for durable consumer goods, (as replacement rather than purchase becomes the norm in advanced capitalist countries) mark a sea change in the world market (Santos 1980). This argues the necessity of extensive technological innovation. However, it is precisely in this respect that British industry generally has been most backward (Pavitt 1979) and, on past performance, there can be little faith in the envisaged national industrial strategy.

For regions such as South Wales, the consequences of this strategy would be especially grave. In addition to the continued vulnerability of the traditional industries, even those sectors which have been relatively successful in terms of job growth would not have an assured future. Hence, further growth is likely to be limited by the changes in the international division of labor, which is bringing problem regions increasingly into competition with parts of the underdeveloped world (Massey 1978). Growth will be limited, too, by technological innovations (such as micro-processors) which may have an adverse impact upon regions like South Wales which have a characteristic industrial organization and consequently low potential for innovation (Oakey 1979). A return, then, to Keynesian/corporatist orthodoxy is simply not enough: a more radical alternative is required.

The AES is directed at sustaining full employment in a modernized and efficient British economy. Its major elements have been discussed extensively elsewhere and may be treated briefly here (CSE London Working Group 1980). These elements are: (a) in the short-term, reflation through an extensive program of public expenditure, thereby reducing unemployment and restoring social service provision; (b) in the long-term, the thorough-going restructuring of the economy through the agency of the state, including the nationalization of key industrial firms (along the lines of the British National Oil Corporation) and the widespread enforcement of planning agreements between government and large private companies, thus enabling the reconciliation of national economic priorities with individual corporate strategies; (c) the public ownership of the major financial institutions; (d) the easing of the pressures exerted on the domestic economy by foreign trade by means of planning agreements with the transnational corporations (for example, Archibugi 1978) and controls over imports and the movement of capital abroad.

Even on technical grounds, the AES has much to recommend it. In the light of the demonstrated inability of either market forces or past policies to achieve the necessary reconstruction of the economy, it sets out a practical program of planning which builds on the reforms which have already resulted from the settlement of 1945 (for example, by extending the scope of nationalization, transforming the roles of the NEB and WDA) (Prior and Purdy 1979). Moreover, it offers the prospect, through modernization, of achieving major advances in productivity, which would enable improved living standards without inflation.

However, for its advocates, the AES is much more than a set of alternative economic policies. At its heart lies the recognition of what earlier sections of the chapter attempted to demonstrate: that the complexities of economic development, and the state strategies designed to shape them, are the outcome of the conflicts and compromises between capital and labor. Hence, for example, even if the policies thus far outlined were wholly successful in achieving the profitability of British industry, this would not guarantee the interests of workers. Indeed, current trends towards jobless growth, the result of the technological changes mentioned earlier, suggest that the provision of adequate employment opportunities would be most unlikely. In consequence, the centerpiece of the AES is the democratization of economic life, ensuring for working people direct access for determining their economic futures. Only by this fundamental shift in the distribution of power over the economy will it be possible to produce a form of planning which is both sensitive to the needs of workers and able to fully utilize their potentialities.

It may be objected that such democratization would simply prevent the necessary industrial restructuring. However, as the fertility of the corporate plans produced by worker groups has already demonstrated, what is in question here is not the merely defensive preservation of an existing industrial structure, but rather the creation of alternatives which will provide fulfilling employment and, very often, socially useful products (Lucas Aerospace Combine Shop Stewarts' Committee 1978).

These arguments would appear to have a special relevance to the problems of declining regions. Hence, it has been shown that South Wales' particular insertion into the wider British economy (and Segal (1979) suggests that this is characteristic of other similar regions) has entailed a persistent inability to adapt to changing economic circumstances and provide adequate employment for the region's population. This inability has reflected a pattern of development which has embodied the predominant interests of the owners of capital, as well as the limited aspirations of organized labor. The balance of power thus implied has manifested equally in the pervasive and highly complex policies which have been pursued by the state. What is required, therefore, is a shift which would break South Wales's chronic vulnerability and utilize its indigenous potential. The implementation of such economic planning in a context like South Wales can only be sketched here. However, it is essential that social accounting methods—taking stock of *total* costs and benefits—be adapted in making investment decisions (Rowthorn and Ward 1979). At its simplest this involves, for example, setting unemployment benefits against the costs of subsidizing a plant to keep it open. By extension, it is important in such a situation to take account of possible alternative products and alternative uses for existing products. The Lucas Aerospace workers, among others, have demonstrated the fruitfulness of full worker participation in such a process. Equally, in negotiating planning agreements, the democratic involvement of workers (through their trade unions) could ensure the control not only of the number, but also the type and quality of jobs to be created by inward investment in the region. These considerations could be offset against the costs of state provision of grants, infrastructure, etc. (through a revamped WDA) for the investing firms. Where it *is* necessary to shed labor from existing industries, as will be inevitable, then alternative ways of utilizing the talents of laid-off workers should be found. Clearly, the state has a key role to play here, particularly as a major direct employer in the tertiary sector. Also, the example of the Mondragon workers' cooperatives in the Basque country, with a total of some 17,000 worker/owners, is instructive in demonstrating the indigenous potential of problem regions such as South Wales. It should be remembered, however, that the protectionism (inter alia) of the fascist regime in Spain provided particularly favorable conditions for the cooperatives' growth. In addition, the Mondragon experience underlines the necessity of a regionally-based source of finance capital, which is capable of developing innovatory approaches for creating jobs (Logan 1981).

The essential point, however, is that adopting this approach to the problems of South Wales appears improbable precisely because the priorities of orthodox development strategies are what they are. However, the earlier arguments with regard to the capacity of a capitalist state to accommodate policies favorable to working people suggest the possibility of adopting strategies with very different objectives. Moreover, the very debating of the AES makes more likely the potential transformation which would make this possibility a reality (Rowthorn 1981).

References

Archibugi, F. "Capitalist Planning in Question." In S. Holland (ed.), *Beyond Capitalist Planning*. Oxford, Blackwell, 1978.

British Steel Corporation. *The Ten Year Development Strategy*. London: BSC, 1973.

Buchanan, K. "The Revolt against Satellization in Scotland and Wales." *Monthly Review* 10 (2), 1968.

Cambridge Economic Policy Group. "Urban and Regional Policy with Provisional Regional Accounts 1966–1978." *Cambridge Economic Policy Review* 6 (2), 1980.

Cameron, C. "The National Industrial Strategy and Regional Policy." In D. MacLennan and J. Parr (eds.), *Regional Policy: Past Experience and New Directions*. London: Martin Robertson, 1979.

Carney, J. "Regions in Crisis: Accumulation, Regional Problems and Crisis Formation." In J. Carney; R. Hudson; and J. Lewis (eds.), *Regions in Crisis*. London: Croom Helm, 1980.

Cooke, P. "Discretionary Intervention and the Welsh Development Agency." *Area* 12 (4), 1980.

CSE London Working Group. *The Alternative Economic Strategy: A Labor Movement Response to the Economic Crisis*. London: CSE Books/Labour Coordinating Committee, 1980.

Davies, G. and I. Thomas. *Overseas Investment in Wales: The Welcome Invasion.* Llandybie: Christopher Davies, 1976.

Griffiths, J.; S. Watkins; M. Philips; and S. Jones. *Unemployment in Wales: The Development of a Regional Programme.* Cardiff: Welsh Counties Committee/Council for the Principality, 1980.

Glyn, A. and J. Harrison. *The British Economic Disaster.* London: Pluto, 1980.

Holmes, G. "The South Wales Coal Industry 1850–1914." *Transactions of the Honourable Society of Cymmrodorion,* 1976.

Jessop, B. "The Transformations of the State in Postwar Britain." In R. Scase (ed.) *The State in Western Europe.* London: Croom Helm, 1980.

Logan, C. *The Mondragon Producer Cooperatives.* London: George Allen & Unwin, 1981.

Lovering, J. "Dependence and the Welsh Economy," *Economic Research Papers* 22, University College of North Wales, Bangor, 1978.

Lucas Aerospace Combine Shop Stewards' Committee. "The Lucas Plan." in K. Coates (ed.) *The Right to "Useful" Work: Planning by the People.* Nottingham: Spokesman, 1978.

McNabb, R. "Segmented Labour Markets, Female Employment and Poverty in Wales," In G. Rees and T. Rees (eds.), *Poverty and Social Inequality in Wales.* London: Croom Helm, 1980.

Massey, D. "Regionalism: Some Current Issues," *Capital and Class,* 6, 1978.

———. "In What Sense a Regional Problem?" *Regional Studies,* 13 (3), 1974

Miliband, R. "A State of De-subordination," *British Journal of Sociology,* 29 (4), 1975.

Moore, B. and J. Rhodes. *Regional Policy and the Welsh Economy.* Cardiff: Welsh Office, 1975.

Morgan, K. "State Regional Interventions and Industrial Reconstruction in Post War Britain: the Case of Wales," *Urban and Regional Studies Working Paper 16.* Brighton: University of Sussex, 1979.

Oakey, R. "Technological Change and Regional Development: A Note on Policy Implications," *Area* 11 (4), 1979.

Pavitt, K. (ed.). *Technical Innovation and British Economic Performance.* London: Heinemann, 1979.

Prior, M. and D. Purdy. *Out of the Ghetto: a Path to Socialist Rewards.* Nottingham: Spokesman, 1979.

Rees, G. and J. Lambert. "Nationalism as Legitimation?/Notes Toward a Political Economy of South Wales," In M. Harloe (ed.), *Urban Change and Conflict.* London: Heinemann, forthcoming.

Rees, G. and T. Rees "Migration, Industrial Restructuring and Class Relations: An Analysis of South Wales," *Papers in Planning Research 23.* Cardiff: UWIST, forthcoming.

Rowthorn, B. and T. Ward. "How to Run a Company and Run Down an Economy: the Effects of Closing Down Steel-Making in Corby," *Cambridge Journal of Economics* 3, 1979.

Rowthorn, B. "The Politics of the Alternative Economic Strategy," *Marxism Today* 25, 1981.

Santos, E. "The Steel Industry: Crisis of Restructuring on a World Scale?" University of Sussex, mimeo, 1980.

Segal, N. "The Limits and Means of 'Self-Reliant' Regional Economic Growth," In D. MacLennan and J. Parr (eds.), *Regional Policy: Past Experience and New Directions.* London: Martin Robertson, 1979.

Warren, K. *The British Iron and Steel Industry Since 1840,* London: Bell, 1970.

Winkler, J. "The Corporatist Economy: Theory and Administration," In R. Scase (ed.) *Industrial Society: Class, Cleavage and Control.* London: George Allen & Unwin, 1977.

Welsh Affairs Committee, House of Commons, Committee on Welsh Affairs, *The Role of the Welsh Office and Associated Bodies in Developing Employment Opportunities in Wales,* vol. 1. London: HMSO, 1980.

9

The Export Base and the Performance of the Local Economy

Norton E. Long and
Jeffrey Wittmaier

The experience of underdeveloped countries strongly suggests that growth in the export base may not be accompanied by a corresponding growth in the local economy and may, in some cases, adversely affect it. It seems possible that a similar process might be at work in at least some American cities. If differently composed export bases have differential effects on local economies, it would be important to know this since the export mix may well be open to the influence of policy. Additionally, magnitudes of export bases may not be a decisive factor for the performance of local economies. Different size export bases may be associated with substantial variance in the growth of local economies. Import substitution, both as a result of local production for local consumption, and local production of inputs for the export sector, can expand the local economy even in the absence of growth in the export base. To get a clue as to the differences in the performance of local economies, Department of Commerce county business data was obtained for twelve cities that comprise counties. This data is not available for cities as such, but only for counties. The cities were Baton Rouge, New Orleans, San Francisco, Jacksonville, Nashville, Baltimore, Indianapolis, Boston, Denver, Philadelphia, St. Louis, and Miami.

The Department of Commerce figures provided information on U.S. percent of total earnings and city percent of total earnings, by the standard classifications: Farm, Non-Farm, *Private;* Agriculture Service for Fish Mining; Construction; Manufacturing-Non-Durables; Durables; Transportation and Utilities; Wholesale Trade; Retail Trade; Finance; Insurance and Real Estate; Services; *Government* federal, civilian federal, military, state and local. Dividing city percent of total earnings by the U.S. percent of total earnings, yields the U.S. Location Quotient which serves as the device to determine industries comprising the local export base. Categories with a figure above unity are considered to be in the export sector, those below in the import sector.

It is recognized that regional variations make the use of national averages to determine local export sectors open to question. However, it seems in the absence of regional data to be the only procedure available. For our exploratory purposes, it appears reasonable to hope that significant variances as demonstrated by the data will at least be indicative and worth further study.

The Commerce data for the cities have been organized to display variances in tabular form. Table 9-1 shows the magnitude of the export base for each of the twelve cities in the years 1973, 1975, and 1978. As appears from the table, the cities have maintained approximately the same rankings, though some have moved slightly. The range of the magnitude of the local export base is from a high in San Francisco of 26.0 percent in 1973, to a low in Indianapolis (Marion County) of 11.5 percent in 1975. It is apparent that the proportion of the export sector in the local economies can vary considerably.

Table 9-2 arrays the cities by difference in percent change in the local economies during 1973-1978 and the percent change in exports. While there is a rough correspondence between the changes in exports and the changes in the local economies, there is a wide range of variance. Denver, in particular, stands out with an increase in exports of only 5.93 percent, but an increase in the total local economy of 55.04 percent. This is the most extreme case. However, Philadelphia shows an increase in exports of 49.41 percent, and this increase is accompanied by an increase in the total local economy of only 33.48 percent. Nashville (Davidson), on the other hand, has an increase in total local economy of 64.91 percent associated with an increase in its export sector of 42.14 percent. St. Louis in the period 1973-1975 had an increase of exports of 22.19 percent, accompanied by an increase in the total local economy of 38.37 percent. The big gain in Baton Rouge (E. Baton Rouge Parish), had an increase in its export sector of 94.01 percent, and an increase in the total local economy of 97.60 percent.

Table 9–1
Magnitude of Export Base

	1973		1975		1978	
Rank	City	Percent Export	City	Percent Export	City	Percent Export
1	San Francisco	26.0	Suffolk	24.3	San Francisco	25.4
2	Orleans	24.2	Orleans	24.3	Suffolk	24.2
3	Suffolk	24.1	San Francisco	24.2	E. Baton Rouge	23.6
4	E. Baton Rouge	24.0	E. Baton Rouge	23.5	Orleans	23.6
5	Dade	23.1	Duval	21.0	Dade	20.6
6	Duval	22.1	Dade	19.7	Duval	20.1
7	St. Louis	18.8	St. Louis	18.5	Philadelphia	18.5
8	Denver	18.4	Denver	18.1	St. Louis	16.6
9	Philadelphia	16.5	Philadelphia	16.4	Baltimore	13.5
10	Davidson	15.6	Davidson	14.3	Davidson	13.4
11	Baltimore	13.3	Baltimore	12.2	Denver	12.6
12	Marion	12.3	Marion	11.5	Marion	11.7

Source: U.S. Department of Commerce.

Table 9-2
Cities Ranked by Percentage Change in Total Economy, 1973-1978

City	Percentage Change, Total	Rank	Percentage Change, Exports	Rank
E. Baton Rouge	97.60	1	94.01	1
Davidson	64.91	2	42.14	7
Orleans	62.44	3	58.41	2
Marion	55.07	4	47.61	5
Denver	55.04	5	5.93	12
San Francisco	54.62	6	51.12	3
Duval	52.79	7	38.85	8
Dade	46.31	8	30.43	10
Baltimore	40.02	9	42.87	6
St. Louis	38.37	10	22.19	11
Suffolk	36.40	11	37.14	9
Philadelphia	33.48	12	49.41	4

1973-1978 Percentage Change in Total Economy

City	1973	1978	Change (dollars)	Change (percent)
San Francisco	$6,037,839	$9,335,753	3,297,914	54.62
Denver	3,946,034	6,118,109	2,172,075	55.04
Dade	6,609,082	9,669,473	3,060,391	46.31
Duval	2,369,712	3,670,669	1,250,957	52.79
Marion	4,451,348	6,902,650	2,451,302	55.07
E. Baton Rouge	1,126,963	2,226,838	1,099,875	97.60
Orleans	2,874,631	4,669,628	1,794,997	62.44
Baltimore	4,708,671	6,593,222	1,884,551	40.02
Suffolk	5,479,022	7,473,408	1,994,386	36.40
Philadelphia	9,399,191	12,546,198	3,147,007	33.48
St. Louis	4,279,708	5,921,876	1,642,168	38.37
Davidson	2,286,744	3,771,108	1,484,363	64.91

1973-1978 Percentage Change in Exports

City	1973	1978	Change (dollars)	Change (percent)
San Francisco	$1,572,263	$2,375,969	803,706	51.12
Denver	729,930	773,215	43,285	5.93
Dade	1,533,195	1,999,726	466,531	30.43
Duval	525,562	729,728	204,166	38.85
Marion	548,721	809,955	261,234	47.61
E. Baton Rouge	270,969	525,705	254,736	94.01
Orleans	698,284	1,106,135	407,851	58.41
Baltimore	627,274	896,177	268,903	42.87
Suffolk	1,320,625	1,811,093	490,468	37.14
Philadelphia	1,558,910	2,329,202	770,292	49.41
St. Louis	806,876	985,909	179,033	22.19
Davidson	357,675	508,391	150,716	42.14

Source: U.S. Department of Commerce

The case of Denver, which stands out most clearly, a 5.93 percent increase in the export sector accompanied by a 55.04 percent increase in the total local economy, suggests the possible importance of import substitution as an explanation for the performance of the local economy. Examination of the Commerce data for the industry and government categories of the city's economy shows a broad and moderate advance, with the exception of mining, which increased explosively. This would be consistent with import substitution as an explanation. The case of Denver indicates the possibility that import substitution may be a more powerful strategy for many cities seeking to improve their local economies than the conventional wisdom of concentrating on the export sector.

Looking at the composition of the local economies of Davidson (Nashville), St. Louis, and East Baton Rouge (Baton Rouge), the reasons for the significant variance is not immediately apparent. The percent of city total earnings from the different industry categories do not vary that much. Thus, for Philadelphia, manufacturing accounts for 23.50 percent, government 10.97 percent, and services 18.41 percent. These are the categories accounting for more than 10 percent of total city earnings. In Davidson (Nashville), manufacturing amounts to 21.73 percent, retail trade 10.72 percent. St. Louis' manufacturing provides 30.24 percent of that city's total earnings, its services 17.35 percent, government 14.57 percent, and transportation and utilities 12.41 percent. East Baton Rouge (Baton Rouge), the city showing the most dramatic growth, has a manufacturing sector accounting for 22.16 percent of that city's earnings. Government provides 17.85 percent, services 16.40 percent, construction 13.28 percent, and retail 11.15 percent.

The magnitude of the export base as a percent of the local economy, is associated with considerable variation in the percent change in the local economy. Thus, while Baton Rouge and New Orleans rank in the top four, both in magnitude of export sector and growth of their local economies, Suffolk (Boston), which ranks in the top three in magnitude of its export sector, ranks number eleven in the percent change of its local economy in 1973–1978. San Francisco, which ranked number one in two of the three measured years in the magnitude of its export sector, was only sixth in the percent change of its total local economy. Marion (Indianapolis), which ranked last in the magnitude of its export sector, was fourth in the percent change of its local economy. It is thus apparent that differences in magnitudes of the export sector, as well as in percent of its change, are associated with varying changes in the total local economies between the cities examined.

To get some idea of the effects of changes in the total local economy, data on median household income were assembled for the cities under review for 1973–1978 (table 9-3). Commerce data not being available, those of the sales and marketing services were utilized. Changes in median house-

Table 9-3
Cities Ranked by Percentage Change in Median Household Export Basic
Income

City	Percentage Change
Davidson	82.44
E. Baton Rouge	79.05
Orleans	71.98
Marion	71.40
Philadelphia	69.88
Denver	69.74
Baltimore	67.37
St. Louis	67.21
San Francisco	62.83
Duval	59.13
Suffolk	56.63
Dade	24.67

Population (000), 1973-1978

City	12/31/73	12/31/75	12/31/78	Percentage Change
San Francisco	671.0	660.2	654.0	(2.53)
Denver	514.4	501.9	500.2	(2.76)
Dade	1,417.7	1,464.4	1,474.1	3.98
Duval	564.0	565.8	574.0	1.77
Marion	803.6	798.2	779.2	(3.04)
E. Baton Rouge	302.9	319.3	337.4	11.39
Orleans	587.2	575.2	565.6	(3.68)
Baltimore	648.5	653.3	649.8	.2
Suffolk	735.8	720.5	701.2	(4.7)
Philadelphia	1,873.1	1,804.1	1,775.7	(5.2)
St. Louis	559.9	520.0	500.7	(10.57)
Davidson	454.7	455.8	464.7	2.20

Source: Sales and Marketing Management.

hold income in the period 1973-1978, ranged from a high of 82.44 percent in Davidson (Nashville), to a low of 24.27 percent in Dade (Miami). Not surprisingly, the cities showing the greatest changes in their total local economies showed the greatest changes in household income. Davidson (Nashville), E. Baton Rouge (Baton Rouge), Orleans (New Orleans) and Marion (Indianapolis), in that order, were the four with the greatest percentage change in household income, and this was associated with the greatest change in the total local economies. However, Philadelphia, ranking just behind Marion (Indianapolis) in percent change in household income, had the lowest percent change in it's total local economy.

While two of the cities with top percentage increases in household incomes showed population increases—Davidson (Nashville) 2.20 percent and

East Baton Rouge (Baton Rouge) an impressive 11.39 percent—the other three in the top five showed losses: Orleans (New Orleans) had a 3.68 percent loss, Marion (Indianapolis) lost 3.04 percent and Philadelphia 5.2 percent. Dade (Miami) which showed the lowest percent increase in median household income of the cities examined, had a population gain of 3.98 percent, ranking next to East Baton Rouge (Baton Rouge).

Looking at the dollar range of median household incomes (table 9-4), they varied in 1973 from a high of Dade (Miami) with $12,227 to St. Louis with a low of $8,091. In 1978, the range ran from Baltimore with a high of $19,490 to St. Louis with a low of $13,529. In the period 1973-1978, Dade (Miami) dropped from first place in 1973 to eight in 1978. While the conventional wisdom of the sunbelt/frostbelt contrast is, to some extent born out, the performance of Baltimore and Indianapolis indicates that the competitive position of some of the northeast quadrant cities may be less grim than commonly supposed. The variation in the performance of local economies is sufficiently greater to suggest that more intensive study might reveal differences among the variables to account for the more favorable outcomes. These differences may be open to policy influence in desired directions. Examining the data for the commerce categories that account for 10 percent or more of total city earnings (table 9-5), no striking single factor or pattern emerges to explain the quite significant variation in local performance. One possibility, in Suffolk (Boston) and St. Louis, is that in these cases a far higher proportion of the city population remains outside the primary labor market. The Commerce data do not desegregate sufficiently to determine whether differences in the composition of the categories might account for differences in the cities' performance. The degree of suburbanization might also, in part, account for variance.

The considerable differences in median household income for the metropolitan area and the central city suggests an industry mix that may work well for the metropolitan area, but not for the central city. Such may be the case with respect of Boston and St. Louis. All that seems safe to say is that the performance of local economies varies quite significantly. If the reasons for the differences could be identified, they might yield dimensions open to policy influence.

Table 9-4
Median Household Income

City	Rank	1973	Rank	1978
Dade	1	$12,227	8	$15,195
Baltimore	2	11,645	1	19,490
Marion	3	10,881	2	18,650
E. Baton Rouge	4	10,397	3	18,616

Table 9-4 continued

City	Rank	1973	Rank	1978
San Francisco	5	9,519	7	15,500
Davidson	6	9,494	4	17,321
Denver	7	9,326	5	15,830
Philadelphia	8	9,259	6	15,729
Suffolk	9	8,912	10	13,959
Duval	10	8,850	9	14,083
Orleans	11	8,102	11	13,934
St. Louis	12	8,091	13	13,529

Total and Household Income

City	12/31/73 Export Basic Income (000)	Per Capita	Medium Household Income	12/31/75 Total Export Basic Income	Medium Household Income	12/31/78 Total Export Basic Income	Medium Household Income
San Francisco	3,841,106	5,724	9,519	4,537,207	11,926	6,056,242	15,500
Denver	2,475,678	4,813	9,326	2,887,184	12,119	3,910,359	15,830
Dade	6,212,590	4,382	12,227	8,100,923	12,087	10,478,023	15,195
Duval	2,079,532	3,687	8,850	2,296,121	10,193	3,345,257	14,083
Marion	3,877,598	4,825	10,881	4,380,803	14,236	5,724,021	18,650
E. Baton Rouge	1,169,199	3,860	10,397	1,552,915	14,669	2,396,833	18,616
Orleans	2,300,125	3,917	8,102	2,800,730	10,660	3,778,493	13,934
Baltimore	3,233,089	4,985	11,645	3,879,773	16,311	4,940,205	19,490
Suffolk	3,011,934	4,080	8,912	3,583,519	11,556	4,411,458	13,959
Philadelphia	7,815,890	4,173	9,259	8,917,847	12,423	11,600,925	15,729
St. Louis	2,119,567	3,786	8,091	2,274,073	9,970	3,039,307	13,529
Davidson	1,974,022	4,341	9,494	2,424,800	14,009	3,316,392	17,321

Per Capita Personal Income by County

	1973	1974	1975	1976	1977	1978
Suffolk County (Boston, Massachusetts)	4,699	5,131	5,472	5,936	6,395	7,077
Philadelphia County (Philadelphia, Pennsylvania)	4,764	5,180	5,614	6,098	6,584	7,222
Orleans County (New Orleans, Louisiana)	4,773	5,231	5,759	6,329	6,987	7,744
St. Louis County (St. Louis, Missouri)	6,171	6,795	7,289	8,024	8,833	9,854
Denver County (Denver, Colorado)	5,967	6,632	7,266	7,857	8,723	9,887
E. Baton Rouge County (Baton Rouge, Louisiana)	4,468	5,092	5,698	6,581	7,230	8,020
Duval County (Jacksonville, Florida)	4,872	5,249	5,708	6,126	6,733	7,484

Table 9-4 continued

	1973	1974	1975	1976	1977	1978
Marion County (Indianapolis, Indiana)	5,492	5,938	6,374	7,015	7,784	8,679
San Francisco County (San Francisco, California)	7,081	7,778	8,800	9,547	10,509	11,878
Baltimore City (Baltimore, Maryland)	4,732	5,118	5,530	6,082	6,518	7,151
Davidson County (Nashville, Tennessee)	5,189	5,744	5,998	6,736	7,575	8,520
Dade County (Miami, Florida)	5,882	6,382	6,501	6,971	7,628	8,567

Source: Sales and Marketing Management.

Table 9-5
Categories of Total Local Earnings of 10 Percent and Over

City	Category	Earnings (present)
E. Baton Rouge	Manufacturing	22.16
	Services	16.40
	Government (state and local)	17.85
	Construction	13.28
	Retail	11.15
Baltimore	Manufacturing	21.14
	Services	19.37
	Government (state and local)	15.66
	Transportation and utilities	11.36
	Retail trade	10.21
Philadelphia	Manufacturing	23.50
	Government (state and local)	19.07
	Services	18.41
Denver	Services	17.26
	Government	15.83
	Manufacturing	15.12
	Transportation and utilities	13.08
	Retail trade	11.06
	Wholesale trade	10.86
Davidson	Manufacturing	21.73
	Services	19.60
	Government (state and local)	14.03
	Retail trade	10.72

Table 9–5 continued

City	Category	Earnings (present)
	1973	
St. Louis	Manufacturing	30.24
	Services	17.35
	Government (federal, state, and local)	14.57
	Transportation and utilities	12.41
Duval	Government (federal, state, and local)	21.35
	Services	16.08
	Manufacturing	11.52
	Transportation and utilities	10.26
	Retail trade	11.17
	Wholesale trade	10.11
San Francisco	Services	20.67
	Government (federal, state, and local)	19.83
	Transportation and utilities	13.37
	Finance, insurance, and real estate	13.04
	Manufacturing	10.65
Marion	Manufacturing (durable)	33.47
	Government	13.67
	Services	13.20
Dade	Services	22.40
	Transportation and utilities	14.07
	Government (state and local)	12.87
	Retail trade	12.24
	Manufacturing	11.88
Orleans	Services	21.11
	Government (state and local)	15.26
	Transportation and utilities	14.31
	Retail trade	10.09
Suffolk	Services	25.20
	Government (state and local)	17.50
	Finance, insurance, and real estate	13.48
	Manufacturing	11.56

Source: U.S. Department of Commerce.

**Part IV
Plant Closings and
Responses**

10 The Incidence and Regulation of Plant Closings

Bennett Harrison and
Barry Bluestone

Introduction

As the American economy enters the 1980s, a great deal of public attention has been drawn to the phenomenon of plant shutdowns. Even before the advent of the most recent recession, newspapers were reporting major closings and cutbacks in a wide range of industries, including (but by no means restricted to) automobiles, steel, and rubber.[1] The conventional explanations for these alleged business failures range from straight-forward competitive disadvantages, both domestically and internationally, to excessive government regulation, for example, with respect to health and safety or environmental protection.

Many U.S. business closings are unquestionably the result of an inability to successfully compete with other enterprises. Yet, building upon the research of a number of other investigators, we have found this explanation to be at best insufficient and often incorrect.[2] The inference that a closing always represents a business failure may be completely misleading in a world of large, multiplant, multilocational corporations, operating under modern management methods. The implications for measuring and regulating capital mobility in such a world are profound.

As one might imagine, the large and apparently growing number of corporate shutdowns and relocations in the United States has generated the beginning of organized resistance. This is due especially to American trade unionists who have learned how other western countries use public authority to regulate private capital mobility, or at least to shelter workers from precipitous closings and cutbacks. This resistance is reflected in the legislative drives in nineteen states and in the U.S. Congress for so-called plant closing laws.

The research upon which this chapter is based was sponsored by the Progressive Alliance, a Washington-based coalition of trade unions, community, feminist, environmental, and public interest groups led by the United Auto Workers. We are grateful to David Birch for making certain of the data available to us, to Maryellen Kelley for helpful criticism, and to Leona Morris and Virginia Richardson for preparing the manuscript.

131

Our objective in this chapter is to analyze the new legislation, together with other complementary approaches to the orderly regulation of private capital disinvestment, especially as it occurs in the form of large-scale plant or store shutdowns. First, however, it will be helpful to put the magnitude of the problem in perspective. We therefore begin by reviewing recent data on the incidence and employment impact of shutdowns during the 1970s, in particular industries, by region, and by form of ownership.

A Typology for Comprehending How Capital Moves

A shutdown is but one, albeit the most extreme, form of the reallocation or movement of capital. It is of course possible for capital to literally move— that is, to be physically shifted by its owners—by closing down operations at one location, selling off the old plant, loading the equipment onto a van, a widebelly jet, or a railroad car, and transporting it to a new site, where a new building is constructed and operations are resumed.[3] This kind of dramatic move gets newspaper and TV headlines, but it is not very common.

Using data from the Dun and Bradstreet Co., a private business credit rating service, David Birch of MIT concluded that, between 1969 and 1976, only about 2 percent of all private sector annual employment change in the United States was the result of such overt physical relocation. During the 1969–1970 recession, the rate was even lower: perhaps 1.5 percent per year, a statistic which has been widely quoted both by academic researchers[4] and by spokespersons for big business, seeking to prove that the growing attempts to restrict capital flight and to make business more accountable to the public "are a solution to a nonexistent problem."[5]

Such explicit physical relocations are undoubtedly infrequent. But admitting this in no way trivializes the problem, for outright plant relocation per se represents only the tip of an iceberg in studying the process of capital shift. There are a number of ways that owners may and do move their capital from one place to another.

1. *Redirect profits.* The multibranch corporation may not, in the short-run, physically remove any of the older plant's capital stock, but will instead reallocate profits earned from that plant's operations to its new facilities, for example, for new product development. Such milking of a profitable plant is especially common among conglomerates, whose managers describe some of their acquisitions as *cash cows.* This most subtle and virtually invisible form of disinvestment is disinvestment nevertheless. The loss of control over its own retained earnings greatly increases the chances that an establishment will run into trouble in the future.[6]

2. *Redirect profits and depreciation (overall cash flow).* Both large and small companies may run down their older facilities (for example, by not

replacing worn-out machinery), and use the savings in the form of depreciation allowances to reinvest in other branches of their own firms, in other businesses, or perhaps in financial instruments.

3. *Remove physical capital.* Multiplant, multistore, and multioffice corporations may gradually shift some machinery, inventories, materials, and so on, from their older to their new facilities located in some other city, state, or country. The old facility remains in operation, at least for the time being. If actual physical capital has been removed, their operations are now subject to a lower level of productive capacity. On the other hand, especially where the labor process is characterized by benchwork assembly, and materials (for example, clothing pieces or electronic components such as silicon chips) are sent to new plants for assembly, the old facility may actually be said to be undergoing a planned reduction in its rate of capacity utilization. The same thing occurs when management cuts back operations domestically and subcontracts various production activities (for example, assembly, or manufacture of particular components formerly made in-house) to other companies.

4. *Shutdown or bancruptcy.* Companies may go the last step, and completely close the older facility. Land and/or buildings may be put on the market, and the machinery sold for scrap to other branches or to other firms. If the owner formally declares bankruptcy, chapter XI of the bankruptcy laws provides a procedure which enables even small businessmen to retain a surplus from their creditors which may then be reinvested in new economic activity or used as a kind of pension. The latter practice is common among small entrepreneurs who want to retire but have no heirs to whom to leave their business or can find no one else who wants to run it.

5. *Actual physical relocation of the facility to a new site.*

In all five cases (which should properly be understood as aspects of a continuum describing capital shift), some form of capital is reallocated from one plant, office, store, warehouse, or hospital to another. Sometimes the transfer takes place among the branches of a single firm and sometimes it occurs across firms, possibly mediated by a bank, insurance company, or local public development authority. In other cases, the transfer takes the form of finance capital (profits or savings reinvested elsewhere). In only relatively few cases does it consist of actually transferring a large volume of capital goods themselves—machinery, equipment, materials, or parts of buildings—within or among firms, over space.

Regardless of the particular form of capital involved, in nearly all cases, the old and new facilities coexist for at least some period of time. This is illustrated in the upper panel of figure 10–1. Often, the older facilities are eventually closed down completely, particularly after the newer ones become fully operational. But the timing can vary enormously. Some corporations like General Electric have operated parallel plants for thirty years or

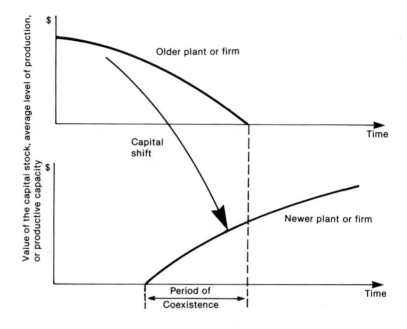

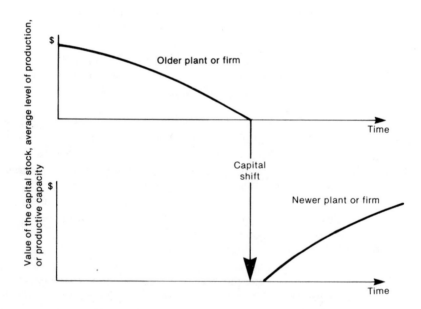

Figure 10-1. Possible Types of Capital Shift between Business Establishments or Plants Over Time

more, while conglomerates like Genesco, Sheller-Glove and Lykes have milked a number of their acquired subsidiaries dry in a decade or less. Alternatively, the old plant may never be shut down entirely.

In special cases, the old closure and the new opening occur more or less simultaneously, or at least in rapid sequence, as shown in the lower panel of figure 10-1. This kind of instant migration of a plant is clearly only a special case of the more general type of capital shift. Not surprisingly, because money, time and effort are necessary to shift capital goods across space, relatively few shifts are of this rather extreme kind.[7] It is these shifts which account for the 1.5 to 2.0 percent employment change noted by Birch and others.

Moreover, since operating a multibranch firm is invariably more costly and difficult than running a single branch enterprise, small businesses with fewer capital resources are least likely to exhibit the parallel plant pattern. Indeed, they are most likely to make simultaneous or rapidly sequential moves when they do actually relocate their own facilities. All of the researchers who have studied the Dun and Bradstreet data agree that the great majority of what can be called simultaneous movers are, in fact, single plant firms, with an average (according to Jusenius, Ledebur, and Birch) of less than twenty employees. This class of runaways has attracted considerable attention and created serious problems for workers in the textile, apparel, shoe, and electronics industries. But as we will see in the next section, when the other forms of capital investment and reinvestment are accounted for, large employers become an increasingly visible part of the process.

The Incidence and Impact of Establishment Shutdowns in the 1970s

Few people have the necessary time, access, or money to pierce the veil of privacy which firms have put around their investment transactions.[9] In this context, the federal government's unwillingness to require companies to disclose the details of their investment activity makes direct measurement of the different kinds of capital movements identified earlier virtually impossible.[10]

Still, even without a systematic, comprehensive picture of cutbacks, rundowns, and the subsidy of new plants at the expense of older ones, the study of plant closings alone is justified because by releasing at least some resources that may be reinvested elsewhere, *every shutdown represents a potential capital shift.*

Because of the lack of other sources, it has been necessary for us to resort to a reanalysis of the same private Dun and Bradstreet data discussed earlier. The 1969-1976 Dun's Identifiers file covers some 5.6 million business establishments, about 3 million of which are independently owned and operated, with the rest being the branches, subsidiaries, and headquarters of corporations. Dun and Bradstreet compiles these data as a by-product of its credit rating and market research activities, and sells them to business groups and researchers. They are expensive, hard to use, and sometimes contain inaccurate information (including, but by no means limited to, the undercounting of migrations). Nevertheless, they are by far the best—certainly the most comprehensive—data available on the subject.

We, like others, have relied on the help of David Birch, who has by now made great headway in mining this valuable source. He has also prepared an extract of the Dun and Bradstreet data for us for New England, in connection with our own ongoing research on regional economic development. This extract provides greater detail than Birch himself has made available in his own publications. What follows draws upon both Birch's published work and our own analysis of this Dun and Bradstreet extract.[12]

Table 10-1 displays the aggregate employment effects of establishment startups, shutdowns and relocations through the mid-1970s for two states in each of the nine census regions. By our estimate, about 31 million jobs were eliminated or relocated in the United States, which comes to an average of 4.4 million jobs per year. Establishments in the northeast destroyed about 118 jobs through closures for every 100 new jobs created through openings, while establishments in the south eliminated an average of only 79 jobs through business closings for every 100 created. The rate of shutdown appears lower than expected in the midwest, but remember that these data do not cover the years after 1976. The great wave of auto, steel, and tire closures occurred during the closing years of the decade.

Not surprisingly, there is particular interest in the shutdown behavior of larger establishments. We should expect that the rate of turnover of capital, as exemplified in this research by startups and closings, is greatest for small business. This hypothesis is confirmed by the figures in table 10-2. In all but one row of the table, for trade and services as well as for manufacturing, given that the establishment started prior to the end of 1969, the odds of shutting down before the end of 1976 show a very strong tendency to fall, the larger the establishment. The only exception is the wholesale and retail trade sector in the northeast, which suffered a number of major closings (for example, in the department store and food wholesaling industries) during this period. In general, though, the largest establishments were the most likely to have survived the two recessions of this highly unstable period. What is of course most astonishing is the overall rate of the aspect of capital turnover which we are measuring. Even among those establishments in the sample that had more than one hundred employees in the base year (1969), as we look across the four regions in table 10-2, between a sixth and a third of them were out of business by 1976.[13]

Let us now concentrate just on the largest manufacturing plants, those with, in 1969, 100 or more employees. Birch's published tables (not shown here) provide us with the sample sizes of each employment size class. With these, we can use the probabilities of closing from table 10–2 to compute the number of closings of established (pre–1969) plants and stores in the sample in each industry and region. Table 10–3 displays the results. We are not surprised to see that by far the largest number of closings of large established manufacturing plants in the sample occurred in the northeast. Moreover, with only 24 percent of the nation's population in 1970, the northeast suffered 39 percent of the shutdowns of large manufacturing plants.

What *is* surprising is the larger number of closings (of this scale) in the south than in the north central region. Even more dramatically, the rate at which large established manufacturing facilities have closed—that is, the probability of a shutdown by 1976, given being in operation in 1969—was actually higher in the south than in any other part of the country. One answer to this puzzle is that there has been a secular acceleration in the propensity of especially multiregional conglomerates to decentralize their operations globally. The south became fully integrated into the modern international capitalist system later than did the north. By the time it did, in the years following World War II, corporate branching, milking, profit target setting, and relocation practices were in far greater use everywhere. The south—precisely because of its latecomer status—was experiencing the effects disproportionately. Thus, for example, it took seventy-five years for the northeast to lose the bulk of its old mill-based industry to the sunbelt (and more recently to foreign countries). Yet already, within a much shorter time span, the sunbelt has undergone extensive restructuring and overseas migration of, for example, textiles, apparel, and electronics assembly. Clearly, we need more research on this intriguing finding.

So far, these results pool the corner grocer, the multinational corporation's branch plant, and the successful family business which has been acquired by a diversified conglomerate. For several reasons, the data should be broken down according to *who owns the business*. Small, independently owned (often family-run) businesses can be expected to have high failure rates. They are generally more vulnerable to the business cycle, have more restricted access to debt finance (and/or must pay more for it), and have no parent or home office to bail them out of trouble. Corporate branch plants presumably have all of these advantages—along with access to the corporation's own internally retained earnings—as, in theory, do the subsidiaries of conglomerates. To the extent that the mode of operation of the modern conglomerate is organized around the acquisition of profitable subsidiaries, conglomerate closings are more likely to be the result of a planned strategy to increase company-wide profits. The closing of an independently owned business is more likely to constitute a truly involuntary failure.

Table 10-1
Jobs Created and Destroyed by Openings, Closings, Relocations, Expansions, and Contractions of Private Business Establishments in the United States, by Region: 1969–1976
(in thousands of jobs)

	Number of Jobs in 1969	Jobs Created		Jobs Destroyed		Ratio of Jobs Destroyed by Closings to Jobs Created by Openings
		By Openings and Inmigrations[a]	By Expansions[b]	By Closures and Outmigrations[c]	By Contractions[b]	
United States as a whole	70,324.3	34,798.0	26,074.8	30,820.5	18,457.3	0.89
Frostbelt	38,758.1	15,288.7	12,518.2	15,237.7	9,577.1	1.00
Northeast	18,669.8	6,480.6	5,641.1	7,719.1	4,701.6	1.18
New England	4,542.0	1,585.4	1,439.5	1,820.8	1,210.3	1.15
Mid-Atlantic	14,127.8	4,895.2	4,201.6	5,898.3	3,491.3	1.19
Midwest	20,088.3	8,808.1	6,877.2	7,518.6	4,875.5	0.85
East North Central	14,756.1	6,282.1	4,711.1	5,340.2	3,514.4	0.85
West North Central	5,332.2	2,526.0	2,166.1	2,178.4	1,361.1	0.86
Sunbelt	31,566.3	19,509.3	13,556.6	15,582.7	8,880.1	0.80
South	19,867.8	12,227.0	8,376.1	9,701.4	5,415.7	0.79
South Atlantic	10,180.8	6,199.9	4,073.9	5,079.0	2,889.9	0.81
East South Central	3,775.8	2,043.9	1,460.2	1,649.5	849.3	0.81
West South Central	5,911.1	3,983.2	2,842.0	2,972.9	1,676.5	0.75

West	11,698.5	7,282.3	5,180.5	5,881.3	3,464.4	0.81
Mountain	2,571.5	1,826.4	1,393.0	1,446.0	716.5	0.80
Pacific	9,126.9	5,455.9	3,787.4	4,435.4	2,747.9	0.82

Source: Our estimates, based on data from David L. Birch, *The Job Generation Process* (Cambridge, Mass.: MIT Program on Neighborhood and Regional Change, 1979), Appendix A. The regional data shown in this table are sums of workforce-weighted aggregates of the figures for each state, which are presented in an appendix to Bluestone and Harrison, *Capital vs. Community*. The basic unit of observation is the establishment (plant, store, or shop). All the data shown are based on a non-probability sample of Dun and Bradstreet (D&B) credit reports. We inflated the D&B counts of openings, closings, etc. by the ratio of U.S. Department of Labor estimates of state employment for 1969 to the D&B counts for the same year. Sample size varied from a low of .30 in Alaska to a high of .61 in Rhode Island.

[a]This column is the sum of two of Birch's categories: *births* and *immigrations*. Technically, a firm moving a preexisting plant into an area would already have an identification (or Duns) number for it, while a true startup would have to be assigned a new number, and that distinction should allow us to tell new plants from movers. Unfortunately, the retention of old identification numbers for movers depends on actions taken by local D&B officers, who are very inconsistent, tending to perfunctorily assign new numbers, thereby coding a *new* activity as a birth when it should have been an immigrant. To be safe, we aggregate births and immigrants.

[b]These columns refer to employment change in establishments that neither relocate nor shutdown during the period of analysis.

[c]This column is the sum of Birch's *deaths* and *outmigrations*, aggregated because movers are so poorly and inconsistently tracked by D&B local offices. Also, it should be noted that at least some of these closed establishments were undoubtedly opened up again at the same site—indeed, often with the same physical plant—under new ownership. That will be captured under our category *openings*, although these data do not allow us to distinguish between such reopenings and the births of wholly new establishments.

Table 10-2

Probabilities of Going Out of Business During 1969–1976 for Businesses Existing in 1969, by Size of Establishment and Region in 1969, and by Major Industrial Sector

Region in 1969 and Industrial Sector	Number of 1969 Establishments in the Sample (000)	Size of Establishment in 1969, by Reported Number of Employees				
		1–20	*21–50*	*51–100*	*101–500*	*501+*
		Probabilities of closing by 1976				
Northeast						
Manufacturing	76	.53	.40	.37	.33	.21
Trade[a]	295	.60	.35	.34	.36	.57
Services	51	.61	.42	.43	.39	.29
Total[b]	514	.59	.37	.36	.33	.26
North Central						
Manufacturing	63	.48	.30	.27	.27	.15
Trade[a]	296	.57	.33	.30	.28	.27
Services	56	.60	.39	.38	.41	.30
Total[b]	519	.56	.32	.28	.27	.17
South						
Manufacturing	49	.53	.36	.36	.34	.28
Trade[a]	335	.59	.33	.30	.23	.23
Services	63	.61	.41	.40	.39	.34
Total[b]	565	.58	.35	.33	.32	.27
West						
Manufacturing	41	.53	.39	.36	.31	.16[c]
Trade[a]	182	.60	.38	.34	.29	.33
Services	35	.62	.41	.40	.42	.36
Total[b]	318	.59	.38	.35	.32	.23

Source: Birch, *The Job Generation Process,* Appendix D.

[a] Includes wholesale and retail trade.

[b] Measures all private sector employment recorded by Dun and Bradstreet: manufacturing, trade, and services, plus other industries not recorded here (farming, mining, transportation, utilities, and finance).

[c] Includes only eighty-six establishments.

Our estimates of startups and closings by type of ownership are unfortunately limited at the moment to Massachusetts and New England. Similar counts could indeed be constructed for other states and regions, but Birch has not done so, and our own extract from the Dun and Bradstreet file is limited to New England. Table 10–4 presents establishment openings and

Table 10-3
Closings Occurring by December 31, 1976, of Manufacturing Plants in Existence on December 31, 1969, with More than 100 Employees at That Time, by Region

Region			Manufacturing Plants with More than 100 Employees in the 1969 Sample			
Name	Number of States	Percentage of U.S. Population	Number of Plants in the Sample in 1969	Number in the Sample Closed by 1976	Probability of Closing by 1976, Given Existence in 1969	Interregional Percentage Distribution of Closings
Northeast	9	24.1	4,576	1,437	.31	38.6
North Central	12	27.8	3,617	904	.25	24.2
South	16	31.0	3,101	1,042	.34	28.0
West	13	17.1	1,155	344	.30	9.2
Total	50	100.0	12,449	3,727	.30	100.0

Source: See table 10-2 (Population statistics are from *1970 Census of Population*).

Table 10–4
Startups (or Reorganizations) and Closures of Private Establishments in Massachusetts and New England, by Type of Ownership: 1969–1976

	Massachusetts			New England		
	Ownership Form[a]			Ownership Form[a]		
	Independent	Corporate	Conglomerate[b]	Independent	Corporate	Conglomerate[b]
Establishments						
Percent distribution of closings	83.4	13.4	3.1	84.5	12.9	2.6
Percent distribution of openings	68.4	29.7	1.9	73.1	25.0	1.8
Ratio of closings to openings	1.6	0.6	2.2	1.5	0.7	1.8
Jobs						
Percent distribution of job destruction	48.8	38.4	12.8	49.6	38.6	11.8

Percent distribution of job creation	29.7	65.4	4.9	34.9	59.1	6.0
Ratio of jobs destroyed to jobs created	1.9	0.7	3.0	1.7	0.8	2.3

Source: Extract from the Dun's Identifiers File, prepared for us by David L. Birch.

Note: Closings includes outmigrations; openings includes inmigrations. See notes to table 10-1.

aOwnership form refers to the relationship of the establishment (factory, office, division, store, hotel, etc.) to its parent firm, if any. Independent establishments operate at only one location, and have no parent. A corporate headquarters or branch facility is an establishment which is part of a multifacility enterprise, and which carries the identification (that is, DUNS) number of the parent corporation. A conglomerate headquarters or subsidiary is an establishment which is part of a family of often quite heterogeneous businesses, all owned by a single parent but each carrying its own DUNS number. These definitions represent our interpretations of file descriptions distributed by Birch. For further discussion, see Birch, The Job Generation Process and Bluestone and Harrison, Capital vs. Community, ch. 2.

bThe conglomerate openings in the table represent either literally new establishments or—probably more commonly, although we have no way to tell—preexisting businesses which have been acquired and then reorganized sufficiently radically to prompt Dun and Bradstreet to assign a new DUNS number to them. (Acquired companies which retain their original identities and DUNS number are not counted as new openings, and do not appear in this table). Analogously, conglomerate divestitures may sometimes appear here as apparent closings, even though they have been bought up and continued to be operated by some other corporation.

closings flows for Massachusetts and for New England, and the associated employment impacts, distributed by form of ownership. Thus, the small family drug store (as well as the not-so-small high technology partnership) are listed as *independents*. The headquarters and branch plants of, for example, General Electric, General Motors, General Dynamics, and Data General are listed under the heading *corporations*. Finally, there is a separate listing for such *conglomerates* as Gulf and Western, Genesco, United Technologies, and all of their many large (and small) subsidiaries.[14]

Between 1969 and 1976, plant closings in Massachusetts cost the state about 937,000 jobs, over 40 percent of the stock of jobs at the beginning of the period. For New England as a whole, closings (and outmigrations) eliminated 1.8 million jobs. Most important, corporations and conglomerates together were responsible for only about 15 percent of the shutdowns, which is consistent with the earlier national finding (table 10-2) that smaller establishments have a higher probability of closing. Yet this relatively small group of corporate and conglomerate establishments was responsible for half of all the jobs lost directly through shutdown. Moreover, we are certain from our fieldwork on subcontracting and procurement networks in the region that a great many of those closings of independently owned businesses were the indirect result of losses of orders and other spillovers generated by the corporate shutdowns.

In particular industries the differences between opening and closing behavior by type of ownership become even more sharply defined. Table 10-5 shows openings and closings (and, because of how we measure them, relocations and reorganizations) for the entire period 1969-1976, for ten important New England industries, both mature and growing. The rate at which conglomerates have closed New England business establishments relative to their rate of openings or acquisitions exceeds that of either independent or corporate owners in eight of the ten industries in table 10-5. For example, take two industries that are very important to (and quite typical of the old and new economic bases of) the region: metalworking machinery and department stores. For every new job created by an independently owned business between 1969 and 1976, 1.6 jobs were destroyed in metalworking and 1 in department stores. But in establishments controlled by conglomerates, for every job created, 4.6 jobs were destroyed in metalworking, while 4 were eliminated in department stores.

While conglomerates controlled a small percentage of all businesses prior to 1976 (although they were responsible for a much larger proportion of all jobs), conglomerate *behavior*—the acquisition of existing facilities in diverse product and service lines bearing little or no relation to the acquirer's original industry—seems to have increased during the closing years of the decade. Thus, for example, U.S. Steel now reinvests a sizeable share of the surplus appropriated from its steel operation into chemicals, nucleonics,

Table 10-5
Startups (or Reorganizations) and Closings of Private Business Establishments in Ten Industries in New England, by Type of Ownership: 1969–1976

Industry and Form of Ownership (Standard Industry Classification Codes in Parentheses)[a]	Startups or Reorganizations		Closings		Rates of Change		
					Ratios of Closings to Openings		Net Percent Change in Employment Associated with Startups and Closings
	Establishments (Percent)	Jobs (Percent)	Establishments (Percent)	Jobs (Percent)	Establishments	Jobs	
Women's apparel (233)							
Total	100	100	100	100	1.9	2.0	−10.1
Independent	56	42	67	53	2.2	2.5	−10.5
Corporate	41	52	28	39	1.3	1.5	−7.8
Conglomerate[b]	3	6	5	8	3.4	2.9	−20.0
Paper mills (262)							
Total	100	100	100	100	1.0	1.3	−2.1
Independent	40	8	39	7	1.0	1.3	−1.8
Corporate	56	89	51	91	0.9	1.3	−2.4
Conglomerate[b]	4	3	10	2	2.0	0.5	+2.0
Commercial printing (275)							
Total	100	100	100	100	1.2	1.2	−1.9
Independent	79	35	89	53	1.4	1.8	−4.2
Corporate	16	33	7	32	0.6	1.1	−2.3
Conglomerate[b]	5	32	4	15	1.0	0.6	+9.9

Table 10-5 continued

Industry and Form of Ownership (Standard Industry Classification Codes in Parentheses)[a]	Startups or Reorganizations		Closings		Rates of Change		
					Ratios of Closings to Openings		Net Percent Change in Employment Associated with Startups and Closings
	Establishment (Percent)	Jobs (Percent)	Establishments (Percent)	Jobs (Percent)	Establishment	Jobs	
Shoes (304)							
Total	100	100	100	100	2.6	4.2	−18.4
Independent	40	17	49	33	3.1	8.1	−24.7
Corporate	54	76	37	51	1.8	2.9	−13.4
Conglomerate[b]	6	7	14	16	6.0	9.5	−28.4
Metalworking machinery (354)							
Total	100	100	100	100	1.6	1.6	−4.4
Independent	74	15	81	24	1.8	2.6	−4.4
Corporate	23	78	15	58	1.0	1.2	−2.3
Conglomerate[b]	3	7	4	18	2.2	4.6	−10.5
Computers (357)							
Total	100	100	100	100	0.9	0.8	+3.3
Independent	43	8	56	10	1.2	1.1	−0.5
Corporate	51	91	36	89	0.6	0.8	+3.9
Conglomerate[b]	6	1	8	1	1.1	1.2	−1.4
Aircraft engines (372)							
Total	100	100	100	100	2.0	3.6	−3.3
Independent	57	7	57	10	2.1	5.3	−4.6
Corporate	37	91	28	55	1.6	2.2	−1.6
Conglomerate[b]	6	2	15	35	4.5	76.2	−22.8

Department stores (531)							
Total	100	100	100	100	0.7	0.5	+11.3
Independent	9	4	14	8	1.1	1.0	0.0
Corporate	82	93	60	69	0.5	0.4	+17.4
Conglomerate[b]	9	3	26	23	2.1	4.0	−27.0
Grocery stores/ Supermarkets (541)							
Total	100	100	100	100	2.3	1.0	+0.3
Independent	75	38	93	64	2.8	1.7	−6.4
Corporate	24	61	6	27	0.6	0.4	+18.4
Conglomerate[b]	1	1	1	9	3.0	12.5	−24.6
Hotels/Motels (701)							
Total	100	100	100	100	1.2	0.8	+3.4
Independent	72	39	87	70	1.5	1.5	−5.8
Corporate	26	59	10	20	0.4	0.3	+4.6
Conglomerate[b]	2	2	3	10	1.7	3.9	−21.5

Source: Extract from the Dun's Identifiers File.

[a]See table 10–4.

[b]See table 10–4.

and real estate. General Electric (also labeled a corporation rather than a conglomerate in the tables) makes everything from toaster ovens to jet engines. And Mobil Oil now owns the Montgomery Ward department store chain.

In other words, the findings on the disproportionate high rate of shutdowns exercised by conglomerates between 1969 and 1976 may be a harbinger of things to come as more and more conventional corporations behave like conglomerates—buying and selling, opening and closing operations in order to meet profit targets. In 1979 alone, acquisitions totaling $40 billion were made by U.S. corporations, more than the total spent on research and development by all private firms nationwide.[15]

Existing Policy Responses

State governments across the country, and the last several U.S. Congresses, have not been completely oblivious to the problems created by shutdowns, relocations, and conglomerate reorganizations. While resisting pressures from public interest groups to directly regulate the pace of private capital disinvestment, governments at all levels have become heavily involved in what we choose to call a welfare strategy for dealing with public demands for help.

The prevailing policy approach consists of tax and other subsidies or incentives to private companies. In a virtual stampede, literally thousands of jurisdictions across the country are adopting tax abatement schemes and other business subsidies in the belief that these are necessary requirements to lure employers to their communities or to retain those companies they already have. The rush has created what *Business Week,* in its May 17, 1976 issue, called "The Second War Between the States." There is now extraordinarily wide agreement in the research community that these subsidies have no demonstrable impact on business location behavior, and what is more, entail high opportunity costs in the form of foregone public revenue.[16] If so, then the policy amounts to regressive income distribution: windfall profits for the corporations, and a deadweight loss to the public.[17]

The other policy is the redistribution of income through federal grants, in order to at least partially compensate workers who lose their jobs as the result of shutdowns. In fact, this welfare approach constitutes the standard government response used since the 1930s to cope with the exigencies of economic development. Limited compensation has been available to the unemployed in the form of state-provided unemployment insurance, job retraining programs, and public assistance. While these programs were never designed to specifically help the victims of plant closings, they have of course been utilized by those who have found themselves in this perilous position. Particularly for non-union workers, these three programs often serve as the first, second, and ultimate lines of defense against poverty. Yet while they are used, none of these programs are particularly well-suited to the task of compensating those adversely affected by plant shutdowns per se. This is because income losses resulting from shutdowns tend to be far more substantial and long-lasting than the personal losses associated with any other cause of unemployment.

Unemployment insurance (UI), for example, replaces only a fraction of weekly earnings, and under normal circumstances is only available for a maximum of twenty-six weeks. The average weekly benefit under UI was a mere $78.60 in 1977, a year in which nearly 2.8 million workers exhausted their benefits before finding new jobs (during the depth of the recession in 1975, almost 4.2 million workers exhausted their benefits).[18] Since a significant minority of plant closing victims are without jobs for more than six months,[19] UI—as presently constituted—provides only temporary, and usually inadequate, relief.

Trade Readjustment Assistance (TRA) augments unemployment compensation for those workers who can prove that liberalized trade relations greatly contributed to the elimination of their jobs. TRA first became law in 1962, as a quid pro quo with organized labor, designed to overcome the protectionist demands of the AFL-CIO.[20] Its provisions and coverage were substantially expanded in 1974, and again in 1977. Nevertheless, "the current adjusted assistance program has been criticized as 'burial insurance' because it provides little more than unemployment-type benefits without enabling the worker to obtain future employment."[21] Except for the cash grants, few workers have demanded the retraining or relocation subsidies. Perhaps this is because comparable jobs, for what are often middle-aged or older workers with very specific skills, are hard to find, so that retraining or migration assistance may be of little practical value. Moreover, many workers who have established themselves in their communities are reluctant to sell their homes, remove their children from the local school system, and move away in search of work.

Collective Bargaining Approaches to Protecting Workers

Of course, for workers who belong to unions, the first defense against precipitous dislocations resulting from plant or store closings is without doubt the negotiated contract between labor and management. In recent years, some unions have made significant breakthroughs in negotiating protection for workers' jobs, wages, or at least severance benefits.

For example, the major electrical unions recently won an agreement from the Westinghouse Corporation for two year's notice prior to any partial or complete plant shutdown. The agreement also covers layoffs connected with changes in product lines and gives the unions limited access to the company's records pertaining to long-term investment and production plans. Other new contracts between the United Food and Commercial Workers and several meat-packing firms prohibit the latter from closing a plant and then reopening it on a non-union basis within five years of the shutdown.[22] A clause in a contract between the Amalgamated Clothing and Textile Workers Union and the Clothing Manufacturing Association of the United States, negotiating on behalf of a certain garment firm, prohibits the employer, during the life of the contract, from removing plants from the city (or cities) in which they are located. In still another case, the Graphic Arts Union recently succeeded in getting the printing industries of metropolitan New York to agree to a provision in its members' contracts according to which: "In the event that an employer shall move its factory, this agreement shall remain applicable to the plant at its new location."[23]

But these stories do not mean that the labor movement has solved the problem. Quite apart from the fact that three-quarters of the American labor force has no trade union protection at all, most of those whose jobs are covered by collective bargaining agreements receive very weak protection from dislocation related to shutdowns or large cutbacks. Table 10–6 displays figures for 1977–1978 on the proportion of American and Canadian contracts which provide for advanced notification to employees of impending shutdowns. In the United States, in 1978, while three-quarters of the 400 contracts surveyed by the Bureau of National Affairs (BNA) made some provision for prenotification to workers (although only 29 percent called for advanced notice to *unions*), 81 percent provided for only one week's notice or less. The Canadian record is much the same.

Moreover, the record for large manufacturing companies is much worse than the BNA averages suggest. According to the U.S. Department of Labor, of 826 contracts active on July 1, 1976 covering 3.4 million workers in manufacturing plants with 1,000 or more employees, only 111 contracts (covering 353,000 workers) provided for any sort of advanced notification. That amounts to only 13 percent of the contracts, covering only 10 percent of the workers.[24]

Table 10–7 shows the incidence of income maintenance provisions in union contracts in 1977–1978 in Canada and the United States. Half of all American workers covered in some respect by a contract receive no income protection of any kind. Only a sixth of all workers were even eligible in 1978 for Supplemental Unemployment Benefits—long-term company-paid unemployment insurance—negotiated as part of their contracts.

Labor Law Reform

The American labor movement has long been unanimous in its opinion that workers need far greater protection than is now available. A key element

Table 10-6
Presence in Collective Bargaining Agreements of Provisions for Advanced Notification of Layoff due to Plant Shutdown or Cutback

	Canada (1977)		United States (1978)	
	Number	Percent	Number	Percent
All contracts surveyed	341	100.0	400	100.0
No provision for prenotification	121	36.0	100	25.0
Some provision	220	64.0	300	75.0
One week or less	180	82.0	244	81.0

Source: Bob Baugh, Department of Research, International Woodworkers of America, "Shutdown: Mill Closures and Woodworkers," IWA, Portland, Oregon, December 3, 1979, p. 8.

Table 10-7
Presence in Collective Bargaining Agreements of Provisions for Income Maintenance in the Event of Layoff due to Plant Shutdown or Cutback

	Canada (1977)		United States (1978)	
	Number	Percent	Number	Percent
All contracts surveyed	341	100.0	400	100.0
No provision	144	42.0	204	51.0
Some provision	197	58.0	196	49.0
Severance	161	47.0	148	37.0
Supplemental Unemployment Benefits (SUB)	81	19.0	64	16.0
Other	—	—	36	9.0

Source: Labor Canada; Bureau of National Affairs; Baugh, "Shutdown: Mill Closures and Woodworkers," p. 11.
Percents may sum to more than 100 because some workers are eligible for more than one benefit.

in enhancing that protection would be removing the fetters that the Taft-Hartley Act placed upon the ability of unions both to organize in businesses and locations where workers are presently unorganized, and to protect themselves from a variety of unfair labor practices by management. The repeal of Section 14(b) in particular—the granting to states of the power to prohibit the closed shop without which union locals' financial survival is made far more precarious—has become something of a crusade in recent years. Our own research supports the view that business is aware of and responsive to the attractiveness of such anti-union jurisdictions as sites for branches of relocated facilities.[25]

A second major area of labor law reform that seems especially pertinent to the subject of capital flight is the clarification of the extremely ambiguous state of affairs that currently prevails with respect to the problem of *successorship*. In 1964, the U.S. Supreme Court ruled that unions had the right to bring grievances before the National Labor Relations Board when an employer disappeared by merger and the new employer refused to recognize the union. For example, this occurred when Perdue, a determinedly non-union employer, acquired three plants from Swift and Company in Delaware and Maryland, all of which had been unionized under Swift.[26] As we saw earlier, this sort of disappearance seems to have become increasingly common in the past twenty years, and another merger wave, led this time by the computer and semiconductor industries, appears to be in the offing. But in 1972, in the *Burns* decision, the Burger Court effectively reversed the previous Warren Court ruling, arguing that a successor's honoring the contract

> does not ensue as a matter of law from the mere fact that an employer is doing the same work in the same place with the same employees as his predecessor . . . a potential employer may be willing to take over a moribund business only if he can make changes in corporate structure, composition of the labor force, work, location, task assignment, and nature of supervision. Saddling such an employer with the terms and conditions of employment contained in the old contract may make these changes impossible and may discourage and inhibit the transfer of capital. . .[27]

Given our own finding that the typical acquisition is anything but moribund, this decision represents a major setback for organized labor. Senator Harrison Williams (Democrat-New Jersey) has submitted legislation to amend the Taft-Hartley Act to make it an unfair labor practice for an employer who assumes ownership or operation of an ongoing business to refuse to assume all of the terms and conditions of a predecessor contract. Thus far, the legislation has had little success.

Plant Closing Legislation

In the past several years, national labor law reform has been thwarted in the U.S. Congress. But even if the various changes being sought by labor were to be achieved, for example, with respect to successorship, common situs picketing, or the repeal of 14(b), there would still be at least three major problems to overcome. First, the case-by-case collective bargaining approach is insufficient for reaching every worker directly at risk, as labor unions are simply not financially strong enough today to organize all employers. Second, protection needs to be extended beyond those workers who are immediately affected by company restructuring strategies, to cover everyone whose income security is threatened. And finally, collective bargaining is obviously incapable of providing for the rebuilding of the local economic base in the wake of major shutdowns. Thus, many have called for legislation that addresses the whole range of problems created by plant and store closings and cutbacks.

The European Experience. In June 1978, a delegation made up of officials from three American unions (the auto workers, steel workers, and the machinists) and several government agencies visited Sweden, West Germany and England to study how those governments—and the unions in those countries—were dealing with what is, after all, an international problem. They found that

> Without exception . . . all three (countries) had programs for coping with the adverse effects of economic dislocation upon workers and communities . . .. In all three countries, corporations are legally obligated to give advance notice (to) workers, unions, and the national employment service before closing a plant or dismissing workers for economic reasons. Before initiating layoffs, moreover, a company must first negotiate the matter with its employees' union or the plant's works joint labor-management council . . . the planned reduction is handled entirely by attrition and no dismissals are necessary. The time gained gives affected workers and potential new employees the chance to arrange for alternative employment . . . advance notice triggers into action labor market boards at the national, regional, local (and in some cases, workplace) levels . . .
>
> Some might argue that Western Europe's statutory programs to protect workers and communities against economic dislocation are costly and burdensome to corporations. [Yet] many of the same corporations which can be counted on to oppose such programs in the United States have been investing heavily over the last thirty years, and for the most part have operated profitably, in the three countries we visited and in others which have long experience with legislation to cope with the effects of economic dislocation.[28]

The Swedes have the most highly developed programs for relocating workers, for example, by bringing employment service computer terminals right inside the old plant as soon as notice of the eventual closing is given, and by statutorily requiring all employees to list vacancies in these computerized files (in strong contrast to the American employment security system, where filing is de facto voluntary and has been shown again and again to be very selective). Moreover, the Swedes have a wide variety of programs for replacing the eroded local job (and tax) base, through direct public enterprise and grants and loans for new private sector startups. In West Germany, a firm contemplating a shutdown is required to give its reasons to the local works council, and to open its books so that the council will have free access to all corporate data relevant to evaluating the reasons for the decision and its likely impact on the region in which the plant is located. Although not yet strictly enforced, the Codetermination Act of 1976 calls for one year advance notice by West German businesses of intended closings.

It is also worth noting that each of these three countries has pushed the welfare approach considerably beyond what is available in the United States. Severance pay, mandatory transfer rights, guaranteed social security credits, health benefits, and adequate income maintenance benefits are provided by the company (or as a last resort, by the government) until the individual is reemployed. Retraining, mobility assistance and guaranteed employer-paid relocation expenses are also mandated in most cases. Through such measures, the governments in these countries have tried as much as possible to fully compensate workers who lose their jobs through no fault of their own.[29]

Legislative attempts in the United States. In 1974, then Senator Walter Mondale (Democrat-Minnesota) and Congressman William Ford (Democrat-Michigan) introduced the National Employment Priorities Act (NEPA) into the U.S. Congress. The act would have created a National Employment Relocation Administration to investigate complaints, rule on whether the plant shutdown or relocation was justified, and, if not, recommend the withholding of various tax benefits. The proposed program has been criticized for being administratively impractical, as well as for lacking criteria for determining justified capital disinvestment. The program constituted an open invitation for every firm to blackmail the government into giving it the various financial subsidies provided for in the bill whenever extra cash was needed. The language of Title VI made any firm, even if it was just *thinking* of closing or transferring operations, eligible for loans, grants, interest subsidies, and technical assistance. In any case, the bill was never reported out of committee.

At this point, the effort to organize plant closing legislation shifted to the states. In late 1975, the Ohio Public Interest Campaign (OPIC) was formed to educate citizens and organize resistance to the wave of plant closings and corporate demands for tax abatements and credits that was sweeping the midwest. OPIC is a coalition of labor unions, senior citizens, civil rights and consumer organizations, and church groups, based in Cleveland, with offices all across the state. In July 1977, a new plant closing bill, the Community Readjustment Act, drafted by OPIC, was introduced into the Ohio Senate by Senator Michael Schwarzwalder (Democrat-Columbus). In spite of a major organizing effort in 1977–1978, the bill died in committee. Through continued effort, and in the wake of a new rash of steel mill closings, the revived 1979 version (Ohio Senate Bill No. 188) began to win more widespread support, including approval by the Senate Finance subcommittee (but not by the entire body) in 1980.

The OPIC-Schwarzwalder bill contains six key provisions, which have come to define the basic agenda for the many similar bills which have followed in many other states:[30]

prior notification of major cutbacks and total shutdowns, varying from six months to two years

discharge or severance payments for all workers, whether or not they are unionized

continuation of health insurance coverage for some period following the layoff, paid for by the company

increased rights of transfer to other plants or stores in the company's system (if any)

lump sum payment to the local municipality, to help finance economic redevelopment

preparation by joint company-union-government committees of economic impact statements, to facilitate the redevelopment effort.

Two other states—Maine and Wisconsin—already have modest plant closing laws on the books (Maine reformers are attempting to strengthen theirs.). In every case, the provisions apply only to shutdowns of (or substantial cutbacks in) the establishments of firms with some minimum number of employees (generally 100, but the details vary from state to state).

Much impressed with what they had learned on their June 1978 tour of western Europe, upon their return to the United States the UAW members of the study group issued a seven-point program for dealing with problems related to plant closings in this country. During the next year, through conferences with the staffs of OPIC and those of other unions, the UAW plan grew into a twenty-seven point program which was published in a joint communique of the three unions that had made the European tour.[31] This statement represents the most comprehensive set of recommendations ever set forth.

The rapid growth of activity at the local level, and the deteriorating economic situation in the country as a whole, made a new initiative in Washington appear more likely in 1979. After long consultations with the UAW Research Department, on August 31, 1979, Michigan Congressman Ford reintroduced his (considerably altered) bill into the U.S. House of Representatives. Co-sponsored by Senator Donald Riegle (Democrat-Michigan) and fifty-eight others, the new National Employment Priorities Act of 1979 (H.R. 5040) has begun to attract attention through hearings around the country, and (more recently) as a result of growing and vocal opposition in the business press. The main provisions of the Ford-Riegle bill cover: prenotification (so workers and communities have time to plan readjustment), severance pay, successorship, transfer rights, the protection of benefits for a period of time following the shutdown or layoff, grants and loans to failing businesses under certain specified circumstances, economic redevelopment assistance to local governments, and grants and loans to workers to help them buy out closing businesses in order to operate them as cooperatives. A companion, but not identical bill, introduced into the Senate by Harrison Williams, is called the Employee Protection and Community Stabilization Act of 1979. And an earlier bill by Congressman Peter Kostmayer (Democrat-Pennsylvania) and Philip Lundine (Democrat-New York), designed to provide federal loans and loan guarantees for worker buy-outs, became a Carter administration-supported amendment to the National Public Works and Economic Development Act of 1979. This legislation sought to renew (with greatly increased funding and authority) the nation's economic programs. Senator Steward (Democrat-Alaska) further promoted this directive toward worker ownership with an amendment to the Small Business Administration Reauthorization Act (S. 918), requiring SBA to extend its entire range of technical and financial services to small worker-owned companies and cooperatives. Finally, still other amendments to the new EDA bill, by congresspersons Dodd (Democrat-Connecticut) and McKenney (Republican-Connecticut), would require advanced notification of military contract cancellations by the Pentagon, and long-term income mainteneance for workers displaced by such cancellations. As of January 1981, none of these bills has been passed.

Corporate Opposition to Plant Closing Legislation

Business executives, lobbyists, management consultants, and their elected supporters seem to be taking these legislative initiatives seriously. In the last two years, books, magazine articles, and public speeches have denounced the efforts of labor and community groups to—as business spokes-people put it—"hold industry for ransom."

Management argues that companies will stop expanding operations in states which pass legislation regulating the mobility of private capital. Moreover, they say, no new companies are likely to build in such places. For example, William McCarthy, an official of the corporate lobbying group Associate Industries of Massachusetts (AIM), warned at the time of the first plant closing legislative hearing in the Massachusetts State House, that even the *consideration* of such legislation "would be raising a sign on the borders of this state that investment isn't welcome here."[32]

In his American Enterprise Institute monograph, Clemson University Professor Richard McKensie, views plant closing legislation as direct support of trade unions and local governments, against the interests of business. By inhibiting companies from shutting down, unions would (he argues) be able to "increase their demands on employers" for higher wages and fringe benefits, while local governments could increase business taxes without improving quality of services.[33]

In the same vein, the editors of the *Wall Street Journal* recently took the position that the new plant closing legislation would give politicians and unions "property rights in the existing distribution of jobs and business activity." Companies' assets could then be "pillaged" by the "featherbedding" and "antiquated work rules" imposed by the unions, and stuck with bills imposed by "vote-buying politicians." Eventually, said the *Journal,* such legislation might actually *increase* job loss, since "shareholders who can't run can be more quickly plundered into bankruptcy."[34]

Andrew Kramer, a partner in a Washington, D.C., labor relations management consulting firm suggests that announcements of plant shutdowns may (1) lower productivity and lead to the loss of skilled and semi-skilled workers and (2) increase the administrative burden on management, while posing a serious danger of protracted litigation. Firms would be tied up indefinitely in court proceedings, as has occurred with respect to the environmental impact statements mandated by the National Environmental Protection Act.[35].

Probably no measure in the proposed legislation is more violently opposed by business than the requirement for advanced notification of major cutbacks or total shutdowns. In a 1977 letter to the study group that subsequently drafted the first Massachusetts bill, the then Acting Commissioner of Commerce and Development asserted that he had "discussed this with several people" and concluded that it would be "impractical" for a firm to be asked to announce such a decision in advance. Besides, he told the group, for most businesses "the decision is often abrupt," so that anything like a six-month to two-year lead time wouldn't even be possible, let alone "practical."

But case studies of a number of plant closings in different industries and different regions make it very clear that a great many shutdowns are either explicitly planned far ahead, or are easily predictable in the light of the parent corporation's measurable disinvestment in the plant or store.[36] Peter Drucker, probably the country's foremost management consultant and analyst, has stated that "there is usually a two-year lead time between the identification of the need to close plants or make reductions and the actual closing."[37]

From our own field notes, we can offer two examples from the women's apparel industry in New England. Its own corporate reports reveal that the Nashville-based conglomerate, Genesco, underwent a major change of management (including its board chairman) in 1977, after which the new team announced that it would close down the entire women's apparel division—sixteen companies operating forty-seven plants. One of these was Girl Town, a sportswear operation in the Dorchester section of Boston, which had been acquired in 1967. Girl Town was not completely closed (the last of approximately 400 jobs eliminated) until mid-1979—two years after Genesco's managers publicly announced that the closing would take place.

One might also look at the even longer-term planned reorganization strategy of a major New England dress company, started in New Bedford in the 1930s. As our interviews with some of the managers disclosed, the firm maintained its headquarters and cutting room in the New Bedford area, and prior to the 1960s, had contract shops (for the sewing and stitching operations) in Rhode Island, Vermont, and upstate New York. In 1963, what had been a family business went public, and with the new infusion of capital that this brought, immediately acquired an industrial building in Tennessee, and another in North Carolina, a few years later. Once these factories were fully operational, the firm sold off its Rhode Island operation and shut down the New York plant. The major clothing conglomerate which acquired the firm in 1971 accelerated the regional shift, opening two more plants in Tennessee in 1972 and 1973, after which it shut down the last of the New England-based assembly plants in Vermont.

In both cases, as with the Lykes Corporation's conglomerate acquisition of the Campbell Works in Youngstown, there is simply no doubt that the disinvestment was planned, and the facilities phased out, over time. Moreover, as we reported earlier, a number of U.S. companies (including the Westinghouse Corporation) seem able to live with prior notification clauses in their labor contracts. And in Europe, virtually all firms have had to come to an accommodation with the principle of prenotification.

Furthermore, for large, often multiplant corporations, the proposition that advanced notice will reduce workers' productivity or lead to the premature loss of the most qualified workers does not seem to be supported by case studies of plant closings or by surveys conducted by the British Manpower Commission.[38] In fact, there is reason to believe that many workers often do hear of an impending closing, but do not know precisely *when* it will occur. As a result, if anything, companies' unwillingness to give advanced notification *induces* quitting because of the free-floating insecurity associated with rumors of a plant closing. Knowing the future date allows the worker to plan rather than merely act out of misinformed apprehension.

Conclusions

Will anything resembling the proposed plant closing and related legislation be passed into law in the foreseeable future? And even if it were, how much real progress toward more orderly economic planning, which necessarily means progress in the planning of investment and disinvestment, would be made without complementary and far-reaching changes in tax, tariff, anti-trust, and *then* economic development policy? These are among the central economic policy issues for the 1980s. Centainly they are crucial to any ser-ious—that is, non-rhetorical—discussion about reindustrialization.

In any case, with regard to all such reforms, it is clear that the business community is adopting a militant posture. In many ways, the clarion call was sounded publicly for the first time in a commentary that appeared in the October 12, 1974 issue of *Business Week*:

> Some people will obviously have to do with less, or with substitutes, so that the economy as a whole can get the most mileage out of available cap-ital . . ..
>
> Indeed, cities and states, the home mortgage market, small business, and the consumer, will all get less than they want because the basic health of the U.S. is based on the basic health of its corporations and banks: the big-gest borrowers and the biggest lenders. Compromises, in terms of who gets and who does without, that would have been unthinkable only a few years ago, will be made in coming years because the economic future not only of the U.S. but also of the whole world is on the line today.[39]

The magazine goes on to observe that the idea that income and resources will have to be redistributed to big business will be a "hard pill" to swallow. To get the American people to swallow it is, they predict, going to require a "selling job" beyond anything that any country has attempted in modern times, to make people accept the "new reality."

As we have seen, the "new reality" includes a high incidence of direct job loss due to shutdowns, in a wide range of industries, and in all regions of the country. Indeed, although the absolute and per capita levels of estab-lishment closings have (predictably) been highest in the northeast, the odds of a pre–1969 large manufacturing plant shutting down sometime before the late 1970s were actually higher in the south than anywhere else. Overall, the country was losing an average of 4.4 million jobs a year to shutdowns (not counting multiplier effects) through the end of 1976. Since then, the inci-dence of job loss has almost surely increased, with the rapid pace of indus-try-wide restructuring schemes in autos, steel, and rubber, and with the growth of conglomerate-like behavior on the part of many corporations.

In all of this, corporate managers' use of industrial location to keep organized labor off guard has helped to destabilize (if not to altogether de-stroy) the consensus between big labor and big business that has formed the basis for more or less orderly private capital accumulation since the early 1950s. Concisely put, the trade unions are under explicit attack once again,[40] with capital "hypermobility" being the newest weapon in the management arsenal.[41]

To us, a key question is therefore whether the unions will respond to the very great need for leadership in the continuing struggle over strategic plant shutdowns, and what that response will be. Will they attempt to restore consensus with (now) global capital? Or will they become an agency for resisting and challenging unregulated capital mobility? The fate of legislation concerning plant closings, labor law reform, and much else may ultimately turn on how these conflicting tendencies within the labor movement work themselves out in the years ahead.

Notes

1. For example, in its November 28, 1979 edition, the *New York Times* reported the closing of fifteen United States Steel Corporation plants and mills in eight states resulting in the loss of 13,000 white and blue collar jobs. This announcement was made in spite of the increased demand for steel.

The near-collapse of the Chrysler Corporation, and major cutbacks in the domestic (but not in the overseas) operations of Ford, are by now too well-known to require documentation. On the other hand, there is still limited awareness of the extent to which the restructuring process has spread, even to non-manufacturing industries. For example, "Food Fair, Inc. (owes) $15 million . . . to . . . employees . . . who lost their jobs when the company closed 212 supermarkets and seventy-nine J.M. Fields department stores (including all its stores in Philadelphia)." *Wall Street Journal,* September 18, 1979, p. 1.

2. Barry Bluestone and Bennett Harrison, *Capital vs. Community: The De-Industrialization of America* (New York: Basic Books, 1982). Related research has been conducted by William F. Whyte and Robert Stern at Cornell University, by Belden Daniels at Harvard University, by Robert Cohen at Columbia University, by Charles Craypo at Notre Dame, by Doreen Massey at the London School of Economics, and by the staff of the North American Congress on Latin America in New York City.

3. In this chapter our interest is mainly in private *dis*investment and its consequences, especially in older regions. But, of course, capital also moves into such areas all the time. It is incorrect to imagine the situation as one in which *everything* is leaving. However, the activities that still do business there, or the new ones that are starting up, may be growing too slowly to make up for those businesses that are cutting back, closing, or leaving. Or the new companies may not want to employ the people who were thrown out of work by the old closings. The jobs that make up the new economic base may pay lower wages and offer less steady or fewer hours of work than did the old base. We estimate, for example, that it takes at least two service

sector jobs to make up in family income what is lost by the elimination of one manufacturing job. These larger questions about economic base transformation (in contrast with decline per se) are examined in detail for one region in Bennett Harrison, *The Economic Transformation of New England Since World War II* (Cambridge, Mass.: MIT-Harvard Joint Center for Urban Studies, 1981).

4. See Carol Jusenius and Larry Ledebur, "A Myth in the Making: The Southern Economic Challenge and Northern Economic Decline", in E. Blaine Liner and Lawrence K. Lynch, eds., *The Economics of Southern Growth* (Durham, N.C.: The Southern Growth Policies Board, 1977); and Bernhard L. Weinstein and Robert E. Firestine, *Regional Growth and Decline in the United States: The Rise of the Sunbelt and the Decline of the Northeast* (New York: Praeger, 1978). In earlier published work, one of us also erroneously cited the 1.5 percent figure as evidence that there is relatively little short-term spatial movement of businesses in the United States; Bennett Harrison and Sandra Kanter, "The Political Economy of State Job-Creation Business Incentives," *Journal of the American Institute of Planners;* November 1978.

5. Richard B. McKenzie, *Restrictions on Business Mobility* (Washington, D.C.: American Enterprise Institute, 1979), p. 5. The basic data may be found in David Birch, *The Job Generation Process* (Cambridge, Mass.: MIT Program on Neighborhood and Regional Change, 1979). Birch's work has been quoted by the *Wall Street Journal* and by many southern researchers to counter the argument that southern growth is occurring at the expense of northern workers. Research papers by regional economists that have cited Birch's famous "one and a half percent" have been similarly used. For example, one study of plant migrations out of the state of Ohio over the period 1970–1974 found that "migrant firms were few in number and mostly small in size." (Jusenius and Ledebur, "The Migration of Firms and Workers in Ohio, 1970–1975," Academy for Contemporary Problems, Columbus, 1977). When this conclusion was announced in late 1977, it was quickly reported by daily newspapers all across the state. At the time, a coalition of trade unionists, community activists, and church leaders was trying to find a way to save the jobs of the 4,100 workers who had been laid off that September when the Campbell works of the Youngstown Sheet and Tube Steel mill was closed down by its conglomerate parent, the Lykes Corporation. In a study by two Harvard Business School economists (Robert A. Leone and John R. Meyer, "Can the Northeast Rise Again," *Wharton Quarterly,* Winter 1979), the authors report that "of the more than 1450 northeast manufacturing facilities that can be definitely identified as making a long distance move from 1971 to 1976 . . . only 128 emigrated to the sunbelt" (p. 23).

6. The fact that more and more large corporations and conglomerates

deliberately milk profitable plants instead of reinvesting in them, or liquidate plants or subsidies that fail to meet arbitrarily set minimum profit targets, represents a culmination of tendencies in the development of modern management with literally epochal effects on the international capitalist system. We present numerous examples in our monograph. Striking confirmation of these developments has now appeared in a most unlikely place: the pages of *Business Week* itself. In a nearly 100-page editorial on the problem of reindustrialization, the editors explicitly accuse modern quantitatively trained managers of not keeping their plants modern; of establishing arbitrary target profit hurdles and then shutting down even relatively efficient facilities which fail to meet them; of pursuing growth for their firms by acquiring unrelated existing businesses rather than by building new plants or expanding existing capacity; and of generally adopting myopic behavior with respect to the investment decision. See "Reindustrialization: Special Issue," *Business Week,* June 30, 1980. See also Robert H. Hayes and William J. Abernathy, "Managing Our Way to Economic Decline," *Harvard Business Review,* July August, 1980; and the series of case studies assembled by the Committee on Small Business, U.S. House of Representatives, *Conglomerate Mergers—Their Effects on Small Business and Local Communities* (Washington, D.C.: U.S. GPO, 1980.

7. This has not stopped business spokespersons from continually *threatening* to move out of town if they don't get their way. In an interview with the trade magazine *New England Business* (October 1, 1979, p. 14), Associated Industries of Massachusetts lobbyist Jim Sledd asserted that Massachusetts high-technology firms are "very mobile" and that "they can be on the back of a flatbed truck tomorrow and be in North Carolina if things don't go the way they want them to."

8. There also appears to be a systematic downward bias in D&B's counts of even what we are calling simultaneous or sequential relocations. That is, D&B almost surely undercounts "movers." Most users of the data seem to agree on this. For details, see Bluestone and Harrison, *Capital vs. Community,* ch. 2 and Birch, *The Job Generation Process.*

9. In this chapter, we report only on job loss as an impact measure. There is a rich literature on the income, earnings, health, community, and labor relations effects of plant closings, which we review in chapter 3 of our monograph. See also Robert Aronson and Robert McKersie, *Economic Consequences of Plant Shutdowns in New York State* (Ithaca, N.Y.: N.Y. State School of Industrial and Labor Relations, Cornell University, 1980); Felician Foltman, *White and Blue Collars in a Mill Shutdown* (Ithaca, N.Y.: Cornell University Press, 1968); Arlene Holen, "Losses to Workers Displaced by Plant Closure or Layoff: A Survey of the Literature," The Public Research Institute of the Center for Naval Analyses, November 1976; Louis Jacobson, "Earnings Loss Due to Displacement," The Public

Research Institute of the Center for Naval Analyses, Working Paper CRC-385, April 1979; Peter B. Meyer and Mark A. Phillips, *Worker Adaptation to Internationally Induced Job Loss: Final Report on a Pilot Study,* Bureau of International Labor Affairs, U.S. Department of Labor, April 27, 1978; Stephen S. Mick, "Social and Personal Costs of Plant Shutdowns," *Industrial Relations,* Vol. 14, No. 2, May 1975, p. 205; James L. Stern, "Consequences of Plant Closure," *Journal of Human Resources,* Winter 1972; and Richard Wilcock and W. H. Franke, *Unwanted Workers: Permanent Layoffs and Long-Term Unemployment* (New York: Glencoe Free Press, 1963).

10. For example, companies now typically select depreciation schedules from a menu offered up by the Internal Revenue Service to fit the former's cash flow requirements. As a result, officially measured differences between gross and net private investment are becoming artifacts of the political process rather than an indicator of disinvestment.

Moreover, the U.S. Bureau of Labor Statistics' and Census Bureau's regularly published figures on changes in employment, no matter how detailed (by industry, occupation, race, sex, age, location), cannot be used to make inferences about what is going on in terms of capital investment. Employment can change due to changing product demand, inventory build-ups (or shortages), seasonality, snowstorms, energy brown-outs, and even unofficial vacation practices traditional to some industries (New England women's apparel manufacturers, for instance, typically complete the production of their fall lines by late spring; some then "invite" their production workers to take off for the summer and return in September, to be supported in the interim by Welfare or Unemployment Insurance). In none of these instances has the facility itself or any of its machinery and equipment necessarily been expanded or contracted.

11. See Birch, *The Job Generation Process,* pp. 3–25 on some of the problems with the data, his own (sometimes controversial) methods for rearranging and editing the raw D&B records, etc.

12. For additional detail on establishment openings and closings in New England, and a more complete description of the methodology, see Bluestone and Harrison, *Capital vs. Community,* chapter 2.

13. Recall that these data refer to individual establishments, that is, stores and plants, *not* to firms. The failure rate of firms is presumably much lower. For some evidence on the latter, see Harrison, *The Economic Transformation of New England.*

14. The criterion used to distinguish a multiestablishment "corporation" from a multiestablishment "conglomerate" is as follows. If the various establishments belonging to a central firm share the same DUNS number (and therefore the same credit rating), and if they do not have legal standing to be sued individually in court, then Birch assigns them to a cate-

gory he calls "headquarters or branch." We call this the "corporate" sector. Otherwise, all of the establishments that make up the multiestablishment firm—each with its own individual DUNS number and court standing—are assigned by Birch to what he calls the "parent-subsidiary" category, which we label "conglomerate." This procedure unquestionably understates the degree of conglomerate-like *behavior* in the sample. For example, a corporation with a famous name may acquire a totally unrelated product or service line, yet treat it as a division rather than as a separate entity, perhaps in order to exploit its own famous name. Birch's and our procedure would classify these as corporate establishments, even though this would be a clear case of conglomerate behavior in the eyes of (say) the Federal Trade Commission. Future researchers will need to develop a more market structure-oriented definition of conglomeration than the essentially legalistic definition used here. Such a definition should explicitly recognize conglomeration as a process of corporate expansion which involves both product (and service) diversity and acquisition of existing facilities as distinct from the construction of new ones. The history of the conglomerate movement in the United States is reviewed in Bluestone and Harrison, *Capital vs. Community,* chapter 6.

15. Cited in *Business Week,* p. 78.

16. For a review of the literature, see Bluestone and Harrison, *Capital vs. Community,* chapter 7. Among the more recent entries are Robert Goodman, *The Last Entrepreneurs* (N.Y.: Simon and Schuster, 1979); Jerry Jacobs, *Bidding for Business: Corporate Auctions and the Fifty Disunited States* (Washington, D.C.: Public Interest Research Group, 1979); Roger Vaughan, *State Taxation and Economic Development* (Washington, D.C.: Council of State Planning Agencies, 1979); and Harrison and Kanter, "The Political Economy of State Job-Creation Business Incentives."

17. Direct financial assistance and tax subsidies are by no means the only major concessions being offered to business to influence their investment decisions. Relaxing business regulation and limiting social wage legislation are advocated as an additional means to create—or at least to advertise—a "good business climate." Because business lobbyists complain most about the compliance costs entailed in environmental protection laws, occupational health and safety regulations, zoning statutes, building codes, and anti-discrimination measures, these have become the prime targets for reform. For example, in Massachusetts, the defeat of a series of 1975 statewide referenda on progressive income taxation, public power, throwaway containers, and "lifeline" electric rates is credited by government officials with restoring business confidence in the Commonwealth. Restrictions on unemployment and workmen's compensation eligibility, labor law reform, minimum wage coverage, and corporate property tax classification are other measures that fall under this category.

18. U.S. Department of Labor, *Employment and Training Report of the President 1979,* (Washington: U.S. Government Printing Office, 1979). Table F-10, p. 372.

19. Bluestone and Harrison, *Capital vs. Community,* chapter 3.

20. For a detailed history of TRA, see *Employment and Training Report of the President 1979,* pp. 243–246; and James E. McCarthy, *Trade Adjustment Assistance: A Case Study of the Shoe Industry in Massachusetts,* Federal Reserve Bank of Boston Research Report No. 58, June 1975.

21. *Wall Street Journal,* October 31, 1977, p. 6.

22. These two cases are reported in *American Labor,* December 1979, pp. 2–3.

23. Reported by Bob Baugh, Department of Research, Education and Collective Bargaining Coordination, International Woodworkers of America, "Shutdown: Mill Closures and Woodworkers", IWA, Portland Oregon, December 3, 1979, page 7.

24. *Ibid.,* p. 9.

25. Bluestone and Harrison, *Capital vs. Community,* chapter 7.

26. Personal communication from David Blitzstein, United Food and Commercial Workers, International Headquarters, Washington, D.C., January 18, 1981.

27. Quoted in Baugh, "Shutdown," p. 32.

28. Labor Union Study Tour Participants, *Economic Dislocation: Plant Closings, Plant Relocations, and Plant Conversion,* UAW, USA, IAM, Washington, D.C., May 1, 1979, pp. 7–8. On the same subject, see also C&R Associates, *Plant Location Legislation and Regulation in the United States and Western Europe: A Survey,* Federal Trade Commission, Washington, D.C., January 1979.

29. Labor Union Study Tour, *Economic Dislocation.*

30. Among the other states with legislation pending as of December 1980 are: Connecticut, Illinois, Maine, Massachusetts, Michigan, New Jersey, New York, Oregon, Pennsylvania, and Rhode Island. The following material is drawn from William Schweke, ed., *Plant Closing Strategy Packet* (Washington, D.C.: Progressive Alliance and Conference on Alternative State and Local Policies, January 1980). This document contains a detailed comparison of the provisions of each state's bill.

31. Labor Union Study Tour, *Economic Dislocation,* pp. 32–34.

32. Quoted by Liz Bass, "Runaway Plants Leave Workers Out in Cold", *The Citizen Advocate* (Massachusetts), March 1979, p. 3. This is hardly a new position for Mr. McCarthy's organization to be taking. As far back as the 1922–1923 legislative sessions in Massachusetts, AIM officials were making the same threats. For example: "By far the most serious menace which confronts the industries of our section today is that growing out of a public misconception of the proper obligation of business enter-

prise to society," Colonel Gow, President of AIM, July 1, 1922; "The community must see to it that legislation shall not unduly hamper business management," Frank Dresser, AIM staffer, December 29, 1923; "It cannot be hoped that, with these great industrial plants once driven out of New England, others would come in to replace them, when competing Sections . . . offer such attractive advantages." AIM editorial, March 3, 1923. All three quotations come from AIM's official magazine, *Industry*. The Dresser statement was part of an article entitled: "What Can We Do To Prevent Unwise Social Legislation?". The "unwise social legislation" being debated on Beacon Hill that prompted these thinly veiled threats included revisions of the minimum wage law, workmen's compensation, and amendments to toughen the child labor laws.

33. McKenzie, *Restrictions on Business Mobility*, pp. 57, 60.

34. "Words and Deeds", *The Wall Street Journal*, November 23, 1979, p. 20. Incidentally, these quotes clearly imply that, precisely because capital mobility is *not* presently regulated, companies *do* run after all, something which McKenzie goes to great lengths to deny in the earlier chapters of his book.

35. Andrew M. Kramer, "Plant Locations (and Relocations) from a Labor Relations Perspective," *Industrial Development*, November–December 1979, p. 4.

36. Cf. the discussion of the shutdown of the Campbell Works of the Youngstown Sheet and Tube Company, in Belden Daniels, et. al., *The Impact of Acquisition on the Acquired Firm* (Cambridge: Dept. of City and Regional Planning, Harvard University, 1980), chapter 4.

37. Quoted in Pennsylvania Public Interest Coalition, *Public Interest News*, vol. 1, no. 2, July 1981, p. 7.

38. Harry J. Gilman, "The Economic Costs of Worker Dislocation: An Overview," prepared for the National Commission for Employment Policy, July 13, 1979. The research to which Gilman refers is by Arnold Weber and David P. Taylor, "Procedures for Employee Displacement: Advance Notice of Shutdown," *Journal of Business*, July 1963; and OECD, *Job Security and Industrial Relations. Report of the Working Party of Industrial Relations*, Paris, May 1977.

39. *Business Week*, October 12, 1974. Copyright © 1974 by McGraw-Hill, Inc. Reprinted with permission.

40. Cf. Donald D. Cook, "Laws to Curb Plant Closings," *Industry Week*, February 4, 1980.

41. This challenge has been reiterated by representatives of the Business Roundtable and the U.S. Chamber of Commerce on several television news programs, for example, the "McNeil-Lehrer Report" of June 18, 1980. Arnold Weber agrees that the challenge to labor is to be understood as corporate *policy:* "Instead of working with unions to solve problems that

might prevent plant closings," Weber is quoted by *Business Week,* "companies increasingly attempt to create a bona fide open shop movement . . . by shifting production overseas or to the Sunbelt." *Business Week,* June 30, 1980, p. 82.

11 Managing and Adjusting to a Plant Closing

Felician F. Foltman

In the diversified and mature economy of the United States, plant closings have occurred and continue to occur with a frequency that is either deplored or commended, depending on the orientation of the analyst. The loss of jobs and income to individuals and to communities is disaster, at least in the short-term; but the economist and the employer, viewing a plant closing in terms of economic criteria, efficiency, cost cutting, productivity, see it as an inevitable and necessary corollary of maintaining a dynamic economy. All would agree that the incidence of plant closings in the 1980s has reached or is reaching crisis proportions.

In this overview we will: briefly review the problems created by a plant closing for management; suggest an appropriate decision-making model; then assay a few general observations and speculations about what the future portends. Given the great disparities in perception and need between the employees (and unions) and employers in a plant shutdown situation, it is obvious that there is no one best solution. It is argued in this chapter that plant shutdowns can and should be managed more humanely and efficiently than they have in the majority of past cases.

First, it is important to define terms and state assumptions and caveats. As used here, plant closings refer to employing organizations which cease or disinvest operations where at least fifty persons will be (or were) permanently unemployed. These criteria happen to be those usually suggested in state-proposed legislation for regulating or ameliorating the effects of plant closings. Second, the circumstances surrounding a particular closing determine the range of responses, whether by collective bargaining, unilateral management action, or to meet the requirements of public policy. Consider, for example, a factory employing 300 persons unaffiliated with any other enterprise, that is forced out of business due to managerial deficiencies, poor products, or changing tastes. There are no other plants, there is no possibility of moving to another location. Consider another example, the plant that also employed a similar number of persons but is closing in one section of the country because of presumed obsolete physical facilities, high taxes or "poor business climate" (a euphemism that covers any number of complaints and criticisms) and plans to relocate in a more attractive setting. To use the pejorative term often used by organized labor, this example could be the runaway shop. On the other hand, consider still another example of a corporation which operates several plants in a number of different locations around the country. One plant is closed, but others are not. Indeed, in many such cases, the obsolete plant is closed but production continues, may even expand, at newer, more modern facilities. The meatpacking industry and the widely reported Armour automation agreement of the 1960s, illustrate this. One other dimension of plant closing will illuminate both the possibilities and the difficulties of ameliorating the effects of closing, that is, the time during which operations must cease and jobs be terminated. If the closing can occur over a period of one year or two years, as some legislative proposals suggest should be required by law, it is obvious that a carefully crafted and managed policy of reducing jobs by attrition would be not only workable but probably cost effective, as well. On the other hand, if circumstances dictate closing over a period of a few weeks, a not uncommon occurrence, there is little possibility of using the attrition model. These examples probably do not exhaust the variety of plant closings, but they do serve to illustrate the need to be precise and factual.

For our purposes we assume there are employers who can and will consider the human, community, and social consequences of a plant closing. Employers who are strict legal constructionists in their definition of responsibility, or employers who are milking a "cash cow" acquisition are likely to view suggestions for providing more advance notice or more liberal severance provisions as simply irrelevant. For such employers the only pertinent question is what are the legal constraints. Without legal compulsion, it can be presumed, such employers will continue to make their decisions on financial/business criteria with humane and social considerations getting secondary or no attention.

Relatively few employers, no matter what their orientation, have demonstrated much interest in planning for layoff, much less a permanent plant closing. The literature on plant closings is characterized by numerous case studies, most, if not all, of which emphasize that employer and/or union assistance efforts were developed quickly, almost desperately, as a response to the impending economic disaster. Truly exceptional are firms like IBM which start from a diametrically opposite premise that regular employees will not be laid-off; that retraining, transfer, and other employer policies can and will ensure full employment security.

Problems in Plant Closings

What problems face an employer who must manage a plant closing? For purposes of understanding plant closing dynamics and potential problems, we will assume that a legally correct decision has been made to permanently close a plant for good and for sufficient reasons of those responsible and authorized to conduct such affairs. No matter how correct the decision there may well be legal complications of various sorts. Legal problems are not covered in this review. Suffice it to say that the decision makers should be alert to the possibility of legal actions by organized labor, by individuals in workmen's compensation cases and perhaps even by suppliers or community groups.

Having come to the conclusion to close, one of the first problems in managing is to clarify what precisely are the objectives to be achieved in the closing. What is the goal with regard to the remaining work force, the unions, the white-collar group, suppliers, future activities, public image or others? It would seem to many at first glance that a plant closing implies simply ceasing activity as quickly as possible, but even a moment's reflection should remind these persons that such a strategy might be counterproductive.

The critical question now facing the planners is how much advance notice of the closing should be given to whom and how? Should the decision be simultaneously broadcast to everyone, or is it necessary to inform union officials before anyone else? What, if anything, should be told to the media, when, and by whom? Similarly, should supervisors and other non-bargaining unit white-collar employees receive notice in advance of others in order to be able to plan and manage the process? The timing and procedure for giving advance notice depends, in turn, on several other strategic and philosophical cosiderations. Is it more humane and perhaps more effective to reduce the work force by a policy of attrition before giving advance notice? Voluntary separations are individual employment decisions that serve a person's self-interest, optimally with a minimum of pain and worry. And quite obviously, a smaller work force at the ultimate closing hour means lower costs for employers, maybe greater benefits for employees or both. With or without advance notice, the underlying problem is whether a maximum effort will be made to alleviate social/human consequences or whether the maximum effort will be made to respond only to the economic criteria. Perhaps this is a false dichotomy; perhaps both objectives might be achieved given sufficient planning time and skill.

On occasion, the notice of a forthcoming plant shutdown has triggered a response by employees to purchase the plant in order to operate under employee ownership. To date the number of such successful transfers of ownership is relatively small (for example, Mohawk Valley Community Corporation, Jamestown Metal Products), but this situation may change since federal legislation supporting such moves to employee ownership (with financial and technical assistance) has considerable support today. The employer who decides to sell to employees instead of closing would still face problems for terminating or transferring insurance and other benefit programs. Advance notice of plant closing might trigger another type of response, that is a union proposal to reduce benefits or even to take wage cuts in order to keep the enterprise from closing. A decision to accept such a proposal would seem to negate the major concerns of this chapter—at least for the short-term.

Another category of problems for management is employee reaction to the official or rumored notice of a shutdown. It can safely be predicted, as a result of recent researches of plant closings, that employers will face aberrant behavior. Some employees simply will not accept the fact. "This plant will never shut down." "Something will turn up or happen." If not disbelief, others will react with resentment, shock, and bewilderment. Plant closing announcements produce reactions that some researchers believe are similar to those observed at the time of death of a loved person. At a very minimum there is a very difficult communication problem for management. And it is very possible that these reactions could also lead to counter-productive employee behavior such as absenteeism, drinking problems, slowdown—all contributing to lowered productivity.

Very early in the plant closing decision-making process management faces the problem of interpreting its responsibilities under collective bargaining agreements. The starting point, of course, is the present agreement. What are the severance, transfer, and other pertinent provisions? What benefits are mandated for whom, when, and how? Is any aspect of the closing negotiable or will the process continue unilaterally? To what extent will the union(s) be involved in planning for and implementing a closing? What should be sought in a closing agreement? The posture taken by any employer with regard to these questions will vary, as has already been emphasized, depending on whether there are other plants that are not shutting down and where the employer must continue to bargain with the same union.

Whether or not there are unions, decisions may have to be made about other matters. What benefits are to be offered to those not in the bargaining unit? If transfers are possible who can transfer? What arrangements are appropriate for relocation? What searching and moving expenses will be made? Will there be flowback rights? And should changes be made in benefit policy? For example, employees who accept other employment may lose a severance benefit which has the effect of being a disincentive to job hunting and work force reduction. Should the policy be changed? Should it be liberalized even further by providing for time off with pay for job hunting? And who will counsel employees about other employment and related matters?

Employers also face the problem of deciding how to deal with the local community. Which community and public leaders should be notified and when? What types of cooperation are feasible and desirable? More specifically, for example, should public employment service officials be invited onto the premises to test and place employees? Should employees cooperate with community leaders in seeking assistance from The Economic Development Administration, Department of Labor, Small Business Administration, or any other government agency? Should other employers be contacted in an effort to find new jobs for those about to be terminated? Should training and retraining be provided?

As is evident these questions are reminders to managers that a plant closing is a problem of managing. The first step is to clarify the objectives to be attained and the second step is to make a thorough analysis of the age and potential benefits distribution of the affected work force. This information, in turn, is the basis for a realistic assessment of the direct costs of the closing. The more intangible costs need also to be factored. And as with any management problem, there is the question of who will have what responsibility during the activity. What will the role of the industrial relations staff and line management, and perhaps outsiders, be?

Historically, relatively few employers who closed plants tried to respond to these questions and problems. More often than not they exercised a traditional right to announce the closing with little or no notice and with similar concern for community plight or human hardship. For every employer, like the Armour Meatpacking Company that negotiated retraining, special relocation, and other policies to help displaced workers adjust, we read about horror stories where an employer gives *no* advance notice whatsoever other than to inform employees at the end of the day that the plant was closing. But this traditional right is being challenged. The lack of regard for human and local community consequences of plant closing has led many legislators to the conclusion that an orderly and smooth transition in these cases will not occur unless the process is detailed by law.

Some Lessons and Observations

Federal and state legislation is being proposed to deal with adjustment problems of individuals and communities. Two different strategies are visible in the proposals. One calls for prenotification, financial and job hunting assistance to affected employees, recognition of local community impact, and penalties for non-compliance. The other model focuses on the possibility of preventing unemployment and local community distress by helping employees and/or the local community to purchase and to operate the plant. Some of the proposals incorporate both prenotification et al. and assistance for employee/community purchase and operation of about to be closed plants. Advance notice of closing or mass layoff ranges from sixty days to two years in order that affected individuals and the local community have adequate time during which to adjust to the change. Additionally, severance and other benefits are provided to tide persons over the transition period. And the penalties for not providing for smooth transition are severe.

For facts and arguments to support such legislative proposals the proponents turn frequently to job security measures in western Europe, where for many years the impact of economic dislocation has been a matter for public policy, not just an impersonal market phenomenon. Although European employers *do* have wide discretion in plant closings, certain actions are required to prevent or to mitigate mass unemployment: (1) prenotifications, employers are required to explain to workers, to unions, to work councils, their future plans for reduction of force; depending on the numbers to be displaced the period of notice varies from two months upward, (2) job training and retraining, usually with income maintenance available during training, (3) job search and relocation assistance, usually through public employment services, (4) compensation to affected workers, usually based on the worker's age and length of employment coupled with liberalized early pension arrangements, and (5) use of national funds to assure adequate compensation. Relatively less emphasis is placed on health benefits, probably because national health programs are well-established in these countries.

Concluding Observations

This brief overview can be thus summarized:

1. Two major human impacts result from plant closings, the one being the psychological and economic difficulties faced by employees who are about to lose their job/income security and the other being the financial/tax problems of local communities.
2. The proposed remedies include prenotification at a minimum and the following features at the maximum:
   a. Advance notice—as long as two years.
   b. Severance and other payments for income and benefits protection of affected employees.
   c. Impact statements which require payroll information, amount of lost tax revenue, effect on other businesses and the community. And, as with environmental impact statements, one can foresee the time when such statements are debated ad infinitum.
   d. Assistance funds for local community adjustment paid for by employers along with grants/loans provided from general public revenues.

e. Establishment of new regulatory/advisory agencies such as a Division of Relocation with an Advisory Council for giving additional responsibilities to established agencies such as a Department of Labor.

f. Providing economic and technical assistance to keep a plant from closing.

g. Facilitating the transfer of ownership to an employee/community organization together with financial and technical assistance.

3. Collectively bargained arrangements for transfer, severance, and other adjustments to plant closing will continue to be made. Assistance provided in proposed plant closing legislation is sometimes a supplement to what is provided in the collective bargaining agreement.

4. Closing or mass layoffs in public agencies are specifically exempted from the closing legislation proposals of the various states. This is a curious omission at a time of local and state government retrenchment and reduction in force. Even with the protection of public sector unions and traditional civil service laws local and state governments can and do layoff with short or no notice and with relatively little regard for individual or community consequences.

5. Whatever the shape and character of future public policy on plant closings it is clear that unilateral action of owners to close will be challenged and such rights reduced in the near future.

6. Longer periods of prenotification are desirable on any and all grounds. Advance notice permits orderly planning and adjustment by individuals, employers, and the community. It relieves some of the tension and anxiety. It forces all parties to make useful complementary plans. It is more beneficial than costly. Similarly, it is clear that two years notice or even six months notice will be impossible to provide in many specific situations. If public regulators take a hard-nosed and dogmatic stance, prenotification will be another onerous provision of a law to be evaded, litigated, or circumscribed. Good faith cooperation in deciding how much notice is feasible is essential.

7. In the few instances when a local plant closing was made with a minimum of individual and social disruption there was a high degree of interaction and cooperation among management, organized labor, community agencies, education officials, and public agencies. Whether the required impact statements and other requirements of the proposed legislation, such as financial and legal penalties, will induce similarly effective cooperation in future closing situations is difficult to predict.

8. Runaway shops continue to be problems for organized labor. Nevertheless, organized labor recognizes that plant closings and relocations are inevitable. When dislocation occurs, they will continue to press for advance notice and adjustment assistance for affected workers.

9. The debate over plant closing legislation is not likely to dwell on individual worker impact. All parties can agree with little difficulty that loss of income means stress, illness, and real trauma. What is likely to be much more controversial are the macroeconomic and social policy questions. Thus, for example, the following issues will be raised: How useful is it to pass legislation at the state level in a situation where states are competing actively for employers to relocate? Shouldn't our public posture be one of supporting *sunrise* industries instead of bailing out *sunset* industries? Haven't we already reached a point of diminishing returns on our public attempts to regulate business? Is it really in the public interest to support unproductive enterprises? Won't business be less able to compete when it is forced to provide impact statement data?

   And the issue of employee ownership and even worker welfare will be translated by some into ideological name-calling rather than rational discourse. It is devoutly to be hoped that this dismal scenario does not come to pass.

10. Finally, and somewhat pessimistically, proactive planning by management has been and is the key to effective and equitable plant closing. But history shows that we give the most rudimentary attention to this until the next disaster strikes and then we scramble to muddle through.

12 Worker Ownership and Public Policy

Joseph R. Blasi and
William Foote Whyte

Introduction

This chapter examines the recent development of broad support for worker ownership in the United States, the problems in starting and maintaining a worker owned firm, the infrastructural and value requirements for worker ownership as a serious phenomenon.

Worker ownership is relevant in the United States because our political leaders, since Jefferson, have recognized that concentrated ownership is a threat to democracy.[1] Stock ownership in America is not broad: 1 percent of the population owns 56.5 percent of the corporate stock. The 200 largest corporations have increased their share of corporate assets and receipts from 47.7 percent in 1950 to 60.5 percent in 1974.[2,3] Nevertheless, this sector which controls so many resources only contributed less than 1 percent of the new jobs created since 1976 and has increasingly placed their investments overseas.[4,5,6] David Birch at MIT has shown that, contrary to popular belief, 66 percent of all new jobs are created by firms employing less than twenty workers, and the crisis in the continuity of small businesses puts further stress on creating jobs by threatening many of these firms.[7,8,9,10] The unions' general approach until now has been to recommend legislation to regulate economic dislocation.[11,12,13] Recently, however, White has shown that some businesses will close profitable operations, and, in these and other cases, the option of worker ownership can save the federal government sizable amounts in transfer payments or job-creation costs.[14,15,16]

Development of Broad Support and Legislation for Worker Ownership

Senator Thurmond: Do you feel legislation should be introduced on this subject and do you feel it would be helpful?

Congressman Kostmayer: Yes, I do.

Senator Thurmond: (referring to worker-owners) They would borrow the money from the federal government?

Congressman Kostmayer: That is right.

Senator Thurmond: What you favor then is to continue that private enterprise, let the government more or less be the banker to finance it?

Congressman Kostmayer: That is right, Senator.

Senator Thurmond: In other words the government wouldn't take it over.
The government would not operate it. It would not be the responsibility
of the government. It wouldn't be socialism. It would just be financing by
the government of a private enterprise in order to keep that enterprise
operating whereas otherwise it was going and the people would be without
jobs.

Congressman Kostmayer: That is right.[17]

Initiatives for legislation on worker ownership began in the spring of
1977. Congressman Peter Kostmayer initiated a series of inquiries to deal
with the growing unemployment caused by plant shutdowns. On March 1,
1978 Kostmayer, together with Representatives Stanley Lundine and Mat-
thew McHugh of New York, introduced the Voluntary Job Preservation
and Community Stabilization Act which was designed to provide loans to
workers to buy factories threatened with a shutdown. The bill provided for
evaluation of the economic feasibility of the firm's continued success and
technical assistance to help in the startup of the new company. It would
have been administered by the Economic Development Administration.[18]
This bill subsequently became part of Title II of HR 2063, the National
Public Works And Economic Development Act of 1979 which passed the
House on November 14 by a vote of 300 to 99 and the Senate on August 1
by a lesser margin. The bill was never to become law because of disagreements in the House/Senate conference committee which arose over the non-
worker ownership section, but Kostmayer demonstrated that sizable support could be garnered for the idea of worker ownership. On the evening of
the bill's passage he outlined its public policy significance:

> The threat of long-term inflation, deficit budgets, government inefficiency,
> burdensome taxation, and the inability of bureaucratic solutions to get at
> the root of certain problems requires that we also encourage efficient and
> sensible nongovernmental solutions. Our current dilemma demands that
> the government begin to utilize alternative solutions that hold out the possi-
> bility of replacing state sanctions in some areas of our social and economic
> programs. We must begin to phase in as much as is possible citizen, cooper-
> ative, and democratically run local solutions involving minimal government
> resources.[19]

His speech and the concluding report on the issue of the Senate[20] comprise
concise summaries of the lessons learned in over two years of hearings on
the areas of benefit and caution with worker ownership. In subsequent
months, the hearings and accompanying coverage in the media began a process of public education on the subject.

At the same time, Kostmayer together with Representative Nowak of New York and Senators Stewart and Long introduced the Small Business Employee Ownership Act which provided for loans up to one half a million dollars through the Small Business Administration (SBA) for employee ownership through buyouts of threatened shutdowns and employee ownership of new startups. This bill subsequently became Title V of the Small Business Development Act of 1980. As a separate bill it passed the Senate by unanimous consent on May 1, 1979. The new bill (S. 2698) passed in the spring of 1980 and was signed into law by the president on July 3, 1980.

It provided for an SBA budget of $1.2 billion in fiscal year 1981 and $1.4 billion in each fiscal year from 1982 to 1984. It authorized SBA to make and guarantee loans for worker owned firms as part of all of its existing programs. This took effect on October 1, 1980 and is guided by a series of definitions and criteria for worker ownership adopted by the Joint House/Senate Conference Report.[21] Because of the strong bipartisan support for SBA and the worker ownership legislation (which was originally co-sponsored in the early phases by Senators Goldwater, Hatch, and Hayakawa) and increasing sensitivity to the importance of small business, there has been no retreat from support of this program by the new administration, nor has SBA suffered any substantial budget cuts. The Congress was quite explicit in outlining its reasons for passing the worker ownership law:

> Sec. 501. This title may be cited as the "Small Business Employee Ownership Act of 1980".
> Sec. 502. The Congress hereby finds and declares that—
>   (1) employee ownership of firms provides a means for preserving jobs and business activity;
>   (2) employee ownership of firms provides a means for keeping a small business small when it might otherwise be sold to a conglomerate or other large enterprise;
>   (3) employee ownership of firms provides a means for creating a new small business from the sale of a subsidiary of a large enterprise;
>   (4) unemployment insurance programs, welfare payments, and job creation programs are less desirable and more costly for both the Government and program beneficiaries than loan guarantee programs to maintain employment in firms that would otherwise be closed, liquidated, or relocated; and
>   (5) by guaranteeing loans to qualified employee trusts and similar employee organizations, the Small Business Administration can provide feasible and desirable methods for the transfer of all or part of the ownership of a small business concern to its employees.

Three other developments in the area of worker ownership legislation should be noted. They are: (1) in union-sponsored economic dislocation legislation; (2) in the states; and (3) in new proposed federal bills.

Union-sponsored Economic Dislocation Legislation. With the mounting crisis of plant shutdowns and increasing use or consideration of the worker ownership option in union locals, the labor movement moved not to oppose inclusion of sections providing loans for worker ownership in the National Employment Priorities Act of 1979 (Senator Riegle and Congressman Ford) and the Employee Protection And Community Stabilization Act of 1979 (S. 1609). Both bills proposed that such loans be part of a series of programs on employee benefits and employer regulations proposed for the Department of Labor's comprehensive program to control plant shutdowns and their effects. Subsequently, increased union support for the worker ownership option has been evident: first, the AFL-CIO's questionnaire evaluating the voting records and stands of members of Congress specifically asked for their opinion on these provisions and rated their support positively.[22] Second, a study of the Worker Ownership Study Group at Harvard University's Project for Kibbutz Studies polled a sample of forty out of 130 national union leaders and found modest but qualified support for worker ownership and the provisions which are currently part of union-sponsored legislation .[22a]

Legislation in the States. Joint Resolution 1 of the 1979 Laws of the State of Maryland asked the Department of Economic and Community Development to study ways in which Maryland could promote employee ownership. The result, a document entitled "An Employee Stock Ownership Plan for Maryland"[23] is a fascinating proposal to encourage worker ownership through a variety of state institutions.

On July 2, 1979 the state of Michigan passed House Bill 4119 which the governor signed into law. It prescribes "the powers and duties of the department of labor and the department of commerce relative to the formation of employee-owned corporations."[24] It is particularly concerned with providing an alternative for the closing or transferring of operations. Employee ownership is part of a more comprehensive bill (House Bill 1251) which was introduced in the General Assembly of the state of Pennsylvania by eighty legislators.[25]

New Proposed Federal Bills. It is without doubt that the right/center/left coalition that consistently supported worker ownership legislation in hearings and in floor votes in the Congress would not support legislation for a comprehensive attack on economic dislocation. The coalition could not support: early warning of plant shutdowns, severance pay, extra health benefits for effected workers, broadened relocation benefits, administrative investigations of plant shutdowns, provision for civil suit against employers, and targeted job retraining, placement, and federal procurement (if a new company buys the firm). Indeed, the public policy success of worker

ownership legislation was that it was not oriented towards a blanket altera-
tion of the economic rules of the game. Rather, it simply introduced a new
position on the board and said that more jobs, more local initiative, less
government, less transfer payments, more small business, and more broadened ownership would result.

It is almost as if the current economic system is saying, "You can have
worker ownership. Now let us see if it works." Surely, the strong support
and sustained attention given to such legislation has come as a surprise to
many people. There was never a strong lobby for any form of worker ownership legislation. A variety of worker-owned firms, unions, and community groups expressed some interest, but as a close reading of the extensive
hearings on the subject indicates, it was the members from the House and
Senate themselves—people of all stripes—who were excited by the idea and
its evident success around the country. The idea combines the conservative
Republican value of small business, private rather than state or public ownership, voluntary citizen cooperation, less government, local control, and
broadened instead of concentrated, ownership with the Democrat's emphasis on economic democracy, community action, expanded role for unions in
American society, improvement in the conditions of workers, and an experimental approach to economic and social problems in the Roosevelt tradi-
tion. Many legislators could point to actual experiments in employee ownership in their districts and some were very much aware that, in the last
analysis, jobs mean votes. More important, however, is that the legislation
created no new bureaucracy and did not involve grants. It simply allowed
and encouraged SBA to provide loans and loan guarantees using its existing
infrastructure. In fact the Senate Small Business Committee made it clear
that they saw this modest loan authority not as an endless funnel:

> Given the success of employee ownership, it seems much the wiser for the
> government to make or guarantee loans, the large majority of which would
> almost certainly be repaid, than to spend money on various programs de-
> signed to ease the impact of unemployment. Of course, such loans would
> only be made to companies with reasonable prospects of success, and the
> government should not strive to make loans in every instance. Government
> encouragement of the concept and practice of employee ownership, how-
> ever, could convince at least some conventional credit sources to treat it as
> just another way of organizing a business.[26]

Problems in Starting and Maintaining the
Worker-Owned Firm

Whether a worker-owned firm is begun on the heels of a threatened shutdown of the old firm or as a completely new business venture there are

several important factors necessary for success. The workers must have access to the idea of worker ownership and have sufficient time to evaluate it, discuss it, learn about it, and judge if it applies to their situation. If a shutdown is involved they must have adequate early warning so that several months of planning, searching for loans and capital, and assessing feasibility can immediately ensue. (If a shutdown is not involved workers must be sure that they have adequate time and energy to see through a lengthy process of simply developing the plan and the resources for the new business.) There must be access to the information, experts, market studies, and potential management leaders to make a feasibility study. If workers are saving a firm, the cooperation of the existing owners and some existing management is crucial. (Getting this cooperation often requires substantial political pressure from local community leaders or members of Congress since many corporations prefer to simply close up and leave the community and the federal government with a big bill of transfer payments and community losses.) Sources of capital from private and public banking institutions, outside community shareholders, workers and managers must be identified and this package must satisfy the requirements of the feasibility study and an operational plan for the firm's future success. Financial and legal advisors (and often political advisors for dealing with institutions) must volunteer their assistance or be paid to conduct the appropriate studies and negotiations and draw up the legal form for a worker-owned corporation. Workers need to be clear about how much control they desire in the new firm in terms of voting rights, participation on the board of directors, involvment in worker participation, quality of working life improvements, finding a role for their union (if one exists) in the new firm, and choosing management. Examples of other worker-owned firms can be examined to identify advantages and disadvantages of various decisions that were made at this early stage and extract the critical lessons. There must be plans to train and educate workers and managers for new skills required in dealing with a worker-owned firm where new opportunities and expectations exist for greater worker participation, improvements in productivity and reduction in waste, involvement of workers in planning, occupational health and safety innovations, and experiments in improving the quality of working life. The group must evaluate whether these actions are likely to be crucial or significant in effecting the economic performance or the success of the new firm. Support of the local community in helping the firm with marketing, development, and capital needs is often necessary. If the firm is unionized, sizable problems of coordination and communication may have to be managed with the national union.

William Foote Whyte has taken the initiative in studying a number of cases of worker ownership to evaluate the salience of these different components of a worker ownership initiative.[27] The Cornell case studies stress the importance of developing explicit plans for worker participation as well as worker ownership. In case after case, workers developed the financial mechanisms to assume responsibility of or start a new company but overlooked the social mechanisms. Next to the availability of capital (once a positive study of feasibility is concluded) this is the biggest threat to the success of a worker-owned firm. Tove Hammer and Robert Stern have systemitized one analysis of the Cornell case studies in an excellent article.[28] Cornell has been heavily involved in applying this knowledge to the current situation at Rath Packing Company in Waterloo, Iowa where a worker ownership takeover became effective on July 7, 1980.[29]

The social mechanisms can be more specifically defined by considering what kind of input is expected on what issues by different levels of the organization. The input could be that of discussion, suggestion, access to information, decision, or confirmation. Possible issues include: work arrangements (shopfloor), technical and professional problems, production plans, choices of candidates for training, investment and development plans, choice of board of directors and management team. Levels of the organization include: board of directors, management team, plant committees, work groups, union representatives, worker/stockholder assembly. As one can readily see, the matrix of possibilities is quite extensive. Some worker owned firms assume that there can be extensive participation but it is ill-planned and little education is provided, while the effect on the economic performance of the firm may not be predictable. Other firms will completely ignore these decisions or possibilities and cause a great deal of conflict once workers realize that they own the firm but have very little say. The recent strike at South Bend Lathe, a 100-percent worker owned firm is a perfect example.[30]

There is no easy answer regarding worker participation and control for these firms. This problem is complicated by a number of considerations. First, few models of such participatory firms exist in the United States. There are approximately 100 worker owned firms in the country. This estimate is based on a telephone survey of all known worker-owned firms and a definition of worker-owned firm as at least 51 percent owned by workers.[31] Blasi and Whyte found little sign of worker participation in these firms. Scarcely more than half provide voting rights with worker's stock, and while many have a worker representative on the board, few if any examples of the possibilities of participation as here noted were identified. While there are thousands of employee stock ownership plans in companies[32] and a much larger number of worker-owned firms exist if one counts minority worker owned companies, Tannenbaum and Conte have found more of a change in attitude than participation in both kinds of firms. The thrust of their report to the Economic Development Administration is basically in agreement with the Cornell case studies and the survey conducted by Blasi and Whyte, with one exception. There may be reason to believe that economic performance was improved.[33]

Second, the United States is in an early stage of evolution as far as worker participation and quality of work life experiments are concerned. It may be true that many such experiments include just small segments and bit parts of the possible social mechanisms for participation and that few programs include a broad spectrum of participatory mechanisms. Also, such attempts seem to be concentrated in those businesses that are large and concentrated in ownership, a further evolution of the anomaly that worker owned firms seem to have little participation. Zwerdling[34] has indicated that change of management, selling of operations, and inability to show consistent effects on economic performance or interest unions are barriers to the development of such innovations in existing firms.

Third, it is clear that worker participation and the experimentation with a series of social participation mechanisms in the worker-owned firm depends on training and education. This cannot be accomplished by ownership or plan alone. It is not automatic and it does not lead to magical increases in productivity and profitability. Therefore, the dilemma of participation, and control, and quality of worklife improvements in the worker owned firm can only be addressed by a patient and realistic stance before, during, and after the firm is established. Probably the safest way to proceed is to emphasize: (1) providing clear and concrete examples of how various participatory mechanisms have worked in other firms; (2) choosing those mechanisms which can be most useful immediately in alleviating tensions and improving economic performance in *some* sectors of the new firm; (3) initiating a process of sharing of information throughout the firm and discussion of problems in plant committees to determine new areas for participation *and* improvement in the operation of the company; (4) develop a modest but regular education and skills training program to provide participatory skills and required content training to more workers and managers so that neither will impede new developments.

The advantages of the worker-owned firm for the worker are obvious; they need not oppose such innovations because they have a stake in improving the company. However, many workers and unions have been suspicious of any innovations where the workers get the satisfaction and participation and the company gets increased profits.

Another problem relates to the legal structures used and the role of the union. Some authors suggest that all worker-owned firms should be organized on the cooperative model, with one vote per worker. This model is seen as more democratic. The economist David Ellerman and the Industrial Cooperative Association of Somerville, Massachusetts have been the main developers of this model.[35] It is a response (in cases where employee ownership exists) to the incompetence of many lawyers, the underhandedness of organizers of employee ownership plans, the lack of clarity of workers and the lack of interest of many unions in protecting workers' rights.

The Employee Stock Ownership Plan (ESOP) was given special tax incentives under the Employee Retirement Income Security Act of 1974. Essentially, the act makes certain types of contributions to pension plans tax deductable. ESOPs are defined as benefit plans and therefore contributions to them are also tax deductible. This certainly accounts for their popularity as a form of worker ownership. Basically, an Employee Stock Ownership Trust buys stock in the company and/or receives contributions of company stock. This stock is distributed to workers according to certain defined schedules and voted by trustees. The company can deduct types of contributions to this trust from its income taxes and is thus provided with a way to simultaneously get cheaper capital and encourage worker ownership.

ESOPs, when used properly can be very beneficial for worker ownership and the fact that Senator Russel Long has worked so hard to establish their position in the law and the Internal Revenue Code (see Section 4975 (e)(7)), and continues to improve their legal definition, validates their usefulness. (Hearings on such plans and worker ownership in general around the country provide a number of case studies of the real-world interplay that ESOPs create.[36])

The ESOP law is very complicated and few lawyers have the social skills, the understanding of financing sources and the organizational problems of worker-owned firms to be able to organize or reorganize a company using an ESOP.[37] Since many employee ownership plans were organized to get cheap capital and not to create a worker owned firm, broadened ownership and financial incentive is usually the only result of such a plan in a firm where there is minority employee ownership. Many large corporations have such plans.

Nevertheless, problems have occurred when majority worker-owned firms are set up using an ESOP and the trust is designed in such a way as to minimize worker rights.[38] For example, mechanisms are available to achieve this purpose which

Minimize workers' involvement in developing and designing the plan in the initial stages by not encouraging examination of pluses and minuses of existing worker-owned firms or choosing the wrong lawyer;

Do not give workers voting rights with their shares of stock;

Do not allow the workers to choose the trustees of the ESOP or to be represented;

Do not allow worker representation on the board of directors;

Do not initiate design of a program of worker participation;

(In the case of large percentages of ownership that is not majority) prevent the initial or the ultimate achievement of 51 percent worker ownership.

The role of the union in the worker owned firm has always been unclear. Are unions suddenly unnecessary? Does employee ownership destroy unions? If worker rights are not safeguarded in the design and implementation of a worker ownership plan then the union (if one exists) has begun in an atmosphere of failure. Surely, union reticence to learn about worker ownership plans and find its place in protecting workers' interests is a major problem. Some unions have raised a specific criticism when, in the case of a plant shutdown, the workers are persuaded to forego their pension plan and rely on the ESOP as their benefits when the new firm is being organized. This was a major issue in the South Bend Lathe strike[30] and has been discussed extensively in hearings.[36] The new SBA worker ownership law speaks against the use of ESOPs in lieu of pension plans.[21]

A survey of worker owned firms showed that the union has an important place and that its role was either maintained or strengthened.[31] Unions are the only traditional structure of firm-wide worker participation. They are thus a useful infrastructure to establish the identity of the new firm. Collective bargaining definitely does become less important, for the managers and the union representatives must still find a forum to discuss firm/worker interests and this must be put in the context of developments in that industry and in the economy in general. Just because most worker owned firms are experimenting with social mechanisms of participation, a union is never negotiating with itself (a very naive stock phrase of union leaders). Instead it is dealing with managers. Unions represent not only firm-specific interests but the workers in a given industry in general. Shared occupational, health, safety, and other common issues, can be effectively addressed through multi-firm unions. Unions, then, provide their members with important services and represent a category of workers, nationwide, in a special way. David Ellerman has provided the historical perspective and the programmatic design for taking these realities into account.[39]

Infrastructure and Value Requirements for Worker Ownership

When one thinks of the future of worker ownership in the United States one may be predisposed to talk about what the government can do. Beyond educating more appropriate officials about worker ownership, making sure it is brought up in plans or legislation which deal with business loans or development, or ascertaining and legislating that in every federal agency that lends money to business it is a fairly represented alternative option, the federal government's role is not extensive. Worker ownership represents an alternative to big government which, at its extremes of bigness, becomes public or state ownership or even state capitalism (dictatorship not of the party but of giant corporations and conglomerates).

The following infrastructural elements are required if worker ownership is to expand:

Consulting groups that can help workers design, establish, and evolve participation (through education) in worker owned firms either out of threatened shutdowns or through new startups, (such as the Industrial Cooperatives Association);

Development of worker ownership programs in all unions, which identify opportunities, advise workers, and aid in finding financing even through union sources such as pension fund mechanisms;

Development of federations of worker-owned firms to identify common problems, work to free up credit sources, and even evolve their own banks for capital;

Economic planning units which can pinpoint the areas, types of industry and services, and training necessary to begin new worker-owned startups;

Management schools which can train managers for worker-owned firms where participation is being developed and train workers to be managers;

Law programs which can train lawyers in orchestrating the successful development of such firms;

Educational programs for children and adolescents which teach this option, provide training in democratic skills, and discussions on organizing work;

Programs in business schools and universities to train economic planners to be sensitive to the development of a worker ownership policy and to promote research on existing firms;

Citizens groups to promote the development of such firms;

Models of successful worker owned firms that can be examined, imitated, and researched;

Media attention and education.

Since the passage of the SBA employee ownership legislation, few groups of workers have applied for loans or loan guarantees. Certainly, the lack of most, if not all, of these infrastructural elements is the prime explanation. The Small Business Administration is the most decentralized federal agency. It surely has not done enough or been prodded enough by Congress, by citizens, by the concerned executive branch to encourage worker ownership. The Farmers Home Administration makes the most sizable loans to businesses in rural areas and farm-related businesses, and represents a fertile area for development. However, it does not make sense to expand legislation or emphasis on worker ownership at the federal level unless new worker-owned firms are set up and existing ones are successfully maintained. An important infrastructural requirement is that university, consulting groups, unions, and other appropriate bodies adopt worker owned firms and work with them to realize the potential of the new ownership.

Worker ownership may have important value requirements. The success of the 250 kibbutz communities in Israel that have the largest concentration of worker-owned factories and agricultural branches in the world is dependent on complex values. The founders and developers of these settings were trying to develop a new form of life, were trying to realize values of fellowship, democracy, and economic cooperation and equality, and were trying to construct the basis for a new nation. We can share Israel's ethical imperative, the need to contribute to nation-building and social development, a commitment explicitly to democratic values that can be applied to daily life, and perhaps even a sense of the immediacy, urgency, and emergency nature of reworking a system. Perhaps this can give vital force to our work.[40] In Israel, this task was assumed by associations, federations, groups, parties, and youth groups. In the United States, worker ownership is already a public policy but with a very weak citizens' base. The Congress has discussed, researched, debated, formulated, evaluated, and legislated extensively but infrastructural associations (such as unions and local Chambers of Commerce) have scarcely seen fit to examine the potential for economic development.

Recently, the National Center For Employee Ownership was established by Dr. Corey Rosen to begin to build this infrastructure. The Employee Stock Ownership Council of America is an association of ESOPs which provides education and public information, but the council is so general an umbrella that it has not been able to take stands on the problematic issues of employee ownership. Rosen's organization promises to include representatives of labor, academia, and business. And to educate the public about employee ownership which develops the benefits of wider participation in shaping the workplace, increased job satisfaction, and improvement in the quality of working life. The question still remains as to whether the social consciousness can be developed in individual firms and in workers so that they will identify with the values implicit in employee ownership for democratizing life and realizing individual potential. If worker ownership is simply *people's capitalism* then it will simply be a structure that broadens ownership and does not realize other social goals. Will worker ownership be a tool for making money and (or) saving jobs among other tools or can it also be a way to improve the quality of life?

Notes

1. Ronald Reagan, "Expanding Ownership." (Washington, D.C.: Reagan-Bush Committee, 1980.) Op-Ed Piece prepared for *Times Picayune.*
2. Mark Nadel, *Corporations and Public Accountability* (Lexington, Mass.: D.C. Heath and Company, 1976).
3. Joint Economic Committee, Congress of the United States, *Broadening the Ownership of New Capital: Esops and Other Alternatives* (Washington, D.C.: Government Printing Office, 1976).
4. Barry Bluestone and Bennett Harrison, *Capital Mobility and Economic Dislocation* (Washington, D.C.: The Progressive Alliance, 1979).
5. Joint Economic Committee, *Broadening Ownership,* pp. 13–14.
6. John Breckenridge, "Employment of the Fortune 1000 and Total U.S. Civilian Labor Force." Congressional Record, March 8, 1978.
7. David Birch, *The Job Generation Process* (Cambridge, Mass.: MIT, 1979).
8. Steve Smith, Testimony on the National Public Works and Economic Development Act of 1979 (Washington, D.C.: Council of State Planning Agencies, 1979).
9. Senate Small Business Committee, Congress of the United States S. 388, *The Small Business Employee Ownership Act Hearings,* February 27, 1979 (Washington, D.C.: Government Printing Office, 1979), p. 12, 16, 65.
10. House Small Business Committee Subcommittee on Equity Capital, H.R. 3056, *Small Business Employee Ownership Act Hearings,* May 8, 15, 1979. (Washington, D.C.: Government Printing Office, 1979), pp. 51, 164, 194, 234.
11. Bill Schweke, *Plant Closings Strategy Packet* (Washington, D.C.: Conference on Alternative State and Local Policies, 1980).
12. Carlisle and Redmond Associates, *Plant Closing Legislation and Regulation in the U.S. and Western Europe: A Survey* (Washington, D.C.: Federal Trade Commission, 1979).
13. Joint Report of Labor Union Study Tour Participants, *Economic Dislocation: Plant Closings, Plant Relocations and Plant Conversions* (Washington, D.C.: AFL-CIO, 1978).
14. Senate Small Business Committee, *The Role of the Federal*

Government and Employee Ownership of Business (Washington, D.C.: Government Printing Office, 96th Congress, 1st Session, 1979).

15. William Foote Whyte, *Confronting the Conglomerate Merger Menace* (Washington, D.C.: Small Business Subcommittee on Antitrust, and Restraint of Trade Hearings on Conglomerate Mergers, 1979).

16. Small Business Subcommittee on Antitrust and Restraint of Trade, *Conglomerate Mergers—Their Effects on Small Business and Local Communites* (Washington, D.C.: Government Printing Office, 1980).

17. Judiciary Subcommittee on Antitrust, Monopoly and Business Rights, U.S. Senate, *Hearing on Failing Company Defense.* (Washington, D.C.: Government Printing Office, 1980), p. 10.

18. EDA is now phasing out of existence and facing an interim administration freeze on its loans.

19. Peter H. Kostmayer, Congressional Record, November 14, 1979, p. H 10698.

20. U.S. Senate, Joint Report of the Committee on Environment and Public Works and the Committee on Banking, Housing and Urban Affairs, "National Public Works and Economic Development Administration Development Act of 1979," Report No. 90-270 (Washington, D.C.: Government Printing Office, 1979), pp. 22, 32.

21. U.S. Senate Small Business Committee "Small Business Development Act of 1980," Report No. 96-1087. (Washington, D.C.: Government Printing Office, 1980).

22. This questionnaire was used during the year 1979 and is available from the AFL-CIO.

23. Granados, Luis, *A Report to the Legislature: An Employee Stock Ownership Plan for Maryland.* (Baltimore: Department of Economic and Community Development, 1979).

24. Michigan Department of Labor, *Management Package for P.A. 44: The Employee-Owned Corporation Act* (Detroit: Job Development Division, Bureau of Employment and Training, Michigan Dept. of Labor, 1979).

25. General Assembly of Pennsylvania, House Bill No. 1251. Session of 1979.

26. See note 14, p. v.

27. William Foote Whyte, *In Support of the Voluntary Job Preservation and Community Stabilization Act.* (Ithaca, N.Y.: Cornell University, 1978). See Whyte's testimony in the several sets of federal hearings cited in this bibliography.

28. Robert Stern and Tove Hammer, "Buying Your Job: Factors Affecting the Success or Failure of Employee Acquisition Attempts," in *Human Relations* (forthcoming). Cited originally in note 9, pp. 225-257.

29. Rath Packing Company, *The Rath Packing Company Employee Stock Ownership Plan* (Waterloo, Iowa: Rath Packing Co., December 10, 1980.)

30. "Worker Owners on Strike," *The New York Times,* September 8, 1980, p. D16.

31. Joseph R. Blasi, Perry Mehrling, and William Foote Whyte, "Worker Ownership in the U.S.," Unpublished manuscript. (Cambridge, Mass.: Project for Kibbutz Studies–Harvard University, 1980. The survey was executed by Robin Jenkins. This article appears in a much shortened version in *Working Papers* in a forthcoming article in 1981.

32. Corey Rosen, "More Than Four Thousand Companies Now Have Employee Ownership Plans, " in *EPIC* 3, no. 4, p. 3.

33. Arnold Tannenbaum and Michael Conte, " Employee Ownership: Report to the Economic Development Administration," U.S. Dept. of Commerce Project Number 99-6-09433 (Ann Arbor, Michigan: Survey Research Center, University of Michigan, June 1976). The data for this assertion must be studied very carefully since adequate controls were not applied to understand whether employee ownership was the main contributing factor, and if so, what aspects of employee ownership. Generally speaking, ESOP advocates of employee ownership make outrageous and often unsubstantiated claims for improved productivity without stating clearly what conditions and components in a firm contribute to this fact. Congressional proponents of worker ownership laws, such as Congressman Peter Kostmayer have been much more careful. Kostmayer's speech on worker ownership (19) is an example of a reasoned scientifically accurate summary of the state of knowledge on the subject.

34. Daniel Zwerdling, *Workplace Democracy* (New York: Harper Colophon, 1980).

35. David Ellerman, "Worker Cooperatives: The Question of Legal Structure," unpublished manuscript. (Cambridge, Mass.: Industrial Cooperative Association, 1980). A number of publications on this topic are available from ICA.

36. House Banking, Finance, and Urban Affairs Subcommittee on Economic Stabilization, *Hearings on Employee Stock Ownership Plans,* February 27, 1979, and November 20, 1978 (Washington, D.C.: Government Printing Office, 1979).

37. Senate Finance Committee, U.S. Senate, *Employee Stock Ownership Plans: An Employer Handbook.* (Washington, D.C.: Government Printing Office, 1980).

38. General Accounting Office, *A Report on Employee Stock Ownership Plans: Who Benefits?* (Washington, D.C.: General Accounting Office, 1980).

39. David Ellerman, *The Union as the Legitimate Opposition in an Industrial Democracy.* (Cambridge, Mass.: Industrial Cooperative Association, 1979).

40. See several books on the kibbutz. Joseph Blasi, *The Communal Future: The Kibbutz and the Utopian Dilemma* (Philadelphia: Norwood Editions, 1979); and Uri Leviatan and Menachem Rosner, *Work and Organization in Kibbutz Industry* (Philadelphia: Norwood Editions, 1980). Leviatan and Rosner suggest the typology of social mechanisms used in this article.

**Part V
Economic Change and
Social Policies**

13 The Behavioral Costs of Economic Instability

Ralph Catalano and
David Dooley

Introduction

Western economic thought has assumed for two centuries that mobile capital and labor are prerequisites to productive efficiency. A less well-known literature has noted that there are social costs of such mobility and that these costs should be considered when judgments are made concerning the efficiency of spatial shifts in infrastructure. Behavioral problems were among the earliest cited social costs of economic change. Steuart, for example, noted in 1767 that emotional trauma was a cost of mobile labor.[1] Durkheim, in 1897, cited economic instability as a source of anomie.[2] In 1894 Adna Weber empirically described the behavioral outcomes of spatial shifts in the system of collection, production, and distribution.[3] In the 1920s, the sociologists of the Chicago School integrated economic, biological, and social theory into a *human ecology* that hypothesized that economic perturbations would increase the incidence of behavioral disorder.[4] Haig provided the economic rationale for internalizing social costs through land use regulation as early as 1925.[5] The theoretical and empirical arguments for accounting the behavioral externalities of mobile capital are, in short, as longstanding as the western concern for economic efficiency.

Despite the longstanding arguments for social cost accounting, rigorous investigation of the behavioral costs of economic change has not been common. This chapter reviews the literature which discusses the connection between economic change and disorder and summarizes the implications for prevention and treatment.

Economic Change as a Cause of Behavioral Disorder

While media-reported links between unemployment and behavioral disorder seem to be recent phenomena, their antecedents date to the case stud-

Preparation of this chapter was supported by National Institute of Mental Health Grant 1EO1MH31494-01.

195

ies from the great depression.[6] Such case studies and reportage reinforce the intuition that economic downturns are stressful. The results of this type of inquiry are, however, not scientifically sound enough to inform debate over policy formation. Unfortunately, the more scientific research remains, as described below, less than definitive.

The most comprehensive review of the quasi-experimental research divides the literature into two types: (1) time-series measurements of the relationship between economic climate and community indices of pathology and (2) studies of individual economic life change and subsequent symptom change.[7] These two types of research partially agree with the anecdotal evidence and with the intuition that pathology rises with unemployment. There are, however, complications and qualifications.

Time Series Analyses. The most common finding in aggregate time-series studies is a large positive association between undesirable economic change (for example, unemployment rate) and subsequent changes in the suicide rate or in the use of mental health facilities. Such results have been produced both by earlier primitive methods and by more recent analytic techniques designed to protect against confounds due to trend, cycle, or other patterns in the data.[8]

The magnitude of the aggregate associations are reported in various ways in this literature making it difficult to summarize the average share of variance in pathology explained by the economy. The association is, for example, often reported as multiple correlation (R) which includes the contributions of several different lags of the same economic variables.[9] If the data have been detrended or deseasonalized, the reported association is for a residual series, the variance of which may be small compared to that of the original series.[10] When the analytic approach is very conservative, the association is apparently reduced in magnitude. For example, Steinberg, Catalano, and Dooley found that child abuse increased following a decrease in workforce size.[11] After controlling for possible regional patterns in child abuse by using a neighboring county's abuse rate as a predictor, the amount of additional variance explained by the economic variable, while significant, was small.

There have been exceptions to the usual pattern of positive association between undesirable economic change and disorder. An attempt to replicate several significant associations of economic variables with surveyed life events and depression was unsuccessful.[12] A number of potentially explanatory differences were found between the metropolitan sample used in the original studies and the nonmetropolitan sample used in the replication.

Another complication for the aggregate literature is the recurring finding that desirable economic change is linked to mental hospitalizations for, at least, some subgroups.[13] Such subgroup differences in the direction of the association are difficult to explain in terms of the intuitive economic stress model.

Still another problem for aggregate time series studies is identifying the causal mechanism which connects economic change and behavioral disorder. A study designed to test whether economic change was linked to mental hospitalization via elevated psychological symptoms or through changes in tolerance for existing symptoms yielded results more consistent with uncovering (existing pathology becoming cases) than with provocation (new pathology being provoked).[14]

Individual Level. In contrast to the aggregate time-series studies, adequately designed, prospective individual studies are few in number and generally reveal weaker positive associations between unemployment and disorder. While there are substantive reasons for this difference, it may, in part, be attributable to differences in levels of measurement. As the reliability of measurement of correlated variables increases, the magnitude of the correlation increases. It is possible that the aggregate measures are more reliable than their individual counterparts to the extent that random individual differences and measurement error have been cancelled in the aggregation.

The relevance of some of the individual studies is reduced by the use of a mild symptom measure such as dissatisfaction with self or sense of powerlessness.[15] Because of the low frequency of suicide and mental hospitalizations, used as dependent variables in most aggregate-level studies, individual-level studies can employ such variables only if very large sample sizes are employed.[16] For example, a panel study of 100 unemployed men did not yield one case of suicide or mental hospitalization.[17] As a result, some researchers have concluded that stress of unemployment may be less than the occupational stress of the work place.[18] It is, of course, possible that changes in the economy of a community influence symptoms by altering levels of occupational stress rather than through job loss or change.

For ethical and practical reasons, most studies of individual responses to economic change are quasi-experimental. The one exception is the evaluation of responses by individuals randomly assigned to income maintenance or control conditions.[19] Surprisingly, guaranteed income appeared associated not with a decrease in symptoms but rather, in some groups, with an increase. This result from an individual-level study echoes the noted aggregate-level finding that desirable economic change is, for some subgroups, positively correlated with disorder over time.

The major obstacle to the interpretative bridging of the aggregate and individual levels of research is the failure to include both aggregate and individual measures of economic change in the same study. Evidence from two such studies indicates that aggregate economic conditions may interact with individually experienced life events to produce symptoms.[20] These studies indicate that individuals cope less successfully with undesirable life experiences when the economy is expanding than when contracting.

Remaining Questions. Evidence for a positive association of undesirable economic change and behavioral disorder is found in both the aggregate and individual levels of research. However, there are studies in both illustrating that this intuitively expected relationship is by no means universal, that its sign may be reversed for some subgroups, and that the causal mechanism of the observed phenomenon is complicated. The research has, in short, raised more questions than it has answered. Studies differ widely, for example, in their temporal unit of analysis. The research has found lags ranging from several months to several years between the economic event and the observed behavioral indicator.[21] In the aggregate studies, the observed lag may be thought of as an average of the various lags exhibited by the individuals experiencing pathology. At the individual level, the lag may depend on numerous variables including individual vulnerability, psychological, social and material resources, and the point in the symptom process at which the disorder is measured (early untreated symptoms or later case identification and admission for treatment). The lag presumably depends also on the mechanism—whether uncovering existing symptoms by converting untreated disorder to treated disorder or provoking new symptoms in previously asymptomatic persons. These mechanisms are not mutually exclusive. Conceivably, undesirable economic change provokes statistically significant but nonpathological changes in the symptom levels of the normal respondents in individual level studies. In the aggregate studies, the observed increases in catastrophic indicators (suicides and hospitalizations) may be due to changes in individuals with symptoms antedating the more recent economic triggering events.

The inconsistencies in sign and lag within the individual and aggregate levels of analysis point to a theory of multiple causal paths between aggregate economic change and psychopathology.[22] The fact that aggregate-level research typically finds larger coefficients of association than the individual-level studies also raises the possibility that different phenomena are being studied in the two approaches. Unemployment in the community (the group effect of unemployment) may include not only individually experienced job loss (individual effect of unemployment) but also the effect of the demoralization of individuals not directly affected. They may fear for their own jobs or worry about friends and family who are losing theirs. Moreover, changes in unemployment may index changes in the level of support from the social environment. In this perspective the aggregate measure of unemployment is a compound variable which carries information beyond that inherent in its individual counterpart.[23] To draw individual level conclusions from aggregate findings would be logical error (ecological fallacy) but to dismiss aggregate-level findings which disagree with individual-level results would be to ignore potentially important evidence.

Implications

Prevention. The suspected link of economic instability to both the incidence of disorder and to the use of facilities has implications for preventive programs.[24] Prevention strategies can be separated into those which preclude the onset of symptoms by either removing the precipitating agent or by inoculating individuals against the agent. The first has been referred to as *proactive prevention* and the latter as *reactive prevention*.

The most intuitive proactive strategy to prevent behavioral disorder induced by the economy is to reduce the number of economic adaptations a population must make. Shaping the economy of communities has been a goal of public planning for several decades, and regulatory as well as decision tools have been devised to further the effort. This manipulation of the local economy could theoretically be pursued in such a way as to reduce economic stress but this would entail major changes in local and national policy.

The most obvious policy change would require that behavioral disorder be accounted in the implicit or explicit cost/benefit analyses which guide choice among alternative courses of action. To ensure that such accounting was at least perfunctorily performed and considered, the environmental impact assessment currently required for many federal, state, and local projects could be expanded to include behavioral costs. The case for behavioral cost accounting as a prerequisite to decision making has been argued on several occasions and has influenced the debate on at least one important piece of federal legislation.[25]

While the behavioral cost accounting concept is consistent with the regulatory and management movements of the past two decades, there are several considerable obstacles to its effective implementation. The first is that the empirical research has not progressed to the point that predictions of behavioral outcomes from policy alternatives can be confidently made.

The second is that economic policy rarely has a uniform effect across geographic areas.[26] These geographic differences create practical as well as political barriers to meaningful social cost accounting. Disaggregation of economic and behavioral data across areas may not be possible. The emergence of special interests defined by geography or industry may further reduce the likelihood of definitive political action.

A third impediment to using regulatory policy as a proactive intervention strategy is that the political tide is going against economic regulation.

There appears to be a growing conviction that productivity has been reduced through attempts to reduce such external costs as environmental
degradation and occupational illness. The suggestion that the private sector
should be further regulated to internalize the behavioral costs of economic
dynamism is not likely to find much favor.

Reactive prevention, or the attempt to increase individual adaptability
to unavoidable shocks, is more congruent with the current political climate
than are proactive strategies. A reactive program would be based on the
growing literature which assumes that theory-based training and counseling
can increase an individual's ability to deal with stressful life situations.[27] A
three-component *stress inoculation* program for job loss has been suggested
by Catalano and Dooley.[28] The first component is educating the target
group about the changes which job loss is likely to cause in personal and
family behavior and emotions. Understanding the general nature of such
changes is thought to increase individual ability to deal with them.[29] The
education component would also provide factual data on employment
opportunities and other services (for example, skill upgrading) available to
the unemployed.

The second component of the reactive program would be to train the
individual to utilize *cognitive restructuring* techniques. These methods are
intended to reduce the loss of self-esteem by deemphasizing the role of individual factors in job loss. Understanding that termination is as much, if not
more, a function of macroeconomic events than of individual ability can
lessen irrationally punitive self-judgments.

The third component is training an individual to recognize early signs
of disorder and to employ appropriate antidotal behaviors. While these
antidotes would include physical relaxation and coping techniques, more
long-term strategies would also be prescribed. Among the most promising
of these is learning to build and effectively use a social support network.[30]
This requires developing interpersonal skills which may also improve employment prospects.

The likelihood of success of reactive prevention programs would be
enhanced if target populations could be identified early. Econometric
models used to forecast the economic sequelae of policy and investment
decisions could be utilized to identify communities or industries likely to experience job loss.[31] Public health agencies could be used to deliver reactive
programs in geographically defined target populations and unions could be
used in industry specific populations.

The major shortcoming of reactive prevention is that it involves identifying a target population that can be organized into a treatment group.
While high probability of future job loss provides a relatively well-defined
and perhaps cooperative population, job loss is probably not the only inter-
vening variable between economic change and behavioral disorder. The

economy may lead to assessment of disorder by affecting tolerance, availability of social support, community mood, and other components of the social ecology.[32] This pervasive influence makes it very difficult to identify the population at risk.

Remedial Services. The suspected connection between economic climate and behavioral disorder has important practical implications for the provision of remedial services. The economic modeling techniques alluded to may allow the identification of communities and industries which will undergo economic dislocation.[33] If current research measuring the association between different dimensions of economic change and the demand for mental health services progresses, it may be possible to extend these modeling techniques to predict which providers of mental health services are likely to be affected. Such predictions could enhance the efficiency of mental health programs by permitting scarce resources to be moved to high risk areas.

Internalizing the Behavioral Costs. As noted, it is not likely that regulatory power will be used to preclude economic dislocation that causes behavioral outcomes. The reason cited is that such regulation supposedly leads to lower productivity and efficiency by impeding the flow of capital and labor to locations where production costs are lowest. The response to such arguments has traditionally been that true efficiency can be achieved only when external as well as market costs are minimized. It is further asserted that the public sector exists to account social costs and to distribute them equitably or to assign them to those whose behavior caused them.[34] If that argument is accepted, the issue becomes who should pay for the services required by those whose problems were precipitated by economic dislocation? If society, through its political institutions, were to decide that treating behavioral disorder is an unavoidable cost of desirable spatial redistribution of productive facilities, then everyone should pay through federal income tax. If, on the other hand, it is decided that those who benefit should pay, then special taxes should be levied on firms that shift location or on locations that are rapid growth areas. The receipts could then be returned to those areas whose declining economies have elevated the demand for service.

The targeting of taxes to the firms or regions assumed to benefit from shifts in labor and capital can act indirectly as a proactive remedial strategy. The cost of the taxes will be passed on to consumers of the products. The smaller the gap between the price of goods produced in declining and in expanding regions, the smaller is the incentive to move. The less movement, the fewer the adaptation demands that are experienced and the lower the demand for service. Proactive prevention is thereby achieved by true-pricing rather than by direct prohibition of spatial shifts.

If the decision were to be made either to nationally distribute the cost of mental health service or to the target firms or regions for special taxes, the situation would be more economically rational than it is now. State and local jurisdictions currently assume most of the cost of mental health services. Given that few, if any, states are likely to experience a zero sum between economically growing and contracting communities, declining areas and their corporate and individual taxpayers bear the cost of treating behavioral disorder. And those who generated the costs move elsewhere to realize the benefit. This situation continues despite the ironic fact that both psychology and economics assume that individuals should bear the costs of their behavior.

Notes

1. J. Steuart, *An Inquiring into the Principles of Political Economy* (London: Millar & Cadell, 1767).

2. E. Durkheim, *Suicide: A Study in Sociology,* G. Simpson, ed., J.A. Spaulding and G. Simpson, trans. (New York: Free Press, 1951, originally published in 1897).

3. A. Weber, *The Growth of the City in the 19th Century* (Ithaca, N.Y.: Cornell Press, 1899).

4. A. Park and E. Burgess, *The City* (Chicago: University of Chicago Press, 1975).

5. R. Haig, *Major Economic Factors in Metropolitan Growth and Arrangement: A Study of Trends and Tendencies in the Economic Activitites within the Region of New York and Its Environs* (New York: New York Regional Plan Association, 1925; reprinted Arno Press, 1974).

6. E. Bakke, *Citizens without Work: A Study of the Effects of Unemployment Upon the Workers Social Relations and Practices* (New Haven, Conn.: Yale Univerisity Press, 1940); R. Cavan and K. Ranck, *The Family and Depression: A Study of One Hundred Chicago Families* (Chicago: University of Chicago Press, 1938); M. Jahoda; P.F. Lazarsfeld; and H. Zeisel, *Marienthal: The Sociography of an Unemployed Community* (Chicago: Aldine-Atherton, 1971); M. Komarovsky, *The Unemployed Man and His Family: The Effect of Unemployment upon the Status of the Man in 59 Families* (New York: Dryden Press, 1940).

7. D. Dooley, and R. Catalano, "Economic Change as a Cause of Behavioral Disorder," *Psychological Bulletin* 87 (1980):450–468.

8. E. Durkheim, *Suicide;* W. Ogburn, and D. Thomas, "The Influence of the Business Cycle on Certain Social Conditions," *Journal of the American Statistical Association* 18 (1922):324–340; M. Brenner, *Mental Illness and the Economy* (Cambridge, Mass.: Harvard University Press,

1973); R. Catalano, and D. Dooley, "Economic Predictors of Depressed Mood and Stressful Life Events in a Metropolitan Community," *Journal of Health and Social Behavior* 18 (1977):292–307; A.S. Hammermesh, and N. Soss, "An Economic Theory of Suicide," *Journal of Political Economy* 82 (1974):83–98; J. Marshal, and D. Funch, "Mental Illness and the Economy: A Critique and Partial Replication," *Journal of Health and Social Behavior* 20 (1979):282–289; E. Sclar, and U. Hoffman, *Planning Mental Health Service for a Declining Economy,* final report to the National Center for Health Services Research, Waltham, Mass.: Brandeis University, January 1978; G. Vigderhous, and G. Fishman, "The Impact of Unemployment and Social Integration on Suicide Rates in the U.S.A., 1920–1969," *Social Psychiatry* 13 (1978):239–248.

9. R. Catalano, and D. Dooley, "Economic Predictors."

10. R. Catalano, and D. Dooley, "Does Economic Change Provoke or Uncover Behavioral Disorder: A Preliminary Test," in L. Ferman and J. Gordus, eds., *Mental Health and the Economy* (Kalamazoo, Mich.: Upjohn Foundation, 1979).

11. L. Steinberg; R. Catalano; and D. Dooley. "Economic Antecedents of Child Abuse and Neglect," manuscript submitted for publication, 1980.

12. D. Dooley, and R. Catalano, "Economic, Life, and Disorder Changes: Time-series analyses," *American Journal of Community Psychology* 7 (1979):381–396; D. Dooley; R. Catalano; R. Jackson; and A. Brownell, "Economic, Life and Disorder Changes: A Failure to Replicate in a Non-metropolitan Community," manuscript submitted for publication, 1980; Catalano and Dooley, "Economic Predictors;" Catalano and Dooley, "Does Economic Change Provoke."

13. M. Brenner, *Estimating the Social Costs of Economic Policy: Implications for Mental and Physical Health and Criminal Aggression,* paper no. 5, report to the Congressional Research Service of the Library of Congress and Joint Economic Committee of Congress (Washington, D.C.: U.S. Government Printing Office, 1976); Brenner, *Mental Illness;* Marshall and Funch, "Mental Illness;" Sclar and Hoffman, *Planning Mental Health Service;* Catalano and Dooley, "Does Economic Change Provoke."

14. Catalano and Dooley, "Does Economic Change Provoke."

15. R. Cohn, "The Effect of Employment Status Change on Self Attitudes," *Social Psychology* 38 (1978):300–314; H. Parnes and R. King, "Middle-aged Job Losers," *Industrial Gerontology* 4 (1977):77–95.

16. T. Theorell; E. Lind, and B. Floderus, "The Relationship of Disturbing Life-Changes and Emotions to the Early Development of Myocardial Infarctions and Other Serious Illnesses," *International Journal of Epidemiology,* 4 (1975):291–2931.

17. S. Cobb, and S. Kasl, *Termination: The Consequence of Job Loss*

(Cincinnati, Ohio: National Institute of Occupational Safety and Health, 1977).

18. S. Kasl, and S. Cobb. "The Experience of Losing a Job: Some Effects on Cardiovascular Functioning. *Psychotherapy and Psychosomatics* (In press).

19. P. Thoits, and M. Hannan, "Income and Psychological Distress: The Impact of an Income Maintenance Experiment," *Journal of Health and Social Behavior* 20 (1979):120–138.

20. D. Dooley; R. Catalano; and A. Brownell, "The Relation of Economic Conditions and Individual Life Change to Depression," manuscript submitted for publication, 1980; Cohn, "The Effect of Employment Status Change."

21. Catalano and Dooley, "Does Economic Change Provoke;" M. Brenner, *Estimating the Social Costs.*

22. Dooley and Catalano, "Economic Change."

23. G. Firebaugh, "A Rule for Infering Individual-Level Relationships from Aggregate Data," *American Sociological Review* 43 (1978):557–572.

24. R. Catalano and D. Dooley, "Economic Change in Primary Prevention," in R. Price, et al., eds. *Prevention in Mental Health* (Beverly Hills: Sage, 1980).

25. R. Catalano; S. Simmons; and D. Stokols. "Adding Social Science Knowledge to Environmental Decision-Making," *American Association for Natural Resources Lawyer* 8 (1975):24–41; R. Catalano, and J. Monahan, "The Community Psychologist as Social Planner: Designing Optimal Environments," *American Journal of Community Psychology* 3 (1975): 324–327; M. Brenner, "Personal Stability and Economic Security, *Social Policy* 8 (1977):2–5.

26. G. Sternlieb, and J. Hughes, "New Regional and Metropolitan Realities of America," *Journal of the American Institute of Planners* 43 (1977):226–241; G. Sternlieb, and J. Hughes "The Changing Demography of the Central City," *Scientific American* 243 (1980):48–54.

27. M. Jarenko, "A Component Analyses of Stress Inoculation: Review and Prospectus," *Cognitive Therapy and Research* 3 (1973):35–48; R. Novaco, "The Cognitive Regulation of Anger and Stress," in P. Kendall and S. Hallan, eds. *Cognitive-Behavioral Interventions: Theory, Research, and Procedures* (New York: Academic Press, 1979).

28. Dooley and Catalano, "Economic Change."

29. D. Glass, and J. Singer, *Urban Stress* (New York: Academic Press, 1972); R. Schultz, "Effects of Control and Predictability on the Physical and Psychological Well-Being of the Institutional Aged," *Journal of Personality and Social Psychology* 33 (1976):563–573; D. Sherrod, "Crowding, Perceived Control, and Behavioral Aftereffects," *Journal of Applied Social Psychology* 4 (1974):171–186.

30. S. Gore, "The Effect of Social Support in Moderating the Health Consequences of Unemployment," *Journal of Health and Social Behavior* 19 (1978):157–165.

31. W. Isard, *Method of Regional Analysis* (Cambridge, Mass.: MIT Press, 1960); W. Isard, *Introduction of Regional Science* (Englewood Cliffs, N.J.: Prentice Hall, 1976).

32. R. Catalano, *Health, Behavior and the Community: An Ecological Perspective* (New York: Pergamon, 1979).

33. Isard, *Methods;* Isard, *Introduction;* A. Isserman, "The Location Quotient Approach to Estimating Regional Economic Impacts," *Journal of the American Institute of Planners* 43 (1977):33–41.

34. K. Kapp, *The Social Cost of Private Enterprise* (New York: Schocken, 1950).

14 Unemployment and Mental-Health Implications for Human-Service Policy

Ramsay Liem

To the economist, the human being is a source of irritating error variance; to the mental health specialist the economy is part of the mosaic background of individual behavior. When one examines the issue of unemployment and mental health, however, it quickly becomes apparent that this disjunction between spheres of interest is a reflection of disciplinary and professional chauvinism and not social reality. Although this discussion of the impact of job loss on mental health is principally directed at implications for human service providers, any conclusions we can draw should have significance for economic policy as well.

The tendency among the mental health professions to underplay the role of socioeconomic factors in mental illness can be traced, in part, to the field's traditional dominance of a biomedical model of illness. Psychiatric impairment has generally been viewed as a personal problem triggered in some instances by life circumstances but largely the manifestation of biopsychological processes. From this perspective, conditions like community economic crises that precede increased need for mental health services are of secondary interest compared to personality and biogenetic vulnerabilities to such disturbances. The biomedical model treats the social contexts of mental illness as largely interchangeable settings for playing out organismic processes.

Developments in mental health theory and practice over the past fifteen years, however, have increased the likelihood that greater legitimacy would be accorded to external conditions (such as economic events) as factors in the etiology or course of psychiatric disorders. Specifically, the prominence of community mental health during this period has led to new interest in preventive interventions as well as more effective treatment modalities. Almost by definition, elevating the status of preventive activities necessitates examining the social context, as well as individual dynamics, for ways to inhibit disease processes. The broad question of how the state of the

Part of the research reported in this chapter has been supported by the Center for Work and Mental Health, National Institute of Mental Health, grant number R01-MH31316. The author would like to thank Tom Atkinson, Joan Liem, Steve McElfresh, and Paula Rayman for their careful reading of an earlier draft of this chapter.

economy bears on mental health should, therefore, have some appeal to those whose thinking has been influenced by the challenge of preventive practice. The brief comments that follow are predicated on this belief and address two issues. First, what is some of the evidence that there are significant personal costs of economic crises, in particular involuntary unemployment, and what progress is being made to understand for whom these costs are greatest? Second, what policy options are sugggested by the available evidence and how do these recommendations relate to contemporary models of practice familiar to mental health practitioners? More precisely, what kinds of actions make sense in light of different conceptions of primary prevention accorded some legitimacy in the clinical professions?

Unemployment and Mental Illness: Research

What mental health research traditions provide a context for current work on the economy and mental illness? As part of its empirical rationale for the community mental health centers movement, the Joint Committee on Mental Illness and Health (1961) drew attention to research on psychiatric epidemiology to capture the scope and distribution of mental illness. What was generally the fruit of the sociologist's labor became a topic of considerable interest among mental health professionals, especially the meaning of the ubiquitous association between measures of social standing and mental illness (Dohrenwend and Dohrenwend 1965). Although interest in this basic relationship has waxed and waned over the past two decades, it has never disappeared entirely, and suggestions as to *how* social class and mental illness are related always stimulate reaction. This has certainly been the case with two recent contributions to the literature on social factors in mental illness, econometric analyses of time-series data reflecting statewide and national economic changes and psychiatric service utilization (Brenner 1973, 1976), and studies of economic and noneconomic stressful life events as precursors to psychiatric symptomatology or treatment (Fontana, Marcus, Noel, and Rakusin 1972; Holmes and Rahe 1967; Myers, Lindenthal, and Pepper 1975). Because of the now well-known findings in both of these areas of research, stress as mediating social standing and psychiatric well-being has achieved a new level of interest with particular attention being paid to economic events as a prime source of personal stress (Liem and Liem 1978).

The line of research initiated by Brenner specifies a gross relation in the aggregate: economic change indexed by employment rates and psychiatric service utilization co-vary with remarkable consistency. What these data do not explain, however, are the underlying social and psychological processes that mediate this relationship assuming, of course, that it is not spurious. If, for example, statewide rates of employment change in inverse relation to statewide first admissions to hospitals, precisely what is happening at the level of personal experience that accounts for this association?

One of several lines of work seeking to address this question has centered on the event of unemployment to determine to what extent job losers or persons close to them are directly accounting for heightened incidence and prevalence of impairment during economic downturns. Without ruling out alternative hypotheses such as the coincidence of enlarged service capacity with periods of recession, one can make a reasonable case for examining directly the impact of job loss on individuals. Unemployment, for example, is virtually always the strongest predictor of hospital use when multiple indicators of economic change are examined. Research on the stress effects of a wide range of discrete life events also tends to indicate that economic events and especially job loss or demotion frequently precede psychiatric impairment (Coates, Moyer, and Wellman 1969). Given that the past decade has also been a time of highly visible threats to employment in the population in general, it is not surprising to find people looking at unemployment as a link between large-scale economic change and mental illness.

With this context for research on the human costs of unemployment, what evidence is there that the stress of involuntary job loss is noteworthy and that there are, indeed, psychiatric casualties associated with this event? Some might wonder why this question need be addressed in the first place. Is it not self-evident that it is catastrophic to lose an activity that is the major source of significant economic, social, and psychological goods? On the contrary, it has become commonplace to think of unemployment in strict economic terms and either to neglect the questions of social and emotional costs entirely or to assume that non-economic outcomes are completely contingent upon economic losses. In the latter case, policy makers often assume that programs like Unemployment Compensation and Supplementary Unemployment Benefits have eliminated the social and personal costs once associated with unemployment, during the Great Depression. That full employment policies are now commonly predicated on uncontested acceptable levels of unemployment is one manifestation of this belief.

In fact, we know little of the complexity of unemployment effects today. The case studies of the Depression have questionable validity for present day experience and there are very few well-controlled contemporary studies of job loss. Most recent work is based on single, brief interviews with relatively small samples. Collectively, this research provides some evidence that unemployment elevates anxiety levels (Fineman 1979), induces withdrawal and secrecy (Briar 1978), produces distortions in the perception of time (Levin 1975), contributes to the deterioration of relationships at certain points during the job loss experience (Powell and Driscoll 1973), and elicits defensiveness and self-criticism with prolonged job loss (Goodchilds and Smith 1963). These findings vary somewhat for different groups of un-employed and are often based on global, qualitative impressions of the investigators or single item survey questions. Research based on a broader assessment of economic and non-economic life stressors as predictors of health also suggests that unemployment is an especially common precursor of psychiatric symptomatology, the need for treatment, and suicidal feel-ings (Theorell, Lind, and Floderus 1975).

There have also been several descriptions of unemployment as consti-tuting a positive experience, generally for white-collar workers and man-agers or professionals (Little 1976; Root and Mayland 1978; Thomas, McCabe, and Berry 1980). These observations are attributed to a range of factors including relative economic security, the opportunity to escape a stressful job situation, mid-career changes in occupational values or ob-jectives, and the opportunity to spend more time with one's family. It should be noted, however, that some of the findings along these lines are based on respondents' disavowals of severe negative consequences of job loss for their families or acknowledgement of positive, as well as negative, impacts of unemployment. In either case, the reporting of positive conse-quences does not necessarily imply the absence of any undesirable effects. What is more likely is that unemployment, like many stressful life events, has complex effects entailing both genuine hardship and strain and positive life changes. Research that is insensitive to this possibility stands to con-struct a particular picture of job loss based on the types of research ques-tions asked rather than to uncover the realities of personal experience and family life that result from the loss of work.

The most comprehensive and careful study of job loss in the current literature has been reported by Cobb and Kasl (1977). For two years this research followed a group of 100 blue-collar workers displaced by two plant closings, comparing it to a sample of matched controls on a variety of in-dices of stress and strain. Data from this study are often cited in support of the claim that plant closings cost workers their physical and emotional health as well as sense of economic security and well-being. The findings are quite complex, however, and, as the investigators have reported recently (1979), the evidence is equivocal, especially as regards mental illness.

While workers with low perceived social support and longer periods of unemployment are significantly more depressed and anomic than other un-employed workers or controls, these differences occur at the anticipation phase prior to actual termination and continue throughout the two year period. Consequently, rather than causing high levels of depression and anomie, longer and more frequent periods of job loss may be *the result* of poor coping and job hunt performance of characterologically depressed, anomic persons. Length of job loss becomes the outcome and the emotional state of the individual, the determinant.

Somewhat more persuasive evidence of an emotional effect of job loss can be found in this research, though, if the experience of urban/rural workers is distinguished. Persons displaced as a result of the closing of an urban plant exhibited greater anger, irritation, resentment, and anomie than unemployed workers from a rural plant closing. Kasl and Cobb note that the urban closing destroyed the major locus of social activity for these workers whereas in the rural area, social networks were not dependent on the life of the plant. The disruption of social and friendship networks for the urban sample may have resulted in a significant loss of social support for weathering the period of unemployment. This post hoc comment is worth noting in view of the fact that perceived supportiveness of spouses and neighbors predicted the severity of the psychological blows of job loss. Here we also gain our first insight into the possibility that the real story of unemployment must be told in different ways for different groups and that closer examination of life circumstances and access to coping resources may be required to understand the variation in response to job loss.

It is also useful to keep in mind that the Kasl and Cobb research deals with relatively short-lived unemployment (median number of weeks of unemployment during the first year was five) occurring in the particular context of whole plant shutdowns. These characteristics of the job loss experience should be associated with minimal self-blame for the unemployment and, perhaps, relatively limited strain on workers' financial resources. Similar conditions of unemployment describe the steel plant closings studied by Buss and Redburn (1980) and may account in part for the limited evidence of severe mental health problems reported for that sample.

Very preliminary results from a survey of workers in the New England aerospace industry are just becoming available (Rayman 1981). These data are retrospective accounts of diverse aspects of the job loss experience, occurring most often during the early-to-mid 1970s recession in this industry. Descriptive summaries of responses to this survey indicate that substantial numbers of individuals experienced stress during their unemployment. Workers commonly report problems with insomnia, increased smoking and drinking, headaches, stomach trouble, and lack of energy. Over half the sample describe themselves as "worrying a lot" and a third report loss of self-esteem. About one fifth of this group report having sought help for emotional or physical problems during their time out of work. Data from follow-up, in-person interviews will also be examined in this research and will hopefully clarify some of the conditions under which these kinds of effects are either moderated or enhanced.

Work and Unemployment Project

The research in which this writer is presently engaged was motivated in part by the dramatic statewide relations between economic change and psychiatric admissions reported by Brenner (1973, 1976). The Work and Unemployment Project is an effort to learn more about how families and individuals react to job loss and is currently in the final stage of data collection. The research involves extensive interviews with about forty blue-collar and forty white-collar families following the involuntary separation from the workplace of male breadwinners. All families have at least one child under the age of eighteen living in the home. The sample also includes an approximately equal number of employed control families matched with unemployed families on such dimensions as socioeconomic status, family life cycle characteristics, and work status of spouses.[1] Two to four hour home interviews are conducted with husbands and wives together four times during the year following job loss. The length of time from the job loss to the first interview is on average one month. Additional interviews are scheduled three, six, and twelve months following the loss of work. These workers were terminated from a broad range of jobs where they had a minimum of one continuous year of tenure.

This research will examine the moderating or exacerbating effects of a range of job, family, social network, and financial resource characteristics on the impact of job loss. It will also describe individual and family coping strategies that respondents employ to manage both the personal and family hardships produced by unemployment and the task of finding a job. Impact is measured by psychiatric and physical illness, sick role behavior, mood states, and perceptions of family climate, relationships, and structure. In other words, we are interested in a wide range of individual impacts measured for unemployed male breadwinners and their spouses, and in the family's response to the job loss, as a social unit.

Based on initial analyses of these data it is possible to comment on several trends appearing in responses from the first two rounds of interviews occurring on average one and three months following termination. These observations are based on a subset of the measures used to assess the psychological functioning of both spouses and their perceptions of the quality of family life. Responses have been examined for blue- and white-collar families unemployed at the time of *both* interviews, blue- and white-collar families unemployed at the first interview but reemployed at the second, and blue- and white-collar control families at both times. The size of the control group at the second interview is substantially less than at the first because of incomplete coding of wave two control interviews at the time of these analyses.

Comparisons of means and variances for husbands and wives are noteworthy in several respects.[2] For husbands, being without work for one and three months is strongly associated with greater psychiatric symptomatology relative to control husbands. These men report greater depression, anxiety, hostility, and psychoticism than controls at the first interview.

These symptoms plus paranoia and somatic complaints distinguish unemployed husbands from controls at the second interview. As expected, husbands who regain employment by the second interview exhibit reduced symptoms in spite of the fact that at the first interview they were indistinguishable from husbands with continuing job loss. Sustained unemployment over both interview periods is accompanied not only by an expanded range of symptom types but also by higher levels of symptoms within each area.

Wives of unemployed men can also be distinguished from women in comparable life circumstances except that their husbands are employed. Although psychiatric symptom differences are negligible, wives of unemployed men appear to be more sensitive to some disruption in their marital relationships than controls. This distinction may also account for the more negative mood states of these wives. By the second interview wives of unemployed as opposed to employed men report significantly greater deterioration in overall family functioning (for example, family cohesion, organization, and conflict) as well as continuing problems in the marital relation. At this point these wives can also be distinguished from controls in terms of their interpersonal sensitivity, levels of depression, and total psychiatric symptomatology.

It is tempting to speculate that wives are indirectly affected by their husband's unemployment via its impact on the quality of family relationships and that mental health effects for wives are mediated by such disruptions in family life. For husbands psychiatric effects could be more of a direct response to the job loss and job hunt experiences. Some caution is warranted, however, in drawing this conclusion prematurely. None of the current analyses directly tests the causal pathways among these several effects. Furthermore, the data suggest that greater differences between wives of unemployed and employed men on symptom and family measures at the second interview are less a function of heightened effects for unemployed wives and more the result of positive changes reported by employed wives. At present a reasonable presumption is that unemployment has negative consequences for both spouses but that the underlying processes associated with these effects may be substantially different.

We cannot conclude without qualification at this time that involuntary job loss precipitates mental illness. Heightened symptom levels in families with unemployment can reflect increased stress relative to control families without indicating clinical level impairment. There are some indications, however, that at least for some families, the stress of unemployment has significant long-term effects. With 80 percent of all interviews completed, six instances of separation or divorce initiated during the study period have been recorded for unemployed families (four blue-collar and two white-collar) while only one separation has been reported in the control sample (a white-collar family). Similarly, problems scheduling interviews due to serious illness or hospitalization of either spouse have occurred fourteen times for unemployed families and seven times for employed families. In several of the unemployed families, it is clear that health problems are associated with suicidal tendencies. Specific instances of extreme despair particularly among husbands still unemployed after twelve months are also evident based on a cursory review of interview protocols for families with extended job loss. Finally, we regret to report that in one unemployed family interviewed during the pilot phase of this research, the husband committed suicide approximately one year after the job loss.

We want to be cautious in making too much of these data in view of their anecdotal nature. However, they are not inconsistent with findings from the initial formal analyses and, if corroborated by subsequent analyses of interview data, paint a rather bleak picture of the impact of job loss. In at least some instances of involuntary job loss it appears that non-economic consequences are both severe and prolonged. Future analyses will be directed at validating these impressions and attempting to specify both social conditions and coping responses that influence the intensity and quality of impact. We already know that the variation in response to job loss on the measures we have reported here is especially large for unemployed husbands in blue-collar families. The consistently larger standard deviations for this group require that we look more closely for shared life circumstances that distinguish those whose responses to the job loss experience is especially severe. We may well discover that present day unemployment is neither as benign nor as universally damaging as has been argued by different camps, but more circumscribed in terms of the social conditions of those who are most distressed by it.

Implications for Human-Service Policy

In spite of relatively limited formal sources of information, the weight of the existing evidence from this and other studies indicates that involuntary unemployment can precipitate psychiatric impairment. At least some of the explanation for the strong state and national level correlations between unemployment rates and psychiatric admissions found by others can be attributed to the response of some individuals and members of their families to the stress of unemployment. What implications does this conclusion have for human service, and especially mental health, policy?

This question can be most meaningfully addressed by reference to the concepts of primary, secondary, and tertiary prevention. The classification of mental health services in these terms implies that legitimacy is accorded not only to remedial activities (tertiary prevention), but also to interventions designed to limit the course of incipient mental illness (secondary prevention) or to prevent entirely its appearance in the first place (primary prevention).

The limiting factor for the design of secondary and tertiary preventive interventions is our knowledge of such things as social and personal correlates of high vulnerability to the stress of job loss, stages of response to unemployment and corresponding degrees of receptivity to outside help, and areas of "natural strength" within families and the social environment. More information in these areas could aid in reducing the stress of job loss. If we knew, for example, that spouses of unemployed workers in fact experience greatest stress several months later than the unemployed person and that such effects reflect a deterioration in family relations, counselors could provide anticipatory guidance (Caplan 1964) to couples and explore with them ways to mobilize new as well as customary coping resources. A broad range of contributions to the planning of secondary and tertiary interventions will follow directly from more reliable and precise knowledge of the mechanisms underlying the psychological impact of job loss.

One service delivery issue, however, whose currency is not dependent on acquiring more data is the generic problem of designing human services in ways that maximally enhance their accessibility to persons in greatest need. The experience of one planning group (Buss and Redburn 1980) reveals that overcoming the stigma, perceived irrelevance, and general lack of knowledge of mental health services is no simple task especially when the potential client population has had limited experience with professional caregivers. The literatures on client-provider style match (McMahon 1964), the placement of mental health services in nontraditional settings (Riessman 1967), and the special utility of indigenous, paraprofessional mental health workers (Klein 1967) are examples of areas of existing knowledge that have a real bearing on the design of meaningful services for the unemployed. The fact that the economic underclasses, as well as the minority work force, carry a disproportionate share of unemployment makes these long-standing issues in the development of mental health services for other than white, middle-class consumers, especially relevant.

The development of relevant and psychologically accessible services should be a priority whether or not a community is actively confronted with wide-spread job losses. One reason why the thoughtful implementation of services described by Buss and Redburn (1980) may have fallen short of its objectives for laid-off steelworkers is that these services were originated in the midst of crisis. Workers had no previous experience with help of this kind (for example, counselors located in union offices) and appeared unable to overcome the common reluctance of many people to be identified as needing mental health services or, in fact, help of any kind. Effective secondary and tertiary prevention for victims of unemployment would surely be enhanced by some prior history of positive contact with mental health services.

Clearly, there is much to be said for more thoughtful design and implementation of secondary and tertiary prevention of mental distress resulting from the experience of job loss. However, without diminishing in any way the importance of this kind of planning, it should be noted that these forms of intervention are largely after the fact. That is, they tend to take the occurrence of a stressor for granted in their focus on minimizing the debilitating *effects* of the stressful event. Whether or not the *occurrence* of stressors ought itself to be a professional concern of mental health practitioners is at the core of opposing views regarding the appropriate conception of primary prevention. In broadest terms, primary prevention involves the minimization of psychiatric risk in the population, that is, the prevention of even early signs of impairment. This objective can be accomplished in theory by directing attention to the persons at risk, the circumstances contributing to the risk, or some combination of both. The real issue is to what extent should mental health professionals be concerned only with helping people cope with or prepare for difficult life situations as opposed to participating as well in efforts to reduce the incidence of social or economic stressors (Albee 1967).

This distinction between approaches to primary prevention can be illustrated concretely in relation to the problem of unemployment. One could, for example, emphasize the need to prepare individuals to anticipate and to be able to cope with increasingly more predictable economic hardships, that is, try to inoculate the public against the ill effects of job loss; or one could advocate serious consideration of the human costs of unemployment on a variety of fronts where economic policy is shaped. In other words, the mental health professions could take it for granted that stagflation, plant closings, layoffs, and reductions in new hirings are present day facts of life and teach the public how to accommodate to this reality. This line of action has already been taken in the area of occupational stress where stress management techniques have recently been proliferated. Similarly, one area of research on primary prevention is devoted to how best to teach problem-solving competency as a general preventive measure. Recent efforts to identify and strengthen "naturally occurring" family and community supports as a means of buffering the stress of everyday life occurrences represent an effort to augment personal competencies with social resources (Hirsch 1980). Helping workers to foresee the hardships of unemployment, to learn new ways to draw on material and social resources, and to acquire basic job hunting skills are examples of prevention through anticipation and skill development.

Primary prevention can also be framed, however, in terms of reducing the incidence of stressors. To some, treating the rate of occurrence or distribution of life stressors (like unemployment as mental health issues) is mixing professional concerns with politics or, at the very least, meddling in things outside one's area of competence. To try to prevent mental illness by minimizing life stresses that contribute to impairment, however, implies only that (1) there is reasonable evidence that a given stressor plays an important etiologic role and that (2) mental health consequences should be considered together *with other* costs and benefits of policies affecting the public's exposure to such stressors. It is especially important to bear in mind that drawing out the real connections between economic decisions influencing the rate of unemployment and the mental health of the public does not mean that these decisions should be based only on this concern. What is being asserted is that the maximization of economic productivity and profit are not the only significant social values nor do they ensure compensation in the long-term for the social and mental health costs of job dislocations. By aligning themselves with this position, mental health specialists are neither stepping outside their professional roles nor raising a concern that is theirs alone. There is every reason to believe that broad segments of the working public would share this concern for a more balanced assessment of economic policy. And who other than the mental health specialist is in a better position to provide the evidence regarding psychiatric outcomes?

Unquestionably, prevention that seeks to alter the occurrence or distribution of external stressors invariably draws one into the ongoing struggle to set public priorities, and to resolve competing interests and social values. Nevertheless, as it has been made clear many times before, avoiding such engagement only affirms the existing ordering of competing interests. Granting that positive mental health is only one of many social values, it is still virtually unheard of in present economic planning and stands to remain so in the absence of outspoken advocates. The mental health professions have a responsibility to help address this problem and to bring into the arenas of public debate the research and experimental basis for doing so effectively.

Notes

1. Unemployed families were screened in Division of Employment Security offices in a major northeastern metropolitan area. Control families were drawn from both town censuses in corresponding areas and local supermarket screenings.

2. Because of space limitations, tables summarizing these analyses have been omitted. These data are available upon request to the author.

218   Public Policies for Distressed Communities

References

Albee, G. "The Relationship of Conceptual Models to Manpower Needs." In E. Cowen, G. Gardner, and M. Zax (eds.), *Emergent Approaches to Mental Health Problems.* New York: Appleton-Century-Crofts, 1967.

Brenner, M.H. *Mental Illness and the Economy.* Cambridge, Mass.: Harvard University Press, 1973.

Brenner, M.H. *Estimating the Social Costs of National Economic Policy: Implications for Mental and Physical Health, and Criminal Violence.* Prepared for the Joint Economic Committee of Congress. Washington, D.C.: U.S. GPO, 1976.

Buss, T., and Redburn, S. "Shutdown: Public Policy for Mass Unemployment." Research report of the Center for Urban Studies, Youngstown State University, Youngstown, Ohio, 1980.

Briar, K. *The Effects of Long-Term Unemployment on Workers and Their Families.* San Francisco, Calif.: R and E Research Associates, 1978.

Caplan, G. *Principles of Preventive Psychiatry.* New York: Basic Books, 1964.

Coates, D.; Moyer, S.; and Wellman, B. "Yorklea Study: Symptoms, Problems, and Life Events." *Canadian Journal of Public Health* 60 (1969):471–481.

Cobb, S., and Kasl, S. *Termination: The Consequences of Job Loss.* Cincinnati, Ohio: OHEW (NIOSH) Publication Number 77–224, 1977.

Dohrenwend, B.P. and Dohrenwend, B.S. "The Problem of Validity in Field Studies of Psychological Disorder." *Journal of Abnormal Psychology* 70 (1965):52–69.

Dooley, D., and Catalano, R. "Economic Change as a Cause of Behavioral Disorder." *Psychological Bulletin* 87 (1980):450–468.

Fineman, S. "Psychological Model of Stress and Its Application to Managerial Unemployment." *Human Relations* 32 (1979):323–345.

Fontana, A.; Marcus, J.; Noel, B.; and Rakusin, J. "Prehospitalization Coping Styles of Psychiatric Patients: The Goal Directedness of Life Events." *Journal of Nervous and Mental Disease* 155 (1972):311–321.

Goodchilds, J., and Smith, E. "The Effects of Unemployment as Mediated by Social Status. *Sociometry* (1963):287–293.

Hirsch, B. "Natural Support Systems and Coping with Major Life Changes." *American Journal of Community Psychology* 8 (1980): 159–172.

Holmes, T., and Rahe, R. "The Social Readjustment Rating Scale." *Journal of Psychosomatic Research* 11 (1967):213–218.

Joint Committee on Mental Illness and Health. *Action for Mental Health.* New York: Basic Books, 1961.

Kasl, S., and Cobb, S. "Some Mental Health Consequences of Plant Closing and Job Loss." In L. Ferman and J. Gordus (eds.), *Mental Health and the Economy.* Kalamazoo, Mich.: The UpJohn Institute, 1979.

Klein, W. "The Training of Human Service Aides." In E. Cowen, E. Gardner, and M. Zax (eds.), *Emergent Approaches to Mental Health Problems.* New York: Appleton-Century-Crofts, 1967.

Levin, H. "Work, the Staff of Life." Paper presented at the Annual Convention of the American Psychological Association, Chicago, 1975.

Liem, R., and Liem, J. "Social Class and Mental Illness Reconsidered: The Role of Economic Stress and Social Support." *Journal of Health and Social Behavior* 19 (1978):139-156.

Little, C. "Technical-Professional Unemployment: Middle-Class Adaptability to Personal Crisis. *The Sociological Quarterly* 17 (1976):262-274.

McMahon, J. "The Working-Class Psychiatric Patient: A Clinical View." In F. Riessman, J. Cohen, and A. Pearl (eds.), *Mental Health of the Poor.* New York: The Free Press, 1964.

Myers, J.; Lindenthal, J.; and Pepper, M. "Life Events, Social Integration, and Psychiatric Symptomatology." *Journal of Health and Social Behavior* 16 (1975):121-127.

Powell, D., and Driscoll, P. "Middle-Class Professionals Face Unemployment." *Society* 10 (1973):18-26.

Rayman, P., Department of Sociology, Brandeis University, Waltham, Mass. Personal communication.

Riessman, F. "A Neighborhood-Based Mental Health Approach." In E. Cowen, E. Gardner, and M. Zax (eds.), *Emergent Approaches to Mental Health Problems.* New York: Appleton-Century-Crofts, 1967.

Root, K. and Mayland, R. "The Plant's Closing, What Are We Going to Do? Worker and Family Response to Job Displacement." Paper presented at the Annual Meeting of the National Council on Family Relations, Philadelphia, 1978.

Theorell, T.; Lind, G.; and Floderus, B. "The Relationship of Disturbing Life Changes and Emotions to the Early Development of Myocardial Infarctions and Other Serious Illness." *International Journal of Epidemiology* 4 (1975):281-293.

Thomas, L.; McCabe, E.; and Berry, J. "Unemployment and Family Stress: A Reassessment." *Family Relations* (1980):517-524.

**Part VI
The Politics of
Redevelopment**

15 Restructuring Local Economies through Negotiated Investment Strategies

James E. Kunde and
Daniel E. Berry

Evidence is accumulating on the detrimental effects that declining firms and plant closings have on urban areas. These negative effects include increased urban apprehension and uncertainty about job availability, and business perception of a poor investment climate.[1] Both of these attitudes can contribute to a vicious cycle of reduced confidence in an area's future that leads to reduced investment and jobs.

The climate of uncertainty and trauma created by declining firms and plant closings has forced public action to deal with these issues. Generally these public actions have focused on short-term considerations. Examples include proposed legislation calling for advance warning to communities of impending plant closures, compensatory payments by closing firms to displaced workers, and for redevelopment fees to be paid by the firms to the communities. State or local governments which adopt such programs create disincentives for the location of new industry or expansion of existing industry within their boundaries.

In several states, legislation has been introduced to halt the loss of industrial jobs by helping ailing firms in economically depressed areas. Some of these states have issued industrial development bonds to create loan-pools, provide loan guarantees, or to provide direct financial assistance to those firms. At the local level, business retention programs have been developed to preserve the existing industrial base. It is unfortunate that the shock of plant closings sometimes has resulted in a preserve it at all costs focus in business retention programs instead of taking into consideration underlying changes in the urban economy. Thus, public funds sometimes are expended in futile efforts to revive dying sectors of the economy. Unwarranted concessions may be given to firms in return for their promise to stay in the community even though it is difficult for public officials to learn the true health and plans of individual firms.

The Need for Process Intervention

Efforts to reverse or mitigate the effects of plant closings require, at a minimum, energetic, open-minded leadership in both the public and private sectors. In many communities such leadership exists, but developing a coordinated strategy is hampered by other factors—including policies of the state and federal governments. In some cases, the local government response to plant closings has been pragmatic recognitions of these policies as well as local political realities and pressures. While the need to restructure a declining economy is apparent, these constraints make restructuring an extremely difficult task. Gaining community acceptance of a posture of triage toward older declining industries is not politically palatable in some communities. However, assistance in the form of outside intervention may trigger a process which allows a community to address long-term restructuring of its economy and to draw on resources both within and outside the community.

This outside intervention can come from any number of sources. For example, most states have resources and authority that they have hardly begun to use in assisting distressed cities. Harnessing these state resources and directing them to communities in need could provide the impetus for revitalization of local economies. It is also possible that considerable progress can be made at the local level by improving relationships between the public and private sectors through the creation of new forums and processes. Such mechanisms can improve the likelihood of compatible public and private investment planning.

Regardless of its source, any process intervention will ultimately encounter the intergovernmental barriers to local economic development. Thus, one of the critical actors in any process intervention is the federal government. There are, at least, two reasons. First, the federal government does have considerable resources which can be applied to the task of restructuring a local economy. Second, it may be that the federal government is the partial *source* of problems faced in communities beset with severely deteriorating economies. For example, Douglas A. Fraser asserts that federal government action or inaction has actually contributed to making the economic dislocation problem worse in the United States.[2]

Unfortunately, the federal government currently is ill-equipped to effectively participate in the local economic development process. A study by the U.S. Office of Management and Budget (OMB), which identifies such situations, concludes that the system impedes rather than assists the formulation and development of approaches to local economic development. Problems cited by OMB include:[3]

Programs and resources are badly fragmented;

Program procedures among departments and agencies conflict;

Delivery systems and criteria diverge widely; and

Authority and responsibility for programs are mismatched.

Some complications resulting from these problems identified by OMB include:[4]

Unnecessary rigidity that leads to a lack of flexibility to respond to local needs and opportunities, and an inability to effectively pool and focus limited funds;

Lack of a policy focus and direction;

Fragmentation of local planning; and

Limited ability to involve the private sector in development assistance programs.

To deal with these problems, the OMB study recommended creation of a new federal agency called the Department of Development Assistance. That department, as it was proposed, would have included elements of the Department of Agriculture and Commerce, all of Housing and Urban Development, the Community Services Administration, the Economic Development Administration, and the proposed National Development Bank. This recommendation was adopted by the Carter administration and submitted to Congress for consideration. It bogged down in the Congressional committee structure. The recommendation never received consideration from the entire Congress and was quietly dropped by the administration.

The fate of the proposed Department of Development Assistance is not surprising in light of the history of attempts to restructure or consolidate the federal economic policy machinery. Twenty-eight such attempts have failed since 1948. As Pat Choate and Gail Schwartz have cogently noted: "The failure of these repeated attempts demonstrates the power of pluralism. This is a modern political reality that should be respected.[5] Often, the chief impediment to structural change is the self-interest of agency bureaucrats. They fear loss of their jobs or programmatic authority, and consequently resist any attempts at reorganization.

Other scholars have argued that attempts to restructure the system through centralized consolidation, even if it were politically viable, might prove ineffective. Catherine H. Lovell, for example, says that such efforts will not work unless they harmonize programs at the precise moment when needed in the local communities. Furthermore, federal programs should also be related to state grant programs and to the local jurisdiction's own public programs and private endeavors.[6]

The Negotiated Investment Strategy as a Process Intervention

Despite the difficulties encountered in attempts to reform governmental structure, the underlying reasons for those efforts remain valid. Recognition of the "power of pluralism" and the need for coordination of federal programs and policies at the community level are two of the realities which guided development of a concept called Negotiated Investment Strategy (NIS). An underlying premise is that the fragmentation and confusion in programs and policies at varying levels of government is likely to continue. Furthermore, it is impossible to deal with fragmentation in the abstract. The NIS proposes that it would be more productive to rationalize the system on a place-by-place basis. Thus, in contrast to structural change, the NIS is designed to improve the processes of interactions among existing institutions and organizations which affect community economies. Because it does not require major changes in the federal structure, NIS can be instituted quickly and tailored to local needs.

In other writings by these authors, the NIS has been described as an approach to developing coordinated strategies for investing public and private resources in communites.[7] The NIS process is based on the assumption that there are legitimate differences between and within levels of government and among private groups about what should happen in a particular community. NIS recommends that it is best to recognize the differences and negotiate agreements on priority issues among the affected parties rather than to proceed on a project-by-project basis. Essentially, the NIS process was designed to deal with the same problems which led to the OMB proposal for the Department of Development Assistance already discussed. NIS is an experimental process designed to test the efficacy of a different approach to dealing with these problems.

The NIS process has six elements:

An impartial mediator:

Three negotiating teams, representing the public and private sectors of the city, the state, and the federal government; each team is small but subject to later expansion to assure representation of important interests;

The opportunity for informal exchange of information before formal proposals are written;

Formal face-to-face negotiating sessions with all teams present;

A written agreement containing mutual commitments; and

Public review and adoption of the agreement, with monitoring of subsequent performance by each team and the mediator.

The NIS procedure begins with the independent development of objectives and proposals by teams representing federal, state, and local interests. The teams are then convened by the neutral mediator to explore areas of potential agreement. The teams participate in a series of meetings until specific written agreements are reached on the priorities for a given area. A second part of the agreement involves committing resources to address those priorities.

Three cities, Gary, Indiana, St. Paul, Minnesota, and Columbus, Ohio, have completed the procedure. The test sites were selected by the federal government which was represented by the Chicago Federal Regional Council (CFRC) with support from the White House. Although economic hardship was not the major selection criterion, each of the cities is dealing with economic transition. Gary, in particular, has been hit hard by plant closings and layoffs in industry. In contrast, the Columbus experiment demonstrates the applicability of the concept of relatively stable communities. In all cases the state and local teams were selected by its governors and mayors. Mediators were selected with the concurrence of all three teams and retained by the Charles F. Kettering Foundation, with assistance from the Ford Foundation and local foundations.

The subjects for negotiation and the specific nature of the process were conditioned by specific local needs and circumstances, as well as public policy objectives of the various levels of government. The St. Paul Agreement, for example, covers fifty-two points involving financial and other commitments on the part of several federal agencies, units of state government, the city, and private interests. Major commitments which were negotiated in St. Paul included the Energy Park, Lowertown Urban Revitalization, East Central Business District Bypass, and the Mississippi River Corridor Plan. It is anticipated that $40 million in public investment in the Energy Park and Lowertown Development will generate private investments amounting to over $260 million in the next five years.

The Columbus process initially focused on reforming the intergovernmental process and cutting constraints. After resolving several basic policy issues, a broad range of items were negotiated, including agreements dealing with human services, fair housing, historic preservation, displacement, minority business development, water quality management, employment and training, and meeting the needs of special populations.

In Gary, negotiations focused on seven major goals, mutually agreed upon by the three teams. Objectives were identified under each of the major goals which, when achieved, would affect the vitality of Gary's downtown and neighborhoods, improve the health and safety of Gary's residents, and enhance the community's amenities. Significant progress was made toward improving relations between the city of Gary and the state of Indiana and steps were taken to improve public/private collaboration in that city.

While not legally binding, the three NIS agreements represent good faith pledges from the signatories to pursue implementation through all available institutional channels—formal and informal. A key question, yet to be answered, is whether the commitments can operate independently of changes in political administrations. It is likely that any new administration will wish to review the agreements; initial indications are, however, that they will transcend political changes. The agreements, containing commitments that were made through a rational and systematic process, represent a document which will be difficult for any administration to ignore. Essentially, the agreements have developed their own momentum. That momentum is being sustained by the active involvement of the mediators in the implementation phase.

NIS Impacts: Coordination of Government Programs at the Federal, State and Local Level

Considerable analysis has been undertaken to determine the effects of the NIS process in the three test sites. Testimony from participants indicates considerable improvement in the processes of intergovernmental relations. Mayor George Latimer of St. Paul, for example, attributes the private sector commitments made in the Energy Park development to the fact that the negotiations proved the three levels of government were serious about "getting their act together."[8] Mayor Tom Moody says that even if Columbus had not received any funds out of the process, it was valuable because of the understandings reached on important policy positions in the three levels of government.[9] Richard G. Hatcher praised the NIS process as "providing the opportunity for the best discussions we've had with the state of Indiana since I've been mayor.[10] The CFRC chairperson, Douglas Kelm, argued that NIS provides a forum where the various programs of the federal government can be integrated, thus creating an aggregate effect that is greater than the sum of individual programs.[11] This effect is greater because of the reduction in conflicting programs and policies that results from face-to-face negotiations. In addition, the internal bargaining that occurred within each federal team allowed federal agencies to leverage each other's programs. The overall effect was to improve the efficiency of federal investments.

Investment Planning. Such accolades indicate the value of the NIS process in improving governmental coordination. Because the negotiations have been completed so recently, however, less information is available regarding what the negotiations actually mean to the cities' future. An earlier articulation of the NIS concept depicted it as a process which would increase a community's capacity to solve local economic problems.[12] In its broadest conception, the public funds negotiated through the process are to be allocated according to an agreed upon investment plan. That plan should be aimed at creating a self-sustaining local economy in conjunction with increased local capacity to improve quality of life. Consideration of NIS steps taken toward investment planning is the focus of the remainder of this chapter.

Harvey A. Garn and Larry C. Ledebur have suggested that, in part, a city can be described by the composition, distribution, and value of its stock of assets. They identify seven major categories of urban assets:[13]

Labor, and the human capital and skills invested in the work force;

Physical capital and the technology embodied within it;

Land and industrial structures;

Entrepreneurial capacity, management skills, and organizational ability;

Public developmental infrastructure and other elements of community infrastructure requisite to industrial activities;

Natural resources, represented by both raw materials and such amenities as location, climate, the quality of air and water, and even the urban ambience;

Claims to assets located elsewhere. These claims can be taken to include claims to funds originating elsewhere such as intergovernmental transfers.

For a city to increase the value of these assets, it is necessary to undertake a two-step process which entails: (1) identification and enhancement of opportunities for asset growth and development; and (2) identification of problem areas impeding such growth and development.

Using their perspective, an urban investment plan would consist of strategies to maximize the value of those assets. Such strategies could include achieving productivity gains from better management of assets, increasing the use of underutilized assets, increasing the stock of assets from internally generated surpluses, and transforming the use of assets by invention and innovation in the face of changing circumstances.[14] Specific investment strategies resulting from negotiations in each of the three cities follow.

Increasing the Use of Underutilized Assets. One of the major assets of Gary is its location. The city's proximity to Chicago represents a development opportunity because there is a need for satellite airports to accommodate overflow traffic from O'Hare Airport and to provide commuter and cargo service to and from the Chicago area. The Gary Airport is located within approximately one hour's drive from downtown Chicago and Gary is serviced by commuter rail service to Chicago. Considerable federal funds are available for airport development.

The principal barrier which impeded realization of the airport development opportunity was the inability of the city of Gary to generate the funds required as a local match to obtain federal funding. The city was unable to raise those funds because it was unable to gain approval from the Indiana State Tax Commission to issue bonds for the purpose of airport development.

During the course of the negotiations, the three teams reached consensus on the importance of the airport bond issue to the future economic vitality of Gary. The three teams then approached the Tax Commission in concert, recommending approval of the bond issue. The bonds were approved and have been issued, consequently enabling the city to obtain federal funding. Private air carriers have already indicated strong interest in locating at the airport, and development of an industrial park adjacent to the airport was subsequently negotiated through the NIS process. Thus, the negotiations process led to investments which allowed the city to obtain better use of an underutilized asset—its location.

Achieving Productivity Gains through Better Asset Management. In the Columbus process, the local team argued that the state of Ohio had failed to acquire and effectively use all of the federal social service support funds at its disposal. As a result, the local human service providers and consumer groups were being short-changed and scarce local resources were being expended on functions that potentially could be paid with federal funds. The state team argued that the piecemeal allocation of federal funds created an unnecessarily complex situation and resulted in inefficiency in the administration of human service programs at the local, county, and state levels. The federal team countered with the viewpoint that the content and implementation of the State's Comprehensive Annual Service Plan was the key to dealing with the issue raised by the local team.

As a result of the negotiations, a joint study was undertaken by the state and local teams to recommend ways to maximize federal reimbursement of state and local welfare expenditures and to increase flexibility in the delivery of those services. In addition, the federal team indicated its support of a waiver to the federal statewide uniformity regulation that would allow several innovative human service delivery demonstrations to proceed within the county. When fully implemented, the agreement will result in productivity gains through better management of the city's asset of claims on intergovernmental transfers.

Transforming the Utility of the Asset Base. All three of the test sites used the NIS to make adjustments to national changes in urban development patterns. Three development trends most relevant to the NIS applications have been identified by Roger Vaughan:[15]

1. Decentralization of employment and population will continue; however, these trends should be viewed as an opportunity for a city to undertake a strategy for redevelopment of central industrial areas into residential and commercial areas.
2. The nation is transforming from a goods producing to a service producing economy. This trend will benefit central cities which have adequate office space and attractive downtowns. However, the ultimate success of a city in adjusting to this shift will depend, in large part, upon its ability to provide residential amenities that attract the highly educated and mobile service work force.
3. The economic transformation of the urban base is creating a demand for new, small, specialized firms. This will require a substantial increase in the birth rate of high technology companies and will require innovative new financing programs.

Recognition of these trends is apparent in the investment strategies negotiated in each city. All three utilized the NIS process to channel investments toward improving transportation to their downtown areas. Gary obtained a state commitment to construct an exit from the Indiana Tollway. Columbus achieved policy agreements on a portion of interstate highway connecting its airport with the downtown and improvements in its mass transportation system. St. Paul negotiated a bypass highway around its downtown, which will relieve traffic congestion.

In addition, each of the cities was able to channel investments into better use of its natural amenities and improvements in its housing stock. Gary was able to coordinate development of a national park with its own plans for housing development on the shores of Lake Michigan. Funding was also obtained by Gary to develop a light industrial park *around* a state-identified nature preserve. Columbus received approvals and funding commitments to expand its network of bike trails along the Olentangy River. St. Paul was able to achieve and begin implementation of an integrated development along the Mississippi River Corridor which includes recreation, housing and light industry, and commercial business.

The Lowertown Development and Energy Park projects negotiated in St. Paul clearly illustrate the potential of the NIS for restructuring a local economy consonant with economic development trends. The Lowertown project, for example, combines the traditional forms of economic development activity, retail, office, and industry with elements of downtown housing, riverfront recreation, and artistic and cultural meeting places.[16] Development in Lowertown also is critical to revitalization of the Central Business District because not enough land and purchasing power is available to support economic functions in the core city.

The Energy Park project represents an innovative attempt to cluster high technology industries involved in energy-related activities. The project also incorporates state-of-the-art techniques in energy conservation, energy production, and energy management. Again, housing and recreation components are included in the development.

Conclusions

Such examples illustrate the potential for restructuring a local economy through a process such as the NIS. It should be noted that, in the main, the commitments to the projects in Columbus and St. Paul represent better use of funds already programmed by the federal and state governments for those cities. The case of Gary is somewhat different. There, the negotiations gave the city access to resources that were previously denied because of an inability to raise local matching funds. Each of the cities was able to improve the timing and phasing of the investments, and to integrate various project elements. The substance of the agreements in each city represents significant progress toward restructuring the local economy, increased capacity to manage that economy, and an increase in the value of city assets.

The NIS, as a process, has proved to be very adaptable. However, further adaptation of the process to situations in other cities is contingent upon several factors. First, and most important, all parties who are to be involved in the process must agree that the system within which they are operating is conflictual. Furthermore, they must all be willing to negotiate over the resolution of those conflicts. Unless the parties are receptive to the concept of mediated negotiations, the process will not work.

Another precondition is the ability of the local area to articulate a bargaining position. Each of the three test cities, had a strong mayor who was able to select local negotiating teams that politically were able to represent a comprehensive local position. In places where no single person can initiate the local agenda development process, it may be necessary to undertake some sort of broadly based community agenda setting exercise. This would be particularly true if the process were attempted in a fragmented metropolitan situation.

Two other characteristics of the NIS might qualify it as a means of restructuring a local economy beset with severe problems. First, the willingness of the federal government to take a negotiating posture with a local community could stimulate a community to address long-term economic problems. Second, the use of neutral mediation, that is, the management of the process by someone who has no vested interest in the outcomes, may facilitate negotiations over issues that appear intractable. Such was the case in each of the initial three-city experiments where issues that had been unresolved for as long as fifteen years were resolved. Thus, skilled mediation, in particular, could assist a troubled community in confronting and resolving its serious conflicts. An effective process intervention could help create a sense of confidence in the community's future.

To speculate on a more widely encompassing view of NIS potentials, it may be useful to examine the recent calls for a federal industrial sectoral policy. The difficulties of major industries such as steel and automobile have evidenced themselves in many U.S. communities, particularly in the northeast and midwest. Gail Schwartz and Pat Choate argue that if these communities are to maintain their economic viability, federal development policies must focus on the needs of the industries and sectors which represent a substantial part of their revenue base.[17]

The involvement of U.S. Steel in the Gary NIS is illustrative of the need. In the main, private sector participation in the NIS, albeit supportive, has been reactive. However, first steps were taken to directly involve private interests in the Gary negotiations. U.S. Steel actually participated in negotiations with the principle objective of protecting its position vis-á-vis its competitors by minimizing its local property tax burden. Lacking in the Gary experiment was any link between the recently announced federal policy toward the steel industry and local concerns of U.S. Steel in Gary.

In order for the federal government to effectively implement a sectoral policy, say Choate and Schwartz, it must be consistent with the nation's regional and community development objectives.[18] The elements of federal policy areas which could harmfully affect local communities and states should certainly involve the affected parties in the policy-setting process. For example, a federal decision to relax air pollution standards to assist a particular industrial sector would have differential effects in U.S. communities. It may be that an NIS, or a similar process, could help tailor federal actions aimed at both the public and private sectors in a particular community.

In conclusion, the concept of organized intergovernmental negotiations seems to hold considerable promise for any number of situations including growing, stable, and declining communities. In addition, a number of experimental variations on the NIS concept are underway to adapt the process to rural development circumstances, to bilateral negotiations between states and their localities, and to negotiations in specific functional areas. However, as an alternative to the current piecemeal, crisis-oriented approach to local economic development, perhaps the greatest potential of an NIS-type process is for distressed communities. It is there imperative that limited investment resources be utilized in the most effective of ways.

Notes

1. See, for example, studies being conducted by Louis Ferman at the University of Michigan which indicate that a plant closing has ripple effects throughout an area's labor force. Workers not directly displaced fear that their plant may also be closed, sometimes resulting in productivity decreases. Preliminary results of these studies were reported in the *Dayton Journal Herald,* October 21, 1980, p. 18. Also see unpublished studies by James Howell, First National Bank of Boston, which show that smaller banks tend to shift their investment portfolios from business loans to safer investments like government securities when negative events occur in an area's economy. The effect is to decrease the availability of high-risk capital at a time when a local economy needs it most. Those findings are based on examination of sixty-three New England bank call statements covering the period of time 1953–1972.

2. Douglas A. Fraser, "Economic Dislocation: Lessons from Abroad," *Urban Concerns,* (February/March 1980):55.

3. Economic Development Division, U.S. Office of Management and Budget, "Reorganization Study of Community Development and Local Economic Development Functions" (Washington, D.C.: O.M.B.), Unpublished mimeo, p. i–ii.

4. *Ibid.*

5. Gail Schwartz and Pat Choate, "A National Policy for Industry: The New Rx for Economic Development," *Commentary* no. 2 (April 1980): 6–7. Published by National Council for Urban Economic Development, Washington, D.C.

6. Catherine H. Lovell, "Coordinating Federal Grants from Below," *Public Administration Review* (September/October 1979):432–433.

7. Carl M. Moore, James E. Kunde, and Daniel E. Berry, "Improving Intergovernmental Relations through Improved Intergroup Relations," *Journal of Intergroup Relations* (December 1980):1.

8. George Latimer, statement to NIS Evaluation Panel, St. Paul, Minnesota, January 16, 1980.

9. Tom Moody, statement to NIS Evaluation Panel, Washington, D.C., July 10, 1980.

10. Richard G. Hatcher, statement made at second Gary NIS negotiating session, Indianapolis, Indiana, July 30, 1980.

11. Douglas Kelm, statement made at Columbus NIS session, March 6, 1980.

12. James E. Kunde; Richard E. Eckfield; James L. Shanahan; and Daniel E. Berry, *Where Does All The Money Go?* (Dayton, Ohio: Charles F. Kettering Foundation, 1979), p. 20.

13. Harvey A. Garn and Larry C. Ledebur, *Economic Growth and*

Development Issues: A Concept Paper (Washington, D.C.:The Urban Institute, 1978), p. 5-6.

14. *Ibid*, p. 4.

15. Roger Vaughan, *Local Business and Employment Retention Strategies: Urban Consortium Information Bulletin* (Washington, D.C.:U.S. Department of Commerce, 1980), p. 3-4.

16. Lowertown Redevelopment Corporation, *Lowertown Projects* (St. Paul, Minn.: Lowertown Redevelopment Corporation, 1979), p. 4.

17. Schwartz and Choate, "A National Policy for Industry," p. 7.

18. *Ibid,* p. 8.

16 Local Economic Planning and Corporate Relocation

Edward M. Bergman

The deepening economic crisis of the 1970s and early 1980s reveals an acceleration in the rate of capital mobility and industry loss in distressed local economies. Researchers and policy analysts have clearly identified the (multi)-national forces which result in corporate disinvestment, plant shutdowns and the relocation of establishments to more hospitable business climates (Bluestone and Harrison 1980). While there is perhaps less agreement concerning the remedies than the causes, nearly every policy proposal requires some form of public intervention at the state or federal level (Carlisle and Redmond 1979a, 1979b; Kanter 1981; Schweke 1980; U.S. Congress, 1979). Even as these proposals are being considered, a variety of narrow tactics is also being pursued at the microlevel by directly affected parties, particularly neighborhoods, workers, and local plant managers (Lindberg 1981; Gunn 1980; Foltman 1981).

Local economic planners are frequently the local intermediaries between the immediately affected parties and federal or state level programs on a case-by-case basis. Planners' intermediate role occasionally goes beyond the broker stage, that is, acting as the conduit for readjustment program resources, to assist in the design and implementation of a proposed economic adjustment project. Missing entirely, however, is a capacity for either local contingency or strategic planning which would include more than the specifics of a particular plant closing and which would express a public concern for the well-being of the area's economy and labor market as a whole. This capacity would include, at minimum, a much improved understanding of potential shifts within the area by specific firms and industry aggregates, a system of contingency plans and local economic adjustment policies geared to vulnerable sectors and workers, and strategic plans to use scarce social resources in developing a local economy which is less susceptible to external disinvestment. Why this necessary and entirely logical planning capacity is not yet in place at the local level deserves comment.

Locally Responsive Economic Planning: Why Not?

Perhaps one of the foremost reasons why locally responsive forms of economic planning have not clearly emerged can be traced to a universal pre-

237

disposition for national economic policy instruments based until very recently on Keynesian theories of aggregate demand. Although sectoral priorities and supply-side policies also gained attention by the early 1980s (Bendick and Ledebur 1981) all tend to devalue the unique attributes of local economies by reinforcing the popular notion that the only economic relationships of note concern macro-aggregates and industry totals at the national level. Some have argued that the political attention paid to conventional measures of macroeconomic goals such as GNP biases economic policymaking because ". . . GNP merely captures the dollar sum of goods and services in trade, and reducing all economic evaluation to cash transactions elevates the national over the local and the quantitative over the qualitative" (Barsh and Gale 1981). The national economy was perhaps the proper focus during the 1930s when the entire economy slumped and when local economies everywhere experienced major layoffs and corporate failures; as Martin and Leone observe, ". . . any regional implications of recovery programs were incidental to the main purpose of reviving the national economy" (1977).

But to continue the one-sided preoccupation with macroeconomic policies in a period when a substantial and growing proportion of all output is produced by mobile, transnational corporations amounts to corporate license at the cost of local dependence. Given this policy perspective, corporate adjustment policies of capital mobility which may devastate local economies are seen as the logical and entirely acceptable consequence of macroeconomic policy. Such a view implicitly argues that local economies have no identity apart from their status as subnational units and that communities should be prepared to bear the impacts of necessary corporate adjustments whatever the costs (Carlisle and Redmond 1978a, 1978b, 1978c). Consequently, little is expected in the way of local economic policies or of the independent need to plan for local economies.

To the degree that space and place do enter the world of economic theory, they are generally considered as measures of market friction which impede the natural equilibrium properties of a market system. Those who hold this view regard equilibrium-seeking ". . . as the more or less spontaneous process of capitalist development, in which the search for increased profits would eventually spin-off growth-inducing industries to the more backward, peripheral regions of a national economy. In this process, the role of government would be limited to offering inducements that would hasten a recovery of spatial equilibrium" (Friedmann and Weaver 1979, p. 55). Although interventions can take many forms, the most frequent practice which localities have traditionally employed is industrial recruitment (Bluestone and Harrison 1980, pp. 212–246; Hunker 1974; Moriarty 1979). Whatever its name, the practice is really focused on policies which facilitate the maximizing behavior of corporations and only secondarily on the economic needs of the affected locality.

Finally, the deluge of area-based assistance programs throughout the 1970s which were initially intended to soften the impacts of local economic distress, probably did more to soften the capacity of planners to deal with inherent problems. The enormous flow of program funds through state and local agencies began long before they were capable of spending it wisely or well. Planners became preoccupied with spending the full annual budget and accounting for expenditures with some acceptable form of a management information system (Bergman 1981). The embarassment of riches stifled independent development of analytically strong and strategically sophisticated planning. Local economic development planning quickly became a form of grants management and planners tended to lose sight of the conditions which gave rise to the need for local economic development initiatives in the first place.

As Martin and Leone (1977) note about local economic development in the mid–1970s, the ". . . choice is whether to develop policies which *facilitate* market forces in rearranging the economic landscape or to pursue policies which *compensate* for the inequities that existing market mechanisms create" (p. 113). It matters little which of the two policies are pursued: each seems to foreclose for different reasons the prospect of locally responsive economic planning.

Toward a Local Economic Planning Practice

The points here presented suggest why a practice of local economic planning responsive to local rather than corporate needs has yet to emerge. A simple typology which summarizes styles of local economic planning may help organize the local consequences of ideas expressed thus far and provide a glimpse of what might yet develop. The following discussion will distinguish the more traditional styles which reflect corporate needs and the styles responsive to local needs that may emerge in the future.

Styles of local economic planning captured in figure 16–1 also reveal obvious differences which reflect the dynamics of a local economy, that is, whether it is growing or declining. The most recognizable styles are (traditionally) responsive to the readjustment strategies of major corporations whose investment policies in turn affect a locality's growth or decline.

Corporate Recruitment Planning

Style I is the traditional form of corporate/industrial recruitment which is found in rapidly growing economies. This style was most visible during the post-WWII period of corporate expansion in the sunbelt regions. Private

Condition of Local Economy	Corporate Responsiveness	Local Responsiveness
Growing Economy: Net inflow of corporate investment capital; new plants and plant expansions	CORPORATE RECRUIT-MENT PLANNING Principal planning style (I) is in industrial or corporate recruitment. Larger local-ities delegate to chamber of commerce and business groups; smaller localities contract an independent industrial recruiter with public funds.	ECONOMIC STRATEGY PLANNING Principal planning style (IV) would include long-range strategic planning to deliberately allocate scarce social resources to develop a local economy which is less susceptible to external disinvestment.
Declining Economy: Net outflows of corporate investment capital; em-ployment cut-backs and plant shutdowns	CORPORATE IMPACT PLANNING Principal planning style (II) is providing program funds for alleviating some episodic economic im-pact. Usually a state or federally funded agency activity which stands apart from locality's main planning and implementation system. Planning for a local arm of the welfare state.	ECONOMIC CONTINGENCY PLANNING Principal planning style (III) would stress the need to anticipate the full extent of potential economic decline, to develop con-tingency plans for specific industrial sectors and workers, and to build a permanent planning and implementation capacity into the structure of local government.

Figure 16–1. Styles of Economic Planning for Localities

sector vitality and initiative tends to displace any local concern for public economic plans and policies. In the words of one observer "For the most part, responsibility for guiding new investment to a locality has been perceived historically as being in the hands of the private sector—the prov-ince of the local chamber of commerce and the area development offices of the utility companies, the major railroads, and banking institutions. For the local government to intervene overtly in those decisions that determine the nature and level of jobs or the mix of economic activity in the community would have been viewed as the unwelcome intrusion (Nathanson 1980, p. 3). As key members of the local growth lobby, these groups—often with appropriated funds from local governments—together or individually employ the services of industrial developers who, in turn, promote the busi-ness climate of the locality, market the area to prospective corporations, and broker the available array of business incentives and subsidies (Blue-stone and Harrison 1980, pp. 214-230; Moriarity 1980; Hunker 1974). While growth in employment is sometimes opposed by major industrialists who wish to reduce wage competition (the growth stability lobby) or by influential citizens who wish to preserve a favored lifestyle (the growth limits lobby), local growth lobby interests generally prevail. This is perhaps the most familiar style of local economic planning and its variants can be found in the majority of localities, even in declining economies which currently experience high levels of corporate disinvestment[1] (NCUED 1977; Nathan, Barnes and Associates 1976).

Corporate Impact Planning

Style II versions of what Bluestone and Harrison call "The Standard Policy Response" (Bluestone and Harrison 1980, p. 14–15) became, in the 1970s another traditional form of local economic planning, particularly in the hardest hit local economies. Funding, mandated requirements and program regulations were derived externally from state or federal program agencies; in the absence of any preexisting form of public economic planning, localities tended to establish free-standing program offices that mirror the structure and concerns of their patron agencies (Yin 1980). Consequently, local program offices do not become permanently integrated into established administrative units of government or within broad political constituencies. Because of this, and the fact that each office is expected to focus its programs on particular target groups or specific instances of economic decline, it is difficult to plan coherent policies for the development of a local economy. The available literature which describes style II planning tends to stress a need for coordination and management improvements between the program offices (NCUED 1977b; NCUEC 1980; Mangum, et al. 1979). Preoccupied with a need for managerial improvement in the operation of specific programs, practitioners of style II economic planning become more attuned to national legislative moods than to local needs. This is particularly true during periods when the public's general disregard for marginally effective welfare state interventions is apparent.

Where styles I and II represent economic planning that is highly responsive to episodic impacts presented by corporate policies, there is some evidence that locally responsive styles are beginning to emerge. That is, traditional styles I and II were suited to situations where infrequent and unexpected instances of capital mobility required some minimal response. But the pace and degree of recent industrial mobility produce effects which go beyond single neighborhoods or groups of workers and begin to affect the area's small businessmen and the fiscal solvency of its municipal governments. Local public officials hesitate to allow corporate decisions determine local action. They will also begin to reconsider whether fiscal policies and development projects should be planned solely for the readjustment needs of corporate sectors to the exclusion of other enterprise types (Stern and Aldrich 1980).

As this chapter and numerous other studies suggest, localities are beginning to rethink their needs and local economic planning can be expected
to more accurately reflect those needs. While initially limited to directly
affected groups of workers or communities, the broadening impact of
plant shutdowns has converted what was earlier seen as a single, interest-
group issue to an area-wide concern. Accordingly, attempts to deal with
major plant shutdowns now find workers and their unions dealing directly
with area bankers, businessmen, and local governments (Gunn 1980). New
demands are placed on planners who had operated in traditional roles, as
they begin to establish styles of economic planning suited to local needs.
This is most clearly visible in areas that have been dramatically affected by
plant shutdowns. In some local economies the outlines of what might be
called planning styles III and IV are beginning to emerge.

Economic Contingency Planning

Economic contingency planning (style III) is perhaps the most fitting description for what is beginning in some declining local economies. The emphasis here is that of permanently establishing a locally responsive planning
capacity to ensure that analyses of the local economy—particularly analyses
of its vulnerability to losses in key industrial sectors—lead to sound contingency plans for stabilizing and rebuilding the local economic base. The
recent establishment of the economic development division within the
American Planners Association (APA Economic Development Division
1980) reveals a professional concern as do a series of monographs distributed to planners and public officials which stress the need for local governments to adopt permanent economic development planning capacity (Bendavid-Val 1980; Conley et al. 1980; Nathanson 1980). As federal programs
which fund planning style II activities change, local governments are likely
to place economic development planning in a permanent setting which isn't
dependent on particular program activities. This setting may be one of several existing agencies (for example, planning departments, development
coordinators, finance division) or perhaps a free-standing unit of local government which would integrate the remnants of federal programs with other
ongoing local functions. Regardless (Thompson 1980, p. 177), it should
allow sufficient contact with the main actors in the local economy (business,
government, labor, and so on) to gain first-hand knowledge of problems as
they arise; it should also be provided sufficient resources to accurately
assess the local economy's vulnerable sectors. Beyond the need to forecast
broad industry trends, many have suggested the need to establish early
warning information systems to anticipate losses of key firms (Nathanson

1980; Smith and McGuigan 1979). In fact, there are even prepared guidelines showing how to apply particular warning models (Tremoulet and Walker 1980). Several urban economic development agencies already rely on some form of this (Nathanson 1980, p. 41) while others try to keep abreast of local business thinking and plans (Conley et al. 1980, p. 19–32).

Preparing contingency plans in the event that plants move or firms fail is another necessary feature of this style. At the broadest level, this entails a review of the full range of alternative industry sectors (based on a sound industry analysis of local consumer demand and business input requirements plus any export production or import substitution potential) and alternative enterprise forms. Alternative industry sectors can be analyzed using a variety of well-known methods, but less is known about alternative enterprises. If conventional private enterprises seem willing to take over, buy out or otherwise reuse existing plants (including their labor), then contingency plans are typically based on specifically coordinated versions of traditional project development plans (Black et al. 1980; Lochnoeller et al. 1975) or on joint public/private ventures (Nathan, Barnes and Associates 1976). But local economic planners in declining areas are seldom able to rely upon firms which shutdown plants to help reopen them, even if the plant is a profitable operation. It is increasingly the case that other types of enterprises must be included as elements of a contingency plan for declining economies. Community-based enterprises such as worker-owned firms, producer cooperatives, and community development corporations have been relied upon in some areas (Bergman, Carlisle and Redmond 1979; Gunn 1980; Miller 1980; Zwerdling 1978) and unsuccessfully attempted in others (Carlisle et al. 1978; Stein 1980). How such enterprises are designed and fostered to participate in the local economy is the concern of students of community economic development (Kelly 1976; Mahmood and Ghosh 1979; National Economic Development Law Project 1974). To the degree that community-based enterprises are not present in every locality, one might expect economic planners to work with community economic development officials and include support assistance for such enterprises in contingency plans (Carlisle 1978). Style III represents a marked departure from traditional styles of local economic planning in tone and in degree of public intervention. It broadens the area of responsibility to include public officials and, indirectly, the system of political guidance in local governments. Once politicized, the economic development issues must be posed in some joint public/private arena where questions of which domain each sector shares and which it controls may be openly resolved. Allowing for differences of scale and level, the initial resolution of these local economic planning issues may resemble proposed structures for industry planning at the macroeconomic level (Rohatyn 1980, 1981).

Economic Strategy Planning

To the degree that planners in declining areas adjust their styles away from corporate and toward local needs, one would also expect to find planners in growing areas to experience similar adjustments. Style IV is based on the assumption that even rapidly growing localities will eventually recognize that corporate-driven growth is neither inevitable nor continuous. Lessons from other areas will be pointed to by those with long-term local interests; workers, small business people, local economic planners, public officials, and so on. This is particularly likely in growth areas whose workers migrated from declining areas or whose planners and economic development officials have had direct experience with declining economies. As they grow, such areas should anticipate their future vulnerability and plan for stability or decline. Accordingly, decisions to commit scarce local resources to economic development programs may become less corporate-dominated and more locally oriented, although this is by no means certain (Bluestone and Harrison 1980, p. 89–98); Dunn 1980; Lindblom 1977; Stern and Aldrich 1980).

As argued, establishment of permanent economic planning capacity would be likely because *no* area is permanently immune to disinvestment and decline (Bluestone and Harrison 1980, p. 60; Bluestone, Harrison and Baker 1981, p. 14–15). Moreover, growing localities are still in a position to establish a strategic style which can anticipate risks and can adopt options which reduce risks and their long-term costs (Bergman 1978; Redmond 1978). This posture affords a planner the opportunity to analyze other areas' experience with various industry sectors and enterprises in terms of their potential for meeting local needs. For example, some sectors or enterprises: require costly infrastructure and services; entail risks to workers and living environments; consume disproportionate amounts of scarce local resources (developable land, water, energy etc.); pay below-average wages and salaries; accumulate and reinvest surplus out of the local economy; purchase relatively few production inputs from local suppliers; or tend to be unstable. They should be evaluated carefully from the community's perspective.

Once the long-term prospects are known, strategic planning for key industries and enterprises can be undertaken. For example, maintaining local ownership of growth industries might be important. If so, local industry and enterprise policies should encourage the incubation of new firms and the continued ownership of existing firms. Such policies will call for imaginative new instruments and institutional arrangements. This sketch of style IV economic planning is intended to suggest the minimal contours of a practice which has yet to emerge.

Prospects for Locally Responsive Economic Planning

The prospects for styles III or IV emerging as serious candidates can only be generally posed.[2] Furthermore, we can speak only of the tendencies which would suggest their emergence, not guarantee it. It can only be argued that, under certain conditions, either could become one of three or four alternatives available to local planners and public officials.

What then are the forces which would produce these tendencies? First, stripping away what Rohatyn calls programs for the padded society will leave declining areas with no means to cushion the impact of corporate relocation (1980). Democrats and Republicans seem to agree with Rohatyn and major cutbacks must be expected. Places denied the programmatic means to soften the impact of job loss and economic decline are likely to be interested in contingency planning for industry loss and may at least consider some version of style III economic planning.

Second, the pursuit of macroeconomic policies which encourage new investment, speed the depreciation of current plant and equipment, and induce a general shift in factor shares from labor toward capital is likely to accelerate capital mobility. The increased velocity of capital mobility could produce an unexpected effect: growing areas will begin to experience noticeable industry loss and declining areas will once again become targets for investment. In both places, the costs and risks associated with future corporate investment plans will be viewed more cautiously, and some variant of economic planning style IV may be called upon to develop longer-term development strategies.

Prospects for the adoption and further elaboration of planning styles III and IV rely heavily on some of these forces. They are certainly among the necessary preconditions, but public officials and planners also play key roles. The extraordinary community stress created by plant shutdowns (and the increasingly prevalent threats to relocate) can quickly politicize the issue. In such circumstances, locally elected office holders and public officials are not necessarily the long-term captives of corporate influence. A reinvigorated form of local political action stimulated by the concerns of affected workers and citizens is possible, as is the responsiveness of public officials to such expression.

Expressions of public concern for the long-term vitality of a local economy can be immediately interpreted as a call for appropriate styles of local economic planning. But local planners must first be prepared to interpret such a call and then to act upon it, by going beyond traditional styles to develop, apply, and test the emerging ones. As discussed, this must include the refinement of stronger planning techniques and analysis. Of equal importance is the willingness of planners to be engaged with all relevant sectors to the local economy and to prepare sensible policies which clearly reflect that engagement. Finally, planners must be willing to participate with public officials and citizen groups in the politically difficult task of permanently establishing a planning capacity within local government which is responsive to the needs of all the area's citizens.

Notes

1. Since low labor costs are frequently the principal, local subsidy, support from the growth lobby for state right-to-work laws is common, but this support is not universal among businesses which must also depend upon wage-based local consumer demand.

2. Styles III or IV could predominate in some communities which are not subject to major corporate influence (for example, Madison or Berkeley) or which adopt public polices similar to those pursued in some American cities during the early part of this century (Stave 1975).

References

APA Economic Development Division. "The Economic Development Division Is Ready for the 1980s," *Newsletter,* vol. 1, no. 1, April 1980.

Barsh, Russel L., and Gale, Jeffrey. "U.S. Economic Development Policy—The Urban Rural Dimension." Chapter 4 of this book.

Bendavid-Val, Avrom. *Local Economic Development Planning: From Goals to Projects.* Planning Advisory Service Report No. 353. Chicago: APA-PAS, 1980.

Bendick, Marc, and Ledebur, Larry C. "National Industries Policies and Economically Distressed Communities." Chapter 1 of this book.

Bergman, Edward M. "New Roles for Local Economic Planners." *Carolina Planning* 2, no. 4 (Fall 1978):8.

Bergman, Edward M. "Review of Job Market Futurity: Planning and Managing Local Manpower Programs, and Evaluating the Performance of Employment and Training Programs at the Local Level." *Journal of American Planning Association* 47, no. 2, April 1981.

Bergman, Edward M.; Carlisle, Rick; and Redmond, Michael. *Employee Ownership and Enterprise Feasibility: A Case Study of Bertie Industries.* Chapel Hill: UNC Department of City and Regional Planning Occasional Paper, 1979.

Black, J. Thomas; Rothstein, Fran; Borut, Allan; Howland, Libby; and Byrne, Robert. *Local Economic Development Tools and Techniques.* Washington: U.S. Conference of Mayors, 1980.

Bluestone, Barry, and Harrison, Bennett. *Capital and Communities: The Causes and Consequences of Private Disinvestment.* Washington: The Progressive Alliance, 1980.

Bluestone, Barry; Harrison, Bennett; and Baher, Lawrence. *Corporate Flight: The Causes and Consequences of Economic Dislocation.* Washington: The Progressive Alliance, 1981.

Carlisle, Rick. "New Strategies for Local Economic Development." *Carolina Planning* 2, no. 4 (Fall 1978):14–81.

Carlisle, Rick; Dopp, Steven; Dowdee, Scott; Perez, Ruby; Redmond, Michael; Schall, Robert; Smith, Lowell; Wilson, Michael; and Bergman, Edward. *Community Involvement in Selecting Worker Ownership as a Local Development Strategy.* Final Report Submitted to NSF-SOS Program. Chapel Hill: UNC Department of City and Regional Planning, 1978.

Carlisle, Rick and Redmond, Michael. "Community Costs of Plant Closings: Bibliography and Survey of the Literature." Unpublished report prepared for Federal Trade Commission, July 1978.

———. "Indicators for Measuring the Community Costs of Plant Closings." Unpublished report prepared for Federal Trade Commission, November, 1978.

———. "Measuring the Community Costs of Plant Closings: Overview of Methods and Data Sources." Unpublished report prepared for Federal Trade Commission, 1978.

———. "Plant Closing Legislation and Regulation in the United States and Western Europe: A Survey." Unpublished report prepared for Federal Trade Commission, January 1979.

———. "Legislation in Western Europe on Mass Dismissals and Plant Closings: A Review of Studies and Commentaries, with Policy Implications for the United States." Unpublished report prepared for Federal Trade Commission, February 1979.

Conley, Gary; Nolan, R.; Schneider, William J.; Shapin, Jan C.; and Yulish, Morton. *Economic Development: New Roles for City Government.* Washington: U.S. Conference of Mayors, 1980.

Dunn, Marvin. "The Family Office as a Coordinating Mechanism Within the Ruling Class." *The Insurgent Sociologist,* 9, no. 2–3 (Fall 1979–Winter 1980):8–23. Special Issues, Power Structure Research II.

Foltman, F.F., "Managing and Adjusting to a Plant Closing." Chapter 11 of this book.

Friedmann, John and Weaver, Clyde. *Territory and Function.* Berkeley and Los Angeles: University of California, 1979.

Gunn, Christopher. "Toward Workers' Control." *Working Papers* 7, no. 3 (May–June 1980):4–7.

Hunker, Henry, L. *Industrial Development: Concepts and Principles.* Lexington, Mass.: Lexington Books, D.C. Heath and Company, 1974.

Kanter, Sandra. "Theory of the Little State." Chapter 17 of this book.

Kelly, Rita Mae. *Community Participation in Directing Economic Development.* Cambridge, Mass.: Center for Community Economic Development, 1976.

Lindblom, Charles E. *Politics and Markets.* New York: Basic Books, 1977.

Lindberg, Mark. "Anticipatory Problem Solving and Community Development." Chapter 18 of this book.

Lochmoeller, Donald G.; Muney, Dorothy A.; Thorne, Oakleigh J.; and Viets, Mark A. *Industrial Development Handbook.* Washington: Urban Land Institute, 1975.

Mahmood, Syyed T., and Ghosh, Amit K. (eds.) *Handbook for Community Economic Development.* Washington: Economic Development Administration, 1979.

Mangum, Garth; Morlock, James; Snedeker, David; and Pines, Marion W. Job Market Futurity: Planning and Managing Local Manpower Programs. Salt Lake City: Olympus, 1979.

Martin, Curtis H. and Leone, Robert A., *Local Economic Development.* Lexington, Mass.: Lexington Books, D.C. Heath and Company, 1977.

Miller, Marc. "Workers Owned." *Southern Exposure* 7, no. 4 (Winter 1980):12–21.

Moriarity, Barry M. (ed.) *Industrial Location and Community Development.* Chapel Hill: University of North Carolina Press, 1980.

National Council for Urban Economic Development (NCUED). *Detroit Michigan Economic Development Delivery System Options: Organizing a Strong Public-Private Partnership.* Washington, D.C.: NCUED, 1977.

———. *Strengthening the Economic Development Capacities of Urban Governments.* Washington, D.C.: NCUED, 1977.

———. *Coordinated Urban Economic Development: A Case Study Analysis.* Washington, D.C.: NCUED, 1978.

———. *CUED'S Guide to Federal Economic Development Programs.* Washington, D.C.: NCUED, 1980.

Nathan, Barnes and Associates. *Strategies for an Effective Public-Private Relationship in In-City Industrial Development.* Vol. A: Model Recommendations; Vol. B: Model Cleveland; Vol. C: Model Milwaukee; Vol. D: Model Indianapolis. Prepared for The Society of Industrial Realtors. Washington, D.C.: Economic Development Administration (NTIS), 1976.

Nathanson, Josef. *Early Warning Information Systems for Business Retention.* Washington, D.C.: Urban Consortium—U.S. Dept. of Commerce, 1980.

National Economic Development Law Project. *A Lawyer's Manual on Community-Based Economic Development.* New York: Berkeley, 1974.

Redmond, Michael. "Roles for Local Planners in Industrial Recruitment." *Carolina Planning* 2, no. 4 (Fall 1978):8–13.

Rohatyn, Felix. "The Coming Crisis and What to Do About It." *New York Review of Books* 27, no. 19 (December 4, 1980):20–26.

————. "Reconstructing America." *New York Review of Books* 28, no. 3 (March 5, 1981):16–20.

Schweke, William. *Plant Closings: Issues, Politics and Legislation.* Washington, D.C.: Conference on Alternative State and Local Policies, 1980.

Smith, David with McGuigan, Patrick. *Towards a Public Balance Sheet: Calculating the Costs and Benefits of Community Stabilization.* Washington, D.C.: National Center for Economic Alternatives, 1979.

Stave, Bruce (ed.) *Socialism and the Cities.* Port Washington, N.Y.: Kennikat Press, 1975.

Stein, James I. "Corporate Failure and the Community: A Case Study of the ILC Steinthal Corporation." Chapel Hill: UNC Department of City and Regional Planning, 1980.

Stern, Robert, and Aldrich, Howard. "The Effect of Absentee Firm Control on Community Welfare: A Survey. In John S. Siegfried (ed.), *Firm Size, Market Structure and Social Performance.* Washington, D.C.: U.S. GPO, 1980.

Thompson, Wilbur. "Urban Revitalization and Industrial Policy." In U.S. Congress, House Subcommittee on the City, *Urban Revitalization and Industrial Policy.* Hearings 96th Congress, 2nd Sess. Washington, D.C.: U.S. GPO, 1980.

Tremoulet, Andree, and Walker, Ellen. "Predicting Corporate Failure and Plant Closings: A Resource for Local Employment Planners." Working paper. Chapel Hill: UNC Department of City and Regional Planning, 1980.

U.S. Congress, Senate Committee on Labor and Human Resources. *Plant Closings and Relocations,* Hearings 96th Congress, 1st Sess. Washington, D.C.: U.S. GPO, 1979.

Yin, Robert K. "Creeping Federalism: The Federal Impact on the Structure and Function of Local Government." In Norman J. Glickman (ed.), *The Urban Impact of Federal Policies.* Baltimore: Johns Hopkins University Press, 1980.

Zwerdling, Daniel. *Democracy at Work: A Guide to Workplace Ownership Participation and Self-Management Experiments in the U.S. and Europe.* Washington, D.C.: Association for Self-Management, 1978.

17 Theory of the Little State: Business-Government Relations on Formation of State Economic Policy

Sandra Kanter

Introduction

With the prospect of reduced federal spending, states are increasingly developing their own economic policy to induce private sector growth and prosperity. But since little research has been undertaken in the past on state economic policy, there is a lack of understanding about the effectiveness of different economic programs. This chapter tries to address one gap in our knowledge—the process by which economic policy gets made. Based on interviews with over seventy public officials and business people in the Commonwealth of Massachusetts between the years 1978 and 1980, this chapter provides an explanation of the formation of state economic policy.[1]

In particular, the research examines the validity of the structuralist theory of the state.[2] While this neo-Marxist theory has many variations and facets, most theorists agree that its main thesis is the relationship between the business community and government. Structuralists, for example, believe that state officials are relatively autonomous from the business community. The two interest groups have different objectives: business leaders want to maintain and expand their level of profits while public officials want to remain in office.

But these seemingly separate objectives are, in fact, inseparable. Clearly, public officials need an expansionary economy because it provides jobs for constituents and public revenues to fund programs that please the electorate who vote them into office. But economic expansion depends upon the production schedule of producers, a function of expected profits, which, in turn, depends upon a positive politico-economic environment. In the end, the process is circular. To stay in office, public officials must find a way of implementing programs that satisfy both the electorate and the business community.

The research tests three hypotheses of a structuralist theory.

The Autonomous Public Official Hypothesis: The first hypothesis restates the main structuralist thesis, that elected officials are relatively

autonomous from the business community, but, nonetheless, implement public programs that assist firms to grow and prosper.

The Competing Business Community Hypothesis: Finding a set of programs acceptable to all parts of the business community is complicated
by heterogeneity in the business sector. Because of these differences,
businesses compete for the power to influence the direction of public policy.

The Conflict Resolution Hypothesis: Since conflict between interest
groups creates controversy that can affect elections, politicians try to
have an economic policy that is accepted by competing groups. This
means that there must be a consensus among members of the electorate,
including union and environmental groups, and members of the business community.

The Autonomous Public Official Hypothesis

Any examination of public policy must begin with an examination of the
public institutions controlling that policy. A critical institution at the state
level of government is, of course, the legislature. In this study, the Massachusetts legislature is examined. The legislature is officially named the
Great and General Court but referred to by people as the *Hill* or the General
Court. The oldest state legislature in the country, the Hill in 1978 consisted
of 40 Senators and 160 Representatives. Despite a relatively low salary
structure, one-half of the Senators and one-third of the Representatives that
year were full-time politicians. Those with other jobs were frequently lawyers with part-time law practices.

While legislatures have numerous reasons for entering public office,
none of those interviewed had any plans for leaving in the foreseeable
future. In addition, because of a desire to remain elected officials, their first
concern was establishing a record of votes and actions that pleased their
supporters. Opinions of party leaders and even personal ideologies were of
secondary importance.

Accordingly, legislation was endorsed which improved the economy
because of constituent rather than business needs. As structuralists correctly
theorized, elected officials in Massachusetts were keenly aware that their
ability to provide public services and employment was dependent upon a
healthy economy. The following remark from one such official was typical:
"There is a limit to how much government can provide in services and
employing people without a healthy economic base from which to derive tax
revenues. Most people are best served by the economy if they are gainfully
employed."

In legislators' minds, their institution, the legislature, had the power to influence the direction of the state's economy. For instance, legislators saw little difference between national and state economic conditions. But even though they thought that the state and nation had similar unemployment and inflation problems, there was a great difference in their perception of the origins of the problems. They viewed external forces like OPEC, drought, and market forces as causing national conditions. In 1978, few legislators blamed national problems on the actions of the national government. At the same time, they were convinced that the state's economic problems were the result of inappropriate state actions.[3] In particular, they blamed high state taxes and government spending for the Commonwealth's difficulties.

To legislators, the key to change was improving the business climate—a term that described the attitude that business had about state and local government. But what did the term really mean? And how could a state's business climate be measured? Legislators had no answer to these questions. Instead, they relied on the opinions of local business leaders in their districts. The fact that several local business leaders claimed there was a bad business climate was prima facie evidence that there was.

In summary, state officials were relatively autonomous from the business community. Their first objective was to implement programs that pleased the electorate. But this required business prosperity. To a great extent, state officials believed their public actions had a major influence on the state's level of private activity. The way to alter economic conditions was to improve the business climate which was the attitude the business community had about the public sector.

The Competing Business Community Hypothesis

If business leaders defined the state of the business climate, then the solution to a bad business climate would be to increase the number of public programs that the private sector liked. But in so doing, legislators were wary not to support anything that would anger the voting citizenry. For instance, since the result might be felt "at the polls", legislators were unwilling to support a reduction in the business income tax rate when they were increasing personal income taxes.

What type of business programs would legislators support? While they wanted to implement programs desired by the business community, this was often easier said than done. Members of the business community had different priorities. For instance, firms growing in employment and or investment (such as high technology companies in Massachusetts) demanded public programs that would eliminate production bottlenecks and make expansion less expensive. Such firms asked the state for programs that reduced the cost or increased the supply of scarce resources (such as trained workers), that improved the transportation network to carry their products to the market, or that made inexpensive capital available for plant expansion. On the other hand, marginal or declining firms simply wanted to survive. To offset inefficiencies, many older companies demanded programs that reduced the cost of doing business and would allow them to compete with more efficient firms that produced the same goods at lower costs. In Massachusetts, older manufacturing firms, often classified as part of the marginal sector, lobbied for lower business taxes and reduced unemployment compensation benefits.

Since elected officials did not discriminate between the needs of different firms in selecting among the various business programs, it was up to business leaders to promote their own priorities. Growth firms, because they (including banks and other financial institutions) were critical to the state's future economic well-being had automatic influence in the legislature. But this did not always translate into an ability to determine the direction of economic policy. While marginal firms were less valued for their economic contribution to the state, their leaders made up for it by being politically useful; they provided technical assistance about bills to legislators during the legislative session and campaign funds at election time. All but the most powerful business leaders also joined trade associations whose members shared similar goals. They hoped, in this way, to increase their legislative access and influence.

In conclusion, firms in the state had different public sector needs. Growth firms desired programs that reduced and eliminated production bottlenecks. Marginal firms wanted cost reductions to offset existing inefficiencies. Because of these differences, the business community competed for the power to influence the public sector.

The Conflict Resolution Hypothesis

Structuralists assert that, in the long-run, it is impossible to satisfy both the business community and the electorate. It was obvious to Massachusetts legislators that there was a basic contradiction between the demands of the business community and the electorate. As one legislator articulated:

> The conflict (between business and the electorate) is inevitable because groups see problems from different perspectives. Business groups are oriented toward the free market system, letting a healthy economy create jobs. Social and labor groups want more government involvement to ensure employment and benefits which lead to increased regulations and decreased profitability of business.

In this connection, Massachusetts legislators, especially members in leadership positions, were convinced that overly liberal past social benefits were the cause of the state's poor business climate and, as such, responsible for the state's postwar economic problems. But while they favored cutting back on social programs, the legislators also feared that tilting too much to business could alienate the electorate and jeopardize their reelections.

Even without the conflict between the business community and the electorate, there was the added problem of satisfying a heterogeneous business community. Since business leaders rarely publicized their differences and preferred pursuing their own agendas, it was difficult for them to agree to a set of programs. Instead, legislators were forced to choose between the programs supported by the various business constituencies. For example, business leaders preferred different types of tax reductions. Leaders of older manufacturing companies wanted tax changes that reduced the cost of doing business, while executives from growth firms advocated lower personal income taxes, an action that would be of greatest benefit to high-salaried employees, such as themselves.

Legislators avoided conflict whenever possible. One way that they did this was to organize legislative committees so that they focused on narrow issues, like unemloyment compensation or labor laws, rather than broader areas, like economic policy. While this system limited the implications of any one legislative action and reduced the number of interested parties, it also resulted in a fragmented policymaking process. Another strategy was to have competing groups meet and develop a compromise solution. With rare exception, legislators passed only those programs agreed upon by competing interest groups. In fact, the favorite type of economic legislation was technical in nature, unlikely to be opposed by the electorate and supported by at least one segment of the business community. This was the reason Massachusetts legislators overwhelmingly favored business tax incentives as the main tool in a development program. Even though there was little evidence that business tax incentives were effective, legislators liked them because they were favored by the association representing the marginal business community and the electorate displayed little interest.[4]

Thus, politicians' main objective was to implement an economic policy accepted by competing interest groups. They preferred economic programs supported by at least one segment of the business community that were technical in nature and thus unlikely to be understood by and consequently arouse the opposition of the electorate. They were similarly reluctant to support comprehensive policies or programs likely to be opposed by the business community.

Dynamics of Economic Policy Making

Even under the best circumstances, developing an economic policy that pleased everyone was a difficult process. But, as some Massachusetts legislators learned, a consensus around the issue of economics was short-lived and had to be continually renegotiated. This was because interest group demands were a function of economic cycles.

The demands of marginal and growth firms were inversely related to turns in the economy. Economic downturns translated into reduced consumer demand, cutbacks in production and employment needs, and often, lower profits. To counteract the effects of a recession, marginal firms turned to the state for programs that reduced the cost of doing business and offset declining profits. Growth firms were less affected by slowdowns and, during such times, had less reason to go to the state for programs to eliminate bottlenecks. This process reversed during periods of economic expansion. Faced with excess consumer demand caused by an expansionary economy, growth firms turned more to the state for assistance while marginal firms, helped by additional spending, were less insistent on public assistance.

But while business conflict was minimized by business cycles, conflicts between the Massachusetts electorate and the business community increased during one part of the economic cycle, when the state was balancing the budget. This meant that state resources were most limited when the needs of the electorate and marginal firms were the greatest.

Upturns in the economy were welcomed periods for legislators. Growth firms had their greatest need for public services during periods of economic expansion while marginal businesses and the electorate had fewer needs in such an economy. But economic expansion was also marked by expanding state revenues that public officials could use to satisfy the demands of competing interest groups. In such prosperity the threat of defeat at the polls was minimal. In contrast, the state budgets declined during recessions. Although growth firms made less demands during downturns, marginal firms needed additional subsidies to offset reductions in sales. At the same time, the electorate wanted more welfare, unemployment compensation, and social services programs. Yet, a balanced state budget meant fewer resources were available to spend on public programs and consensus, especially between marginal firms and the electorate, regarding the direction of public policy, was consequently almost impossible to achieve.

Threatened with political defeat in a time of rising constituent dissatisfaction, state politicians obviously found it in their interests to maintain the condition of prosperity. Unfortunately, as we will see, their actions were often counterproductive.

Effectiveness of State Economic Policy

There are several reasons why state economic policy in Massachusetts (and elsewhere) is not likely to succeed. Most theorists who write about structuralism assume that public officials maintain their independence from the business community. This implies that they can implement programs that go beyond and sometimes against the interests of any individual member but advance the interest of the economy as a whole. Yet the research conducted in Massachusetts provided overwhelming evidence that state-elected officials were more interested in minimizing conflict than in developing reforms that might induce economic prosperity. Even if policies might be in the state's economic interest—such as plant closing legislation or community-controlled energy companies—they were ignored or rejected on the grounds that one or more segments of the business community opposed it.

This is an important conclusion. Are structuralists wrong when they say that policymakers can judge independently of existing business demands? Or is the structuralist framework simply more appropriate for the nation than the little state?

Why would the structuralist framework be inappropriate at the state level of government? One possibility is that the intensity of business involvement may not be the same at the two levels of government. Existing businesses may find it easier to control a small state legislature, with a limited staff, than a larger U.S. Congress and, as a result, may have more power at the lower tier. It might also be true that state officials believe that they have fewer options than their federal counterparts. Certainly, state officials are aware that capital flows unimpeded between regions of the country.[5] Since states do not have the power to control the movement of capital, state officials are more reluctant than federal officials to alienate the private sector. As long as the potential for capital or firm relocation is present, it does not matter to state officials that the actual amount of firm expansion and relocation is small and contributes a small share of new jobs in the state.[6]

The consensus-building model described herein has one other important negative effect. The effectiveness of a state's economic policy is, in large measure, dependent upon the state's ability to offer a comparative advantage—some combination of inexpensive inputs or accessible markets that give firms an economic advantage over companies making similar products elsewhere.

One outcome of the process of minimizing conflict is the continued presence and ability of marginal firms to influence economic policy. In the short-run, it is conceivable that many marginal firms can forestall bankruptcy by prudent use of public subsidies. This means that inputs, normally available for growth firms, remain employed by marginal firms. This may not be a problem during recessions, when growth firms limit their production. With economic expansion, however, marginal firms' employment of labor, capital, and other inputs make it more difficult for growth firms to acquire similar resources at a reasonable cost. To compensate, growth firms will either pressure the public sector for more programs that increase the supply of needed resources or they will grow elsewhere. In either case, the result distorts the allocation of resources in the market. Most significantly, it means that state economic policy actually has the effect of limiting future growth and prosperity.

In conclusion, the following observations can be made about state economic policy. First, state legislators are relatively autonomous from the business community. But that does not mean that they are able to go beyond the interest of the private sector. The reason for this is a perceived or real lack of power at the state level of government. Legislators fear that antibusiness actions will result in the outflow of capital. They, therefore, implement policy that represents consensus between competing interest groups. The result of this process, however, is counterproductive and ends up limiting, not assisting, growth and development.

Notes

1. The *little* state is a term for one of the fifty states of the United States. It is called *little* to separate it from the Marxist term, the *state,* a reference to the nation-state.

2. For an example of a structuralist framework, see N. Poulantzas, *Political Power and Social Classes,* (London: New Left Books, 1973).

3. Legislators' opinions about the cause of regional business cycles are not shared by the vast majority of economists. The accepted wisdom is that a state's prosperity is largely explained by national economic conditions. By themselves, state actions cannot induce demand. See Albert Hirschman, *The Strategy of Economic Development,* (New Haven: Yale University Press, 1958).

4. See Bennett Harrison and Sandra Kanter, "The Political Economy of States' Job-Creation Business Incentives," *American Institute of Planners Journal,* October 1978.

5. The analysis implies that the flow of capital determines the flow of labor, and this is why public officials are more concerned about firm relocation than skilled labor migration. Actually, there is a great deal of controversy about this finding. For an example of a contrary finding see Richard Muth, "Differential Growth Among Large Cities," in J. Quirk and A. Zarley, eds., *Papers in Quantitative Economics,* (Lawrence, Kansas: University of Kansas Press, 1968).

6. For an estimate of job generation that comes from firm relocation, see David Birch, *The Job Generation Process,* (Cambridge, Mass.: MIT Program on Neighborhood Regional Change, 1979).

18 Partnership for Community Problem Solving: Failure and Promise

Mark Lindberg

Introduction

Efforts to stabilize and develop urban economies in America have been characterized by unintended consequences and failure. The policies of federal, state, and local government, as well as private lending institutions, insurance companies, and real estate firms have accelerated the cities' loss of population, loss of industry, and declining tax bases. In addition, economic crises have stimulated non-economic problems.[1] As wealthier whites fled to the suburbs, poorer blacks, browns, and ethnics were trapped in an urban apartheid. Economically drained city governments were pressured to increase police, fire, and human services at a time when they could barely maintain the sewers and streets.[2] City residents suffered from increased unemployment, mental illness, family distress, delinquency, crime, pollution, insufficient services, and deterioration of local mediating institutions.[3]

Before these trends were even viewed as an urban crisis, the white and wealthy reformers muted the inner-city interest groups by implementing reforms such as nonpartisan, at large elections for city councils. By eliminating ward-based politics, and ensuring that campaigns would be expensive, citywide, and media efforts, the inner-city minorities and poor were moved farther from access to power.

Clearly, these economic shifts, demographic trends, political changes, and social problems were interdependent. However, recognition that problems are interrelated has rarely translated into actions which treat the solutions accordingly. Recently, officials with federal, state, and local perspectives have been blessed with the insight that urban economic problems cannot be adequately addressed without some communication and shared decision making among economic, political, and social sectors of the community. They have responded through policies and a new rhetoric about

The author would like to acknowledge the help and support of Peter Ujuagi, commissioner, National Commission on Neighborhoods; David Beckwith, staff to The National Commission on Neighborhoods; and Bryan Downes, associate dean, University of Oregon. Many of the ideas herein were developed when the author was writing for The Governance Task Force, National Commission on Neighborhoods.

259

partnerships between different community sectors. However, the history of partnerships has been no more productive than the history of economic development. This chapter attempts to clarify why constructive partnerships are so difficult to achieve, and to identify principles for ensuring their success.

Partnerships: Easier Said Than Done

For most of U.S. history, clear role distinctions, or at least the pretense thereof, separated the roles of public, private, and community sectors. The shock of the Great Depression and the response of The New Deal blurred those role distinctions, since the public sector took on the task of crisis intervention, and the private and community sectors openly accepted some degree of assistance. With the exception of the 1940s, each decade since the Depression has marked a new stage of cooperation as well as new heights of frustration.

During the 1950s, inner-city slums were acknowledged as a ghastly problem. In response, Congress expanded its Urban Renewal policy. Cities could participate if they fulfilled components of a *workable program,* including a mandate for citizen participation. Unfortunately for the slum dwellers who were poorly organized, most cities responded by forming blue ribbon citizen committees dominated by real estate, construction, and business groups, as well as members of the chambers of commerce. The community sector, especially the residents of Urban Renewal target areas, were effectively kept out of the partnership. As a result, many dwellings were demolished but not replaced, poor residents were displaced into even more densely populated tenements, and many centrally located slums became prairies, waiting for eventual commercial or upper-income developments. The narrowly defined Urban Renewal intervention had disastrous, although unintended, consequences.

In the 1960s, the Kennedy-Johnson Community Action Program mandated local partnerships via the *three-legged stool* of public, community, and private sector representation on local Community Action Agency boards. At last, the government sought to involve those people who were the mandated beneficiaries of the programs. Unfortunately, local politicians felt threatened by the federal government's attempts to form direct ties with the urban ghettos, as they felt rejected from the partnership.[4] The low-income communities who thought they had been offered control found themselves struggling against unfriendly mayors, congressmen, and wealthy civic leadership. In spite of some local gains, city governments eventually captured the right to run the agencies through the Green Amendment, 1967, while internal conflict and inexperience often led to allegations of program mismanagement. The partnership was doomed, as the minority and low-income communities lacked the capacity, in terms of power, skills, financial resources, and organizational experience, to maintain independent and effective programs. The local public and private sectors, feeling their roles had been eroded, would not help the community sector gain in strength.

The policy and politics of partnerships evolved again in the 1970s. In 1974, the Nixon administration compromised with the Senate to form the Community Development Block Grant program (CDBG), a system designed to help cities revitalize low- and moderate-income areas. CDBG stimulated many cities to work with either existing or new neighborhood organizations, especially after federal regulations tightened requirements for citizen participation in 1978. The same year, Jimmy Carter articulated his urban policy, calling it a New Urban Partnership. Other federal programs, such as EDA's Special Projects and HUD's Urban Development Action Grants were designed to stimulate public/private, and community sector partnerships. ACTION's VISTA program, LEAA's Community AntiCrime Program, and HUD's Self Help Development Fund were examples of federal efforts to build the capacity of neighborhood-based organizations. In concept, these community groups would gain resources to enter partnerships more effectively.

Meanwhile, on the local level, an awareness emerged that neighborhoods were important economic, social, and political units. Local governments realized that citizen organizations could be used effectively, especially for planning efforts. Eugene, Oregon, for example, developed a system of *refinement planning* through which neighborhood teams, with the help of city staff, could develop their own housing, transportation, recreation, zoning, and commercial development plans. The refinement plan would be approved by City Council and incorporated into the city's comprehensive plan. In theory, residents, business people, and city officials would be working together to design their own futures.

Again, unfortunately, many innovations of the 1970s changed the physical landscape of neighborhoods but failed to build genuine partnerships. Some of the federal programs were exploited at the local level, diverting the benefits from their intended recipients.[5] As a result, plans and projects lacked broad community support. In addition, such programs often relied on small numbers of activists who failed to attract new volunteers or to provide participants with experiences of empowerment. The converse was also true. Many citizens assumed that they had decision-making authorities which they did not. The outcome in both cases was frustration and anger.

If the neighborhood planning teams are not supported by independent democratic community organizations, they are left with no base of followers to back them. As a result, the bureaucratic processes and goals prevail and citizen teams become unpaid extensions of city hall.

Principles of Effective Partnerships

In spite of this legacy of ambivalence towards partnerships, each era has produced information which can be accumulated into a set of principles. Enacted in isolation, they are unlikely to overcome the barriers between sectors. Taken as a whole, they should increase the potential for effectively solving community problems.

Start Small. One clear failure of urban renewal was its delusions of grandeur. In hindsight, it seems evident that cities could not expect instant cooperative relationships between government, business, and neighborhood residents when the three sectors have such divergent self-interests and a history of overt or covert conflict. Success requires a degree of trust and respect, gained over time through disagreement, negotiation, and compromise.

For example, by the early 1970s, the residential and business districts on the east side of Toledo, Ohio, were in decline. Starting with a fight to keep open a branch library, the residents built a multineighborhood coalition, the East Toledo Community Organization (ETCO). From a small storefront painting project, the business people established the River East Redevelopment Corporation. Over the years these organizations often agreed on goals, disagreed on implementation, and alternatively fought and cooperated with the city government. However, they developed effective working relationships which stabilized the neighborhood and brought in over $15 million in private and public investments for the commercial district.

The key to success was carefully pacing the issues and projects, starting small, building relationships, allowing each sector to take responsibility of the plans. By the final hearing before the Toledo City Council, only two people testified against the project.

Clarify the Role of Each Sector. Trends in recent decades, the internal dynamics of each sector, as well as incompatible characteristics between organizations in each sector have led to a confusion of roles in solving community problems.

Dealing with the public bureaucracy is one frustration. Its management style tends to emphasize routinization, stability, and long-range planning for the public good which many outsiders view as impenetrable, inflexible, and unresponsive. A private business, on the other hand, is often focused on short-term cycles of cash flow problems, and may be viewed by outsiders as efficient but trapped in a tunnel vision of profit. Since community organizations often operate with diffuse goals on small budgets and volunteer labor, they are perceived by some as poorly organized, unsophisticated, and unable to plan ahead. When government, business, and community groups try to work together, cooperation is made difficult by the incompatibility of goals, time orientations, structures, and reputations.

The internal dynamics of each sector also restrict the potential for well-functioning partnerships. Both private and community sectors often seemed atomized, since citizens, voluntary associations, human services, small businesses and corporations usually act as individuals without regard for any mutual interests. In contrast, the public sector often seems monolithic, organized into fewer and better integrated structures known as the government.

The differences between such sectors have become more salient as the pressures on them to cooperate have increased. As the size of bureaucracies and the complexity of urban problems increased, citizens demanded greater access to unelected officials, public administrators sought to build their own constituencies through citizen participation,[6] and the private sector alternately welcomed and condemned public intervention.

The pressures for partnership came from all sides, yet the expectations between citizens, business people, and public administrators differed and each came with individual interests and goals. Each expected more control and more benefits than were received. The confusion of roles and responsibilities led to mutual subversion, breakdowns in communication, and inequitable decision-making. The partnerships became zero-sum games.

One remedy to role confusion involves the formation of umbrella organizations which are expressly formed to engage in networking, communication, advocacy, and partnership. Common examples include merchants' associations and neighborhood coalitions. When networks receive strong support from and participation by their member organizations, the private and community sectors improve their ability to interact with the comparatively monolithic public sector.

An extreme variation of this strategy was adopted by The Cherry Hill Coalition, a group of neighborhood councils in Seattle.

> The Cherry Hill Coalition has inherited a legacy of organizing efforts in the Central District, as well as the whole of Seattle. As the city's "poor" and "minority" neighborhood, Central has been deluged with agencies, researchers, planners and programs. Many of them left trails of frustration and broken expectations.[7]

As a method of breaking dysfunctional alliances and unproductive dependencies on governmental programs, the Coalition severed ties with others. By concentrating on democratic issue-oriented advocacy, they established a clear role in the community, increasing their potential to enter future partnerships with less fear of misunderstanding and overdependence.

Independence before Interdependence. Role clarity is difficult unless each partner has a significant level of independence. The history of the War on

Poverty illustrates the point, since the local Community Action Agencies were dependent on federal funding. This left them vulnerable to angry mayors who were threatened by direct federal subsidy to community organizations. In addition, many communities had little experience with boards, budgets, planning, programming, and organizing. They were ill-equipped to take over these large bureaucracies, parachuted into their neighborhood. They were forced to violate principle number one: Start small. As a result, the local programs were often torn with controversy, and after the Green Amendment many were subsumed by city hall.

In contrast, hundreds of independent neighborhood organizations, funded through local churches and private foundations, rose to grass roots power in the 1970s.[8] A prototype, the Hartford Areas Rally Together (HART), grew strong maintaining a small paid staff, building a coalition out of block clubs, and developing leaders through confrontations with city officials.

In recent years, HART and its counterpart have spun-off development corporations and social service agencies creating political, economic, and social partnerships controlled by the community sector.[9] The power organizations have formed coalitions at city, state, and national levels. For example, the Home Mortgage Disclosure Act of 1975 was conceived of and fought for by neighborhood organizations.

Because of their power and independence, many of these citizen groups have the capacity to enter fruitful partnerships with the public and private sectors. They are respected for their achievements and their ability to hold others accountable. Because of this respect, power, and independence, they enter partnerships that are genuinely reciprocal.

Reciprocity. Among the best-known, successful partnerships are dozens of Neighborhood Housing Services (NHS), which bring together city officials, bankers, and neighborhood residents. The success of NHS is based on reciprocity—every sector gives something and every sector gets something.

NHS organizations are generally started through local invitation to a federal agency, the Neighborhood Reinvestment Corporation. A field officer then facilitates the partnership agreement, in which the public and private sectors agree to commit resources to the target neighborhood. The neighborhood, in turn, must demonstrate an adequate level of community organization, so local leaders and residents can play strong yet sensitive decision-making roles.

The level of community organization spells the difference between success and failure for NHS. Unfortunately, the process of physical decline often correlates with the erosion of human networks and institutions, so the neighborhood residents in greatest need often have the least capacity to participate. The most prevalent criticism of NHS is their unwillingness to work in severely deteriorated areas. Nevertheless, the NHS partnership formula has produced effective partnerships in dozens of U.S. cities.

Reciprocal Technical Assistance and Training. Once the joint problem-solving venture begins, each participant can benefit by sharing the unique knowledge and perceptions held by each sector. For example, Baltimore Mayor William Shaeffer asked Vincent Quale of the St. Ambrose Housing Aid Center how the city could be responsive to neighborhood needs. Quale replied that his community organization would like to train newly hired city housing personnel working in that neighborhood. Mayor Schaeffer agreed, and now city workers are more able to spot problems and be more sensitive to the area's needs. Such technical assistance is a valuable part of reciprocal relationships, and could be pursued more extensively with sectors alternating as trainers and trainees. Various mechanisms for assisting the community sector are discussed further in the next section.

Capacity Building for Neighborhood Organizations. It is their human scale which makes neighborhoods crucial. They are immediate in people's experience. Participants know each other on a face-to-face basis. They nurture confidence and a sense of control. They have built-in adapting mechanisms: churches, PTAs, Boys' Clubs, Girl Scouts, ethnic clubs, civic associations, merchants' associations, fraternal groups, YMCAs and YWCAs, settlement houses, community development credit unions, alternative community technology groups. Even the most devastated neighborhoods have networks and support systems, whether formally incorporated or informally centered at a corner store, tavern, or storefront church. Neighborhoods are the building blocks of cities, because they are meaningful units of participation.

In spite of their human resources, the voluntary groups which form the backbone of neighborhoods often have comparatively little in terms of financial and technical resources. If urban partnerships are to survive as reciprocal relationships between interdependent peers, then attention should be paid to building the capacity of these organizations.

There are constructive ways for city governments to help build neighborhood capacity. The simplest is to recognize the need, and to avoid obstructing independent efforts to support it, such as direct federal funding.

Former Buffalo City Councilman William Price called the best city governments "neighborhood competent." These are city governments that serve their neighborhoods by stimulating volunteerism, developing flexible structures to adapt to diverse neighborhood needs, engaging in educational exchange with the neighborhoods, and developing mechanisms that link citizens with government, ensuring communication and accountability. Of course, even the best city structure cannot be effective without strong leadership. Baltimore, for example, has been fortunate to have three succesive mayors with sensitivity to neighborhoods, as well as innovative community development administrators, and the backing of civic leaders.[10]

Several cities have encouraged building neighborhood capacities through programs and policies that stimulate volunteerism. Cincinnati received a grant from the Mott Foundation to fund neighborhood councils that developed programs to involve more residents. Baltimore set aside one million dollars of its Community Development Block Grant allocation to fund experimental or exemplary projects of neighborhood organizations. Buffalo helped establish community controlled corporations, such as FLARE, so the city could delegate large portions of its Block Grant money to people who knew its neighborhoods best, the residents.

At the federal level, both Presidents Carter and Reagan expressed an interest, at least, in building neighborhoods. The Carter administration's initial commitment was expressed when the president appointed Msgr', Geno Baroni, longstanding proponent of neighborhood policies and founding director of the National Center for Urban Ethnic Affairs, to head the HUD Office of Neighborhoods, Voluntary Associations, and Consumer Protection (NVACP). In 1978, NVACP opened the Office of Neighborhood Development (OND), mandated to establish a network of self-help neighborhood development organizations to foster self-determination. HUD states that OND was to organize the necessary supports in policy, funding, access to resources, and skill development. It was hoped that as the number of such organizations increases, they would be able to maintain themselves, and build successful partnerships with local governments and the private sector. To these ends, the Office of Neighborhood Development attempted to develop networks, to build capacity, and technical assistance.

Two acts of Congress have supported the goals of HUD's neighborhood offices. The Neighborhood Self-Help Development Act would fund neighborhood development organizations to prepare and implement housing rehabilitation, commercial revitalization, weatherization, and the like. The projects must serve low- and moderate-income people; they must be controlled by local residents, businesses, and institutions; and they must be run by nonprofit entities.

President Ronald Reagan is expected to abolish these programs as well as the Office of Neighborhood Development. Consistent with his philosophy of tax-cut incentives, Reagan's best known alternative to neighborhood capacity-building is the Enterprise Zone, as proposed by Jack Kemp (Republican-New York) and Robert Garcia (Democrat-New York). The zones, encompassing distressed neighborhoods, would receive various breaks in taxes and depreciation schedules. Whether such incentives will actually stimulate reinvestment or relocation decisions, and to what extent the benefits will trickle down to local residents remains to be seen. It has been suggested that neighborhood organizations be involved in the selection, development, and monitoring of the zones.[11] However, Mr. Reagan's aversion to federal regulations makes this unlikely.

Conclusion

Problems in different sectors of a community are interrelated. Economic crises can stimulate social crises. Social problems can stimulate political crises. However, communities and the individuals who reside in them cannot deal effectively with serious problems or crises unless they are both willing and able, that is, have the capacity to solve problems. Hence, anyone concerned with economic development and with communities in economic crisis must first concern themselves with community development. Communities which are effectively organized and led are in the best position to proactively engage in successful economic development. They are also the communities which anticipate and deal with problems, such as deterioration of the economic base, before it becomes a crisis.

Notes

1. *People, Building Neighborhoods. The Final Report to the President and the Congress from the National Commission on Neighborhoods,* Washington, D.C., 1979.

2. Stanley Hallett, paper written for the National Commission on Neighborhoods, Washington, D.C., 1979.

3. Peter Berger and Richard Jolin Neuhaus, *To Employer People: The Role of Mediating Structures in Public Policy* (Washington, D.C.: American Enterprise Institute for Public Policy Research).

4. Martin Rein, *Dilemmas of Social Reform* (Reading, Mass.: Addison-Wesley, 1967).

5. *Carter's "Urban Action" Lacking Disclosure* (Chicago: National Training and Information Center, May/June 1979).

6. Stuart Langton (ed.), *Citizen Participation in America* (Lexington, Mass.: Lexington Books, D.C. Heath and Company, 1978).

7. Mark Lindberg, "Cherry Hill Coalition," *People, Building Neighborhoods,* Case Study Appendix, vol. 1, p. 353 (Washington, D.C.: The National Commission on Neighborhoods).

8. J. Perlman, "Grassrooting the System," *Social Policy* 7 (1976).

9. Stan Hold, "Community Organizing v. Community Development," *Just Economics.*

10. *People, Building Neighborhoods.*

11. Brigid Flanigan, "Analysis of the Free Enterprise Zone." Unpublished paper, 1981.

Name Index

Abernathy, William J., 132
Agee, James, 64
Aldrich, Howard, 239, 241, 244
Alpert, Irvine, 71
Archibugi, F., 113
Aronson, Robert, 135
Arvola, T.F., 67
Austin, Phyllis, 70

Baker, Lawrence, 244
Bakke, E., 196
Baran, Paul, 18
Barbe, Nancy, 94
Barnet, Richard, 71
Barsh, Russel, 41
Bass, Liz, 156
Baugh, Bob, 150, 151
Bearse, Pete, 94, 95, 97
Bendavid-Val, Avrom, 242
Bendick, Marc, 238
Berger, Peter, 259
Bergman, Edward M., 239, 243, 244
Berry, Daniel, 226, 288
Berry, J., 210
Birch, David, 6, 87, 97, 132, 135, 136,
    139, 140, 143, 177
Black, J. Thomas, 243
Blasi, Joseph R., 183
Blitzstein, David, 152
Bluestone, Barry, 131, 136, 144, 147,
    148, 149, 151, 177, 237, 240, 241
Borut, Allan, 243
Bradford, Calvin, 83
Breckenridge, John, 177
Brenner, M. Harvey, 20, 196, 199, 208,
    212
Briar, K., 209
British Steel Corporation, 110
Brittan, Samuel, 11
Brownell, A., 196, 198
Buchanan, K., 109
Buckdrop, Deborah L., 7

Burgess, E., 195
Burggraf, Shirley, 5
Burton, Dudley, 71
Business Week, 132, 148, 159
Buss, T., 211, 215
Butler, Stewart, 98
Byrne, Robert, 243

Cambridge Economic Policy Group,
    111
Cameron, C., 110
Caplan, G., 215
Carlisle, Rick, 237, 238, 243
Carlisle & Redmond Associates, 177,
    237, 238, 243
Carney, J., 108
Case, John, 22
Catalano, R., 196, 200
Cavan, R., 196
Choate, Pat, 4, 224, 233
Coates, D., 209
Coates, Robert N., 67
Cobb, S., 197, 210, 211
Cohn, Robert, 131, 196, 197
Committee on Small Business, 6, 132
Conley, Gary, 242, 243
Conte, Michael, 184
Cook, Donald D., 159
Cooke, P., 110
Council for Northeast Economic
    Action, 33
Craypo, Charles, 131
CSE London Working Group, 113

Daniels, Belden, 94, 96, 98, 100, 101,
    131
Daunton, 107
Davidson, Steven, 100
Davies, G., 109
Dayton Journal Herald, 223
Denison, Edward F., 3, 30
Department of Commerce, 66

269

Subject Index

About the Contributors

Irvine Alpert is a graduate student in the Department of City and Regional Planning at the University of California, Berkeley. Mr. Alpert and Dudley Burton are working on a detailed history and analysis of the Redwood National Park controversy and its consequences.

Russel L. Barsh is associate professor of business, government, and society at the University of Washington Graduate School of Business Administration and is a member of the Washington State Bar. He serves as a legal and economic advisor to several North American tribal governments, including the Union of Nova Scotia Indians and Oglala Sioux Tribe, and he has published numerous studies of U.S. and Canadian Indian political and economic-development strategies. His recent books include *The Washington Fishing Rights Controversy: An Economic Critique* (rev. ed. 1979) and (with James Youngblood Henderson) *The Road: Indian Tribes and Political Liberty* (1980).

Marc Bendick, Jr., is senior research associate at The Urban Institute. Dr. Bendick specializes in problems of poverty, economic development, human-resources development, and the management of social-assistance programs.

Edward M. Bergman is associate professor of planning at the University of North Carolina, Chapel Hill.

Daniel E. Berry is program associate with the Urban Affairs Program of the Charles F. Kettering Foundation. His primary responsibility is that of project director of the foundation's experimental work with the Negotiated Investment Strategy. He also serves as project officer for the Local Elected Officials' Capacity Building Project, administered by the National League of Cities, and coordinates the foundation's research activities relating to neighborhood economic development. Mr. Berry received the bachelor's degree in political science and the master's degree in urban studies from Kent State University.

Joseph R. Blasi is lecturer in social studies and director of The Project for Kibbutz Studies, an institute at the Center for Jewish Studies, Harvard University. As a social-policy advisor from 1975–1979, he worked to develop federal legislation on worker ownership with William Foote Whyte. Mr. Blasi has been academic advisor to the Task Force on Business Continuity, Small Business Administration.

Barry Bluestone is associate professor of economics and director of the Social Welfare Research Institute, Boston College.

Dudley J. Burton is assistant professor of social theory and planning at the University of California, Santa Cruz.

Ralph Catalano is associate professor of social ecology at the University of California, Irvine. Professor Catalano, who received the Ph.D. in social science from the Maxwell School of Syracuse University, is also associate director of the university's Public Policy Research Organization. He is currently coprincipal investigator on two NIMH-sponsored projects measuring the social costs of economic change.

Philip Cooke is a professor in the Department of Town Planning at the Institute of Science and Technology, the University of Wales, Cardiff. He is the author of several articles on Welsh development.

Steven D. Davidson is an economic and financial consultant employed by the Policy Project on Development Finance, whose objectives are to develop and advance public-policy recommendations designed to meet the credit-and-capital needs of economically disadvantaged communities. The Policy Project is sponsored by the National Rural Center and the Opportunity Funding Corporation under a grant from the Rockefeller Brothers Fund.

David Dooley is associate professor in the Program in Social Ecology at the University of California, Irvine. He received the B.A. in economics from Harvard University and the Ph.D. in psychology from the University of California, Los Angeles. His research interests include the relationship of economic change in behavioral disorder and the role and facilitation of nonprofessional mental-health agents, including support from naturally occurring social networks. He is research associate with the Public Policy Research Organization at the University of California, Irvine, where he is currently coprincipal investigator of an NIMH-sponsored longitudinal survey of economic change, stressful life events, social support, and behavioral symptoms in Los Angeles.

Felician F. Foltman has been professor of industrial relations at the New York State School of Industrial and Labor Relations at Cornell University since 1950. His principal interests are human-resources management from an organizational and public-policy perspective. His publications have covered plant shutdowns, labor-management committees, apprenticeship training, and human-resources information and management systems.

Jeffrey Gale is assistant professor of business, government, and society and adjunct assistant professor of social management of technology at the University of Washington. His research and teaching interests are in the fields of government regulation, urban development, and public-private planning. He has served as a consultant to private and public organizations in health planning and urban development. His current research is in the structure of the environmental-review process and housing.

Bennett Harrison is an associate professor of economics and urban studies in the Department of Urban Studies and Planning at the Massachusetts Institute of Technology.

Sandra Kanter is assistant professor at the University of Massachusetts, Boston. Dr. Kanter is a text specialist and is currently writing a book on state business taxes for the Council of State Planning Agencies.

Martin T. Katzman is professor of political economy and environmental sciences at the University of Texas, Dallas. He is a specialist in regional development, municipal finance, and energy.

James E. Kunde is director of the Urban Affairs Program of the Charles F. Kettering Foundation. He has directed the foundation's research program in the area of urban affairs since 1974. Mr. Kunde has served as city manager of Dayton, Ohio, as county administrator of Jackson County, Missouri, and as city development director for Kansas City, Missouri. He received the bachelor's degree in mathematics from Wittenberg University and the master's degree in public administration from the Fels Institute at the University of Pennsylvania.

Larry C. Ledebur is director of the Urban Economic Development Program at The Urban Institute. Dr. Ledebur's research has focused on urban and regional development, industry and firm performance, and industrial incentives.

Ramsay Liem is associate professor of psychology in the Department of Psychology, Boston College. He is also coprincipal investigator for the Work and Unemployment Project, a longitudinal study of personal and family impacts of unemployment.

Marc Lindberg is a city councilor in Eugene, Oregon, and assistant professor of community development at the Wallace School of Community Service and Public Affairs, University of Oregon. He has also been on the faculty of Springfield College, Springfield, Massachusetts, and Holy Cross

College, Worcester, Massachusetts. Dr. Lindberg has been director of research and program development for the New England Training Center for Community Organizers, Providence, Rhode Island. Before moving to Oregon, he worked for President Carter's National Commission on Neighborhoods, writing case studies of urban neighborhood organizations, a policy paper on Federally Mandated Citizen Participation, and the final report of the Task Force on Governance, Citizen Participation, and Empowerment.

Norton E. Long is Curator's Professor in Political Science at the University of Missouri, St. Louis.

Paul Pryde is the president of Janus Associates, an economic development and finance consulting firm. He also serves as director of the Policy Project on Development Finance.

Gareth Rees is professor in the Department of Town Planning, Institute of Science and Technology, University of Wales, Cardiff.

Elliott D. Sclar is associate professor of urban planning and chairman of the Division of Urban Planning at Columbia University and is an economist specializing in economic development. He is currently completing a study on the impact of regional economic stagnation on mental health in a small industrial city in north central Massachusetts. Dr. Sclar was formerly on the faculty of Brandeis University and chief of economic research and health planning at the Veteran's Administration's out-patient clinic in Boston. He has written several books and articles exploring various aspects of economic change and its individual and social costs.

June A. Sekera has received the B.A. in sociology from California State University. She is a manpower-development specialist in the Employment and Training Administration of the U.S. Department of Labor in the Private Sector Initiatives Program.

Roger J. Vaughan received the Ph.D. in economics from the University of Chicago. He has been an economist at The Rand Corporation and at Citibank, NA, New York. He is now deputy director of the Office of Development Planning, New York State. He is the author of several books and articles on economic development.

William Foote Whyte is professor emeritus at Cornell University's New York State School of Industrial and Labor Relations. He has directed the school's New Systems of Work and Participation Program and is currently president of the American Sociological Association. Whyte's case studies on worker-owned firms set the stage for federal legislative initiatives in this area, which he began with Joseph Blasi.

Jeffrey Wittmaier is a member of the Department of Political Science at the University of Missouri, St. Louis.